Communications in Computer and Information Science 416

For further volumes:
http://www.springer.com/series/7899

Łukasz Bolikowski · Vittore Casarosa
Paula Goodale · Nikos Houssos
Paolo Manghi · Jochen Schirrwagen (Eds.)

Theory and Practice of Digital Libraries – TPDL 2013 Selected Workshops

LCPD 2013, SUEDL 2013, DataCur 2013
Held in Valletta, Malta, September 22–26, 2013
Revised Selected Papers

 Springer

Editors
Łukasz Bolikowski
Uniwersytet Warszawski
Warszawa
Poland

Vittore Casarosa
Paolo Manghi
Istituto di Scienza e Tecnologie
   dell'Informazione
Consiglio Nazionale delle Ricerche
Pisa, Pisa
Italy

Paula Goodale
University of Sheffield
Sheffield
UK

Nikos Houssos
National Documentation Centre
Athens
Greece

Jochen Schirrwagen
Bielefeld University
Bielefeld
Germany

ISSN 1865-0929   ISSN 1865-0937 (electronic)
ISBN 978-3-319-08424-4 ISBN 978-3-319-08425-1 (eBook)
DOI 10.1007/978-3-319-08425-1
Springer Cham Heidelberg New York Dordrecht London

Library of Congress Control Number: 2014942569

Printed on acid-free paper

Springer is part of Springer Science+Business Media (www.springer.com)

Preface

This volume contains the papers presented at three different workshops, held in connection with the 17th International Conference on Theory and Practice of Digital Libraries (TPDL 2013). The TPDL Conference Series (formerly known as ECDL, European Conference on Digital Libraries) started in 1997 in conjunction with the activities of the first DELOS Working Group (which later became the DELOS Network of Excellence) and has evolved into the leading scientific forum in Europe, focusing on digital libraries and associated technical, practical, and social issues, meeting the needs of a large and diverse constituency, which includes practitioners, researchers, educators, policy makers, and users.

TPDL 2013 took place during September 22–26 in Valletta, Malta. The conference exhibited the traditional mix of events, which usually include tutorials at the beginning and workshops at the end. TPDL 2013 started with six tutorial sessions, on topics ranging from linked data to preservation to text digitization, to metadata. In parallel with the tutorials, a Doctoral Symposium was held, where PhD students, selected after a call for proposals, had the opportunity to present and discuss their research topics with a panel of experts. Alongside the tutorials, for the first time the Global Workshop of iSchools was held, whose aim was to foster the development of a global iSchool community by inviting delegates from information schools to discuss their academic programs and research strengths/interests so as to allow them to identify areas of possible collaboration.

The conference attracted about 300 delegates from over 40 countries, who presented and discussed challenges and opportunities in digital library architecture, interoperability and information integration, digital library interfaces, user behavior, data re-use and open access, linked data, data visualization, long-term preservation, the Semantic Web in digital libraries and digital curation. The presentations and discussions were continued in a number of workshops held at the end of the conference.

This volume is organized in three chapters, containing the accepted papers of the three workshops LCPD-2013, SUEDL-2013, DataCur2013. A short description of each workshop is given here.

LCPD-2013: Linking and Contextualizing Publications and Datasets

Today's scientific communities are faced with data-driven requirements of e-science and new kinds of research methodologies and approaches inspired by e-research. In particular, these trends led to a new data-centric way of conceptualizing, organizing, and carrying out research activities and, consequently, revolutionized scientific communication. Scientific communities and funding bodies are eagerly discussing and investigating the need for scientists to publish their raw datasets—e.g., experimental details, analytical methods, and visualizations—alongside scientific publications or using novel types of data publication. Data are becoming a first-class citizen of the modern scientific communication, being published for discovery and re-use together with literature to a greater extent. More specifically, linking and contextualizing publications and datasets in a meaningful way is increasingly becoming a key requirement not only for the scientists, but also for their organizations and ultimately for funding agencies. For example, dataset-publication linking allows researchers to better verify the quality of scientific outcomes, e.g., by reproducing the experiments, and greatly improves dataset availability, discoverability, interpretability, and re-usability. Moreover, contextualizing such information, by adding further interlinking with research funding information and affiliations, would allow funding agencies and organizations to measure their research impact in order to assess the quality of their investments and their activities.

Modern scientific communities and their research infrastructures serve for discipline-specific activities whose input and output affect and are affected by scientific communication. To cope with the increasing speed of such activities and the growing volumes of research outcome, communities need to be facilitated in publishing, interlinking, contextualizing, preserving, discovering, accessing, and reusing their research outcomes. Achieving such objectives would foster multi-disciplinarity, generate novel research opportunities, and endorse quality research. However, researchers rely on different technologies and systems to deposit and preserve their research outcome and their contextual information. Datasets and publications are kept into digital libraries and data centers together with descriptive metadata. Contextual information is scattered into other systems, for example, CRIS systems for funding schemes and affiliations, national and international initiatives and registries, such as ORCID and VIAF for people and authors. The construction of *modern scientific communication systems* capable of collecting and assembling such information in a meaningful way has opened up several research challenges in the fields of digital library, e-science, and e-research.

The goal of this workshop was to provide researchers and practitioners in the fields of digital library, e-science, and e-research with a forum where they could constructively explore these topics. Ten contributions and two invited papers report on theoretical, systemic, and foundational work targeting popular topics of linking and contextualizing datasets and publications. The quality of the contributions was ensured by a rich and qualified Program Committee.

SUEDL-2013: Supporting Users Exploration of Digital Libraries

There is a pressing need to better exploit valuable resources in cultural heritage digital libraries through improved access and support for users in information discovery and use. Current challenges in information access include: raising awareness and discovery of the availability of collections; helping users to understand the overall content of a digital library and gain an overview of the collection as a starting point for information discovery; and, enabling more exploratory modes of information seeking, such as open-ended browsing and serendipity. In cultural heritage contexts, especially when domain and collection knowledge is limited (e.g., novice users, the general public, and students), the simple search box approach often delivers less than satisfactory results, and there is therefore a need to offer new ways of discovering and engaging with digital libraries in this environment.

Many different approaches to these challenges are being taken, bringing together knowledge and expertise from research areas as diverse as interactive information retrieval, human–computer interaction, data visualization, guided paths and trails, personalization and recommendation, NLP and content enrichment, among others. There is also broad acknowledgment that support for more complex tasks may require a more holistic approach to the design of digital library systems, with the provision of tools that extend user interaction into areas such as sensemaking and information (re)use. Furthermore, as solutions and results begin to emerge, there is a need to consider how to evaluate these novel systems and how to interpret results beyond the typical IR measures of precision and recall, including aspects of user experience such as exploration, task performance, user engagement, and satisfaction.

At this second SUEDL workshop, we once again aimed to bring together academic and practitioner perspectives, and to promote discussion and collaboration in addressing some of the issues outlined above, with a strong focus on users and solutions to support their needs. The workshop comprised five research papers and five demonstration papers, covering topics as diverse as human–computer interaction, digital library and archive evaluation techniques, linked data, image similarity, visualization and recommendations, in a variety of digital library contexts including national libraries, museum, archival and special collections, sound and vision, and oral history. The program of papers and demonstrations was enriched further by a keynote speech from Professor Ann Blandford of University College London, on "Exploring the Information Landscape: The Digital Library in Context", and a lively panel-led discussion on the topic of "Supporting Users' Exploration of Digital Libraries: Priorities and Future Directions."

DataCur2013: Moving Beyond Technology: iSchools and Education in Data Curation. Is Data Curator a New Role?

The increase of digital content in the broad areas of institutional and domain-specific repositories, libraries, archives, and museums and the increased interest in the sharing and preservation of research data have triggered the emergence of some buzzwords that more and more often appear in the literature, such as *convergence, digital curation, and data curator.*

Convergence, in this context, is related to the merging of the education curricula for information professionals in the disciplines of library science, archival, and museum studies, under the assumption that the digitization of the collections is blurring the traditional boundaries between those three professions.

Digital curation is a term generally used to indicate those activities that add value and knowledge to the collections, and the added value is usually given by the curator or manager of the cultural institution. The term digital curation is also used to describe the actions needed to maintain digital material, including digital research data, over their entire life-cycle and over time, for current and future generations of users. Assuming that there is a set of core competencies needed by a digital curator, it is yet to be understood how these competencies could at the same time play in favor of the convergence (given the digital nature of the resources to be curated) and in favor of a professional identity (given the different focus and mission of the three disciplines, where the value adding and the access to the collections would remain different).

Data curator is used here in the context of the storage, management, and preservation of digital research data, since more and more scientific research, in almost all disciplines, ends up being based on digital sources. There are a number of good reasons for preserving research data, but today it is not (yet) clear which of the existing professional roles are best suited for this activity. Should there be a data librarian, or a data archivist, or a data museum curator? Or is this a new role to be invented from scratch? Or should the responsibility of curating research data be given to the data producers, i.e., the researchers themselves?

In the context described above, the DataCur2013 main goal was to debate ideas and concrete examples of research projects, educational programs and training initiatives in digital curation and research data management, illustrating approaches, methodologies, and success stories addressing the need for an increasingly qualified *information workforce* in the data library, data center, archive, museum, and cultural heritage sectors. Specific objectives were to provide additional insight into the complex interplay between education, research, and curation (including long-term preservation) of digital data, and how these needs could be addressed in curricula for the education and training of the information professionals; and to gain a better understanding of the level at which a convergence of the three traditional professions could be achieved, contributing to a more global view of the access and preservation of research outcomes, which today are very often scattered in libraries, archives, institutional repositories, data bases, etc.

This workshop was the ideal continuation of a series of workshops and events that started in 2005 with a workshop on "Information Technologies Profiles and Curricula for Libraries" (held at the University of Parma), and has continued through five more events up to the last one in February 2013 with the workshop "iSchools Building on the Strengths Found in the Convergence of Librarianship, Archival, and Museum Studies to Improve the Education of Managing Digital Collections" (held in connection with the iConference 2013 at Fort Worth). A detailed descriptions of these events and an analysis of their results can be found in the volume edited by A.M. Tammaro,

V. Casarosa, and D. Castelli: *Closing the Gap: Interdisciplinary Perspectives on Research and Education for Digital Libraries* (IRCDL 2013, Rome, Italy), in the series *Communications in Computer and Information Science*, published by Springer.

September 2013

Łukasz Bolikowski
Vittore Casarosa
Paula Goodale
Nikos Houssos
Paolo Manghi
Jochen Schirrwagen

Organization

Committees

LCPD Organizing Committee

Paolo Manghi

Łukasz Bolikowski

Nikos Houssos

Jochen Schirrwagen

LCPD Program Committee

Eloy Rodrigues

Brigitte Mathiak

Stefan Kramer

Richard Cyganiak

Petr Knoth

Sarantos Kapidakis

Asunción Gómez-Pérez

Philipp Cimiano

Anna Clements

Dragan Ivanović

Jane Greenberg

Brigitte Joerg

Johanna McEntyre

Miguel-Angel Sicilia

Brian Matthews

Cezary Mazurek

Keith Jeffery

SUEDL Organizing Committee

Paula Goodale

Mark Stevenson

Eneko Agirre

Kate Fernie

SUEDL Program Committee

Maristella Agosti

Donatella Castelli

Paul Clough

Jillian Griffiths

Mark Hall

Gareth Jones

Jaap Kamps

Birger Larsen

Séamus Lawless

Johan Oomen

Arantxa Otegi

Juliane Stiller

Tinne Tuytelaars

Max Wilson

DataCur Organizing Committee

Vittore Casarosa
Donatella Castelli

Seamus Ross
Anna Maria Tammaro

DataCur Program Committee

Kevin Ashley
Christoph Becker
Toni Carbo
Paul Conway
Kate Fernie
Mariella Guercio
Carolyn Hank
Cal Lee
Jens Ludwig

John McDonald
Nancy McGovern
Mary Molinaro
Andy Rauber
Michael Seadle
Stefan Strathmann
Manfred Thaller
Terry Weech

Contents

**Second International Workshop on Supporting Users Exploration
of Digital Libraries**

**Moving Beyond Technology: iSchools and Education in Data Curation:
Is Data Curator a New Role?**

First Workshop on Linking and Contextualizing Publications and Datasets

Datasets: From Creation to Publication

Sarah Callaghan[✉]

STFC - Rutherford Appleton Laboratory, British Atmospheric Data Centre,
Chilton, Didcot, Oxfordshire OX11 0QX, UK
sarah.callaghan@stfc.ac.uk

Abstract. This article describes a case study of a small research group collecting and managing data from a pair of long-running experimental campaigns, detailing the data management and publication processes in place at the time of the experiments. It highlights the reasons why publications became disconnected from their underlying data in the past, and identifies the new processes and principles which aim to address these issues.

1 Introduction

Data are increasingly being acknowledged as a crucial output of the research process, and as a valuable resource to the community in their own right. Yet often the dataset as an entity lacks the crucial extra information to contextualise it and make it usable by other researchers, as that information is generally only made available through the medium of a journal article (or even grey literature), which may or may not be linked back to the dataset.

Datasets are also difficult to publish in the traditional scientific sense, as their size and complexity makes it difficult to understand them when just presented as pages or tables of numbers. Hence the data that underlies a research publication is often disconnected from the publication itself. However, if the results and conclusions given in a paper are to be verified and confirmed, the data that supports them must be available for examination.

The industrialisation of data production has resulted in some scientific domains where data production is valued and credited, and the mechanisms for archiving, curating and quality controlling the data are well established. Unfortunately, at this time, these Big Data enclaves are the exception rather than the rule, meaning that the majority of data production is done on a dramatically smaller scale. Datasets are created in a bespoke fashion by individual researchers, or small groups, with only one purpose or project in mind. These dataset creators often lack the funding, ability, or motivation to spend the significant amounts of time required to standardise the datasets, document them for other users, and to archive them for the long term, meaning that these datasets may very well be lost to the rest of the scientific community and the scientific record when the project that creates them finishes, or the researcher retires or changes jobs.

This paper outlines a case study of a small research group (of which the author was a part), from the creation of a dataset, through their thoughts and processes in managing, archiving and documenting it, to the final publication of the dataset in a trusted

Ł. Bolikowski et al. (Eds.): TPDL 2013, CCIS 416, pp. 3–9, 2014.
DOI: 10.1007/978-3-319-08425-1_1, © Springer International Publishing Switzerland 2014

data repository and its documentation, complete with peer-review, in a data journal. It highlights the reasons why publications became disconnected from their underlying data in the past, and identifies the new processes and principles which aim to address these issues.

2   The Experiments and Datasets

The Radio Communications Research Unit (RCRU, now the Chilbolton Group), at STFC Rutherford Appleton Laboratory, UK, was investigating the effects of rain, clouds and atmospheric gases on the received signal levels from radio beacons aboard geosynchronous satellites, to determine the best way of counteracting the signal fading experienced by radio frequencies above 10 GHz when a rain storm blocks the path between the satellite transmitter and the receiver in the ground station. To do this, the RCRU installed and operated a number of receivers at different locations in Hampshire, UK. Table 1 gives information about the experiments including their names, their measurement period and their primary publication.

It is important to note the significant delay between the completion of the Italsat experiment and the primary publication from it. This was due to the significant amount of processing that had to be done to the dataset due to the motion of the satellite in its geostationary orbit which caused a diurnal variation of the received signal. Also, the primary work of the staff involved in the Italsat and GBS experiments was to run and manage long term measurement campaigns, meaning that writing up the experiments for publication often was often of a lower priority.

3   Linking the Publications to the Datasets

The Italsat raw and processed data was stored on the RCRU's servers, with a backup on CD on a shelf in the author's office. Ventouras et al. 2006 [1] does not make any statement on data availabilty or location of the raw data. It does publish some of the

Table 1. Key characteristics of the ITALSAT and GBS datasets

Experiment	Italsat	GBS (Global Broadcast Service)
Frequencies studied	49.5, 39.6, and 18.7 GHz	20.7 GHz
Receive sites	Sparsholt (51° 04′ N, 01° 26′ W)	Sparsholt (51° 04′ N, 01° 26′W)
		Chilbolton (51° 08′ N, 01° 26′ W)
		Dundee (56.45811° N, 2.98053° W)
Measurement period start	April 1997	Chilbolton: August 2003
		Sparsholt: October 2003
		Dundee: February 2004
Measurement period end	January 2001	August 2006
Primary publication(s) about the experiment	Ventouras et al. 2006 [1]	Callaghan et al. 2008 [2]
		Callaghan et al. 2013 [3]

derived data in the form of tables and figures of cumulative distribution functions, but there is a crucial disconnect between the paper and the dataset on which it bases its conclusions.

Similarly, for the GBS dataset, the Callaghan et al. 2008 [2] paper does not provide any figures or tables of the processed data, instead only presenting figures showing the curves resulting from the analysis. This paper does have a comment about the location of the underlying data:

The database collected as part of the GBS experiment has been submitted to the International Telecommunications Union (ITU-R) Study Group 3 for inclusion into its databanks.

These databanks are available on-line at [4] but it is not clear where the GBS experiment data can be found within them.

Both Italsat and GBS datasets have now been archived in the British Atmospheric Data Centre (BADC) and have been assigned digital object identifiers (DOIs) to enable formal data citation to occur [5–11]. It is worth noting that the DOIs for the GBS dataset were only assigned in April 2011, and the Italsat data DOIs were assigned in 2012 – a long time after the completion of the datasets and their primary publications.

Figure 1 shows a schematic diagram of the processes involved in the Italsat and GBS experiments, in rough chronological order. Note that for both experiments, a final step (archiving the data, or publication in a data journal) took place some time after the experiment was officially concluded.

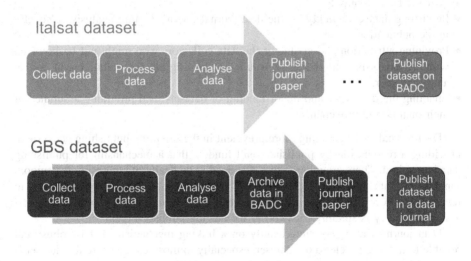

Fig. 1. Comparison of the processes involved in the Italsat and GBS experiments, highlighting the fact that for the Italsat data, archival in the British Atmospheric Data Centre (BADC) took place several years after the dataset's creation, while for the GBS experiment, archiving took place regularly during the experiment.

Both the Italsat and GBS experiments had details project reports written about them which were provided to the funders of the experiments. These reports are are a valuable resource as they are significantly longer and more detailed than the journal publications, but as grey literature access to them is limited. For the GBS experiment the report is marked as "commercial in confidence" and so therefore can't be made public. For Italsat, the documentation has fallen foul of changes in word processing software and key figures in the document can't be viewed on screen. This just goes to show that data curation applies to supporting documentation as much as it does to the datasets themselves!

4   Formal Data Publication and Data Journals

The GBS dataset differs from the Italsat dataset (and many others) in that it has been formally published in a data journal [3]. A data journal is an on-line journal which specialises in the publication of scientific data in a way that includes scientific peer-review. Most data journals publish short data papers cross-linked to, and citing, datasets that have been deposited in approved data centres.

A data paper is a short article which describes a dataset, and provides details of the dataset's collection, processing, software, file formats etc., allowing the reader to understand the when, how and why data was collected and what the data-product is. The data paper does not require novel analyses or ground breaking conclusions, instead the dataset is presented "as-is", allowing the publication of negative results.

Data journals support the development and enchancement of the scholarly record by providing a mechanism for:

- Peer-reviewing datasets.
- Publishing datasets quickly, as the data journal doesn't require analysis or novelty in the publication.
- Providing attribution and credit for the data collectors who might not be involved with the analysis, and therefore would not be eligible for author credit for an analysis paper.
- Enabling the discovery and understanding of datasets, and providing assurance of their quality and provenance.

Data journals are becoming more prevalent in the scientific publishing ecosystem, providing a recognition by publishers and funders that a mechansim for publishing data is required. There are many issues that need to be dealt with to ensure the smooth running of data journals, including (but not limited to) providing guidance to reviewers on how exactly to go about peer-reviewing a dataset, and how to certify that a data repository is suitably trustworthy for hosting published data.

Data journals also rely significantly on a linking mechanism that is robust and reliable to link the article to the dataset, especially in those cases where the dataset is archived in a repository outside of the journal publisher's control. Linking between digital objects is commonplace on the internet, but for the scholarly record to be maintained, the links between articles and datasets must be held to a higher standard of stability and reliability.

5   On the Importance of Data Citation

Thankfully, there is no need to teach researchers a new method of linking between datasets and papers as the current mechanism for linking between papers (citation) is equally as applicable to datasets. The main blocker preventing data citation from becoming standard practice is the simple fact that researchers aren't used to thinking of datasets as things which are citeable. Many international organisations such as DataCite [12], CODATA [13] and the Research Data Alliance [14] are working together to promote data citation as part of the business of doing research. The CODATA Task Group on Data Citation has recently released a report on the current state of practice, policy and technology for data citation, in which it outlines ten first principles for data citation [15].

Citation is just one mechanism for linking data and publications. Journal publishers are increasingly working closer with repository managers to enhance articles by adding links to the underlying data, as well as data repository banner ads, plotting the data on geographical maps, and allowing the reader to click on a graph to download the data that created it (sometimes called "data behind the graph").

The Jisc and NERC funded PREPARDE (Peer REview for Publication & Accreditation of Research Data in the Earth sciences) project has investigated various methods of cross-linking between journal articles and datasets, and a report on the topic will be published soon on the project webpage [16].

6   Conclusions

It is acknowledged that data are increasingly important and valuable, not only for researchers, but also for a far wider range of the population including funders, policy makers and members of the general public.

However, the conclusions and knowledge provided in publications are only as good as the data they're based on, and without access and review of the data it is not possible to reproduce or verify the science. Scientists take great efforts in collecting and analysing the data in their experiments, but due to the lack of reward structures for publishing their data, often fail to manage or archive the dataset appropriately. This was unfortunately common pactice over the past few decades, though this does seem to be changing in a number of disciplines, including the atmospheric sciences.

Data publication is becoming more widespread, though it is acknowledged that there are still issues (both cultural and technological) that need to be overcome [17, 18] to ensure that making data available in a structured and useful way becomes the norm rather than the exception.

This paper provides a short case study describing how experiments were (or were not, in most cases) linked to journal papers in the past decade, and provides an example of how data should be published in the future.

References

1. Ventouras, S., Callaghan, S.A., Wrench, C.L.: Long-term statistics of tropospheric attenuation from the Ka/U band ITALSAT satellite experiment in the United Kingdom. Radio Sci. **41**(2), RS2007 (2006)
2. Callaghan, S.A., Boyes, B., Couchman, A., Waight, J., Walden, C.J., Ventouras, S.: An investigation of site diversity and comparison with ITU-R recommendations. Radio Sci. **43**, RS4010 (2008)
3. Callaghan, S.A., Waight, J., Agnew, J.L., Walden, C.J., Wrench, C.L., Ventouras, S.: The GBS dataset: measurements of satellite site diversity at 20.7 GHz in the UK. Geosci. Data J. (2013). doi:10.1002/gdj3.2
4. http://www.itu.int/ITU-R/index.asp?category=study-groups&rlink=rsg3&lang=en
5. Science and Technology Facilities Council (STFC), Chilbolton Facility for Atmospheric and Radio Research, [Ventouras, S., Callaghan, S.A, Wrench, C.L.] ITALSAT radio propagation measurement at 20 GHz in the United Kingdom. NERC British Atmospheric Data Centre (2012). http://dx.doi.org/10.5285/3158D138-D592-4045-ADE4-B76CF9F42129
6. Science and Technology Facilities Council (STFC), Chilbolton Facility for Atmospheric and Radio Research, [Ventouras, S., Callaghan, S.A, Wrench, C.L.] ITALSAT radio propagation measurement at 40 GHz in the United Kingdom. NERC British Atmospheric Data Centre (2012). http://dx.doi.org/10.5285/4A60EE2F-0FD1-4141-9244-7BEBF240BB49
7. Science and Technology Facilities Council (STFC), Chilbolton Facility for Atmospheric and Radio Research, [Ventouras, S., Callaghan, S.A, Wrench, C.L.] ITALSAT radio propagation measurement at 50 GHz in the United Kingdom. NERC British Atmospheric Data Centre (2012). http://dx.doi.org/10.5285/597C906A-B09E-4822-8B60-3B53EA8FC57F
8. Science and Technology Facilities Council (STFC), Chilbolton Facility for Atmospheric and Radio Research, [Ventouras, S., Callaghan, S.A., Wrench, C.L.] ITALSAT radio propagation measurement at 50 GHz in the United Kingdom (2012)
9. Science and Technology Facilities Council (STFC), Chilbolton Facility for Atmospheric and Radio Research, [Callaghan, S.A., Waight, J., Walden, C.J., Agnew, J., Ventouras, S.] GBS 20.7 GHz slant path radio propagation measurements, Sparsholt site. NERC BADC (2009a). http://dx.doi.org/10.5285/E8F43A51-0198-4323-A926-FE69225D57DD
10. Science and Technology Facilities Council (STFC), Chilbolton Facility for Atmospheric and Radio Research, [Callaghan, S.A., Waight, J., Walden, C.J., Agnew, J., Ventouras, S.] GBS 20.7 GHz slant path radio propagation measurements, Chilbolton site. NERC British Atmospheric Data Centre (2009b). http://dx.doi.org/10.5285/639A3714-BC74-46A6-9026-64931F355E07
11. Science and Technology Facilities Council (STFC), Chilbolton Facility for Atmospheric and Radio Research, [Callaghan, S.A., Waight, J., Walden, C.J., Agnew, J., Ventouras, S] GBS 20.7 GHz slant path radio propagation measurements, Dundee site. NERC British Atmospheric Data Centre (2009c). http://dx.doi.org/10.5285/db8d8981-1a51-4d6e-81c0-cced9b921390
12. DataCite. http://www.datacite.org
13. CODATA: International council for science: committee on data for science and technology. http://www.codata.org
14. Research Data Alliance. https://rd-alliance.org/
15. CODATA-ICSTI Task Group on Data Citation Standards and Practices. Out of cite, out of mind: the current state of practice, policy, and technology for the citation of data. Data Sci. J. **12**, CIDCR1-CIDCR75 (2013). doi:10.2481/dsj.OSOM13-043
16. PREPARDE: Peer REview for Publication & Accreditation of Research Data in the Earth sciences project webpage. http://proj.badc.rl.ac.uk/preparde/wiki

17. Lawrence, B., Jones, C. Matthews, B., Pepler, S., Callaghan, S.A.: Citation and peer review of data: moving towards formal data publication. Int. J. Digit. Curation **6**(2) (2011). http://dx.doi.org/10.2218/ijdc.v6i2.205
18. Parsons, M.A., Fox, P.A.: Is data publication the right metaphor? Data Sci. J. **12**, WDS32-WDS46 (2013). http://dx.doi.org/10.2481/dsj.WDS-042

Towards Facilitating Scientific Publishing and Knowledge Exchange Through Linked Data

Sören Auer[1(✉)], Christoph Lange[2], and Timofey Ermilov[3]

[1] Enterprise Information Systems, University of Bonn and Fraunhofer IAIS,
Bonn, Germany
auer@cs.uni-bonn.de
[2] School of Computer Science, University of Birmingham, Birmingham, UK
math.semantic.web@gmail.com
[3] AKSW Research Group, University of Leipzig, Leipzig, Germany
ermilov@informatik.uni-leipzig.de

Abstract. In this position paper, we describe our vision of an architecture of participation for semantic linking and contextualizing of research articles. We discuss requirements of such an architecture and showcase an early first prototype.

The Linked Data paradigm has recently evolved into a powerful enabler for integrating structured information and data on the Web and within Enterprise intranets. It is based on the RDF data model and de-referenceable URIs, which not only allows for describing resources and linking to them, but also accessing them using the HTTP protocol to retrieve structured information.

Scientific knowledge exchange (cf. Fig. 1) often involves structured information, such as experimental results, collected data, taxonomies or formulas. Data portals can be used to publish data underlying a certain publication. However, even the actual text of scientific publications often contains structured information currently hidden in prose. Examples include (a) claims and supporting evidence for these, (b) related approaches with their advantages and disadvantages, or (c) a taxonomical classification of the approach described in a certain publication. Such information could easily be expressed and represented in a structured way in RDF. Once scientific publications are increasingly represented in a way that preserves the structure of information, related or similar information from different publications can easily be interlinked and integrated. A survey on a certain research area, for example, could then possibly be generated almost automatically, by collecting the taxonomic classifications as well as advantages and disadvantages of various approaches from different structured publications. As a result, scientific knowledge sharing would be improved substantially, since researchers and other stakeholders would be enabled to search and discover research results not only by using keyword search and following citations, but by formulating sophisticated queries such as "List me all Named Entity Recognition approaches published in the last 5 years, together with the corresponding precision and recall they achieve on a certain benchmark corpus". Currently, answering such a

Ł. Bolikowski et al. (Eds.): TPDL 2013, CCIS 416, pp. 10–15, 2014.
DOI: 10.1007/978-3-319-08425-1_2, © Springer International Publishing Switzerland 2014

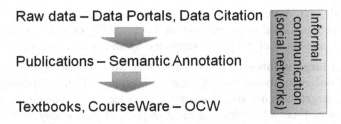

Fig. 1. Different means of scholarly communication.

relatively simple question costs a researcher several weeks or even months of research. Especially for young researchers its currently extremely difficult to navigate through the jungle of research related to their research question.

Although a general solution for this problem is relatively straightforward to realize – researchers could simply publish some RDF Linked Data describing their research along with a paper – the main challenge is to create a network effect through an architecture of participation. This is required, since very few researchers would spend the additional effort of creating a semantic description in addition to a paper if the benefit of doing so would not be immediate. We discuss some requirements, challenges and possible solutions for realizing this vision of truly semantic scientific knowledge exchange.

1 Requirements for Linking and Contextualizing Research Articles

With increasing provision of linked data vocabularies for representing knowledge in specific fields of science[1] but also across science[2], we no longer see the bottleneck on the side of representing and publishing scientific papers as linked open data, but on the side of knowledge acquisition from readers and authors.

For obtaining a critical mass of Linked Data from research papers, we are interested in an approach that is practically feasible, that attracts a large number of users, and that poses a low entry barrier to them.

Practical feasibility means that we do not currently expect a strong natural language processing (NLP) algorithm to fully automatically extract a sufficient RDF graph from

---

[1] For mathematics and all sciences involving mathematical formulas, see, for example, [1]. Pointers to vocabularies for further scientific domains, particularly including biology and medicine, a long-standing stronghold of semantic web applications, can be found in the Linked Open Vocabularies dataset (http://lov.okfn.org/dataset/lov/).

[2] See, for example, the BIBO bibliographical ontology (http://bibliontology.com/), and the SALT ontologies for rhetorical structures and claims [2], and the more recent SPAR family of Semantic Publishing and Referencing ontologies (http://purl.org/spar/), whose Document Components Ontology DoCO reuses the SALT Rhetorical Ontology and whose FaBIO ontology is more expressive while at the same time computationally more efficient than the still widely used BIBO (cf. [3]).

a paper's full text. Instead we rely on the partial application of well-tried NLP techniques such as named entity recognition, but primarily expect users to manually complete the annotation of the paper, supported by an assistive user interface.

Attracting a large number of users means that we have to work with the most widely used document format for scientific publications, which at this point is PDF, and that our target audience should comprise all readers of publications rather than just their writers. From a knowledge acquisition point of view it may be of advantage to tap the author's stream of consciousness by an invasive editing approach, where semantic annotation facilities seamlessly integrate into the author's preferred editor. Invasive editing solutions (cf. the Related Work section below) promise to reduce the author's effort of inserting frequently occurring structures into the document, while at the same time capturing the precise semantics of these structures. However, solutions would have to be as diverse as the editors that authors prefer, and invasive editing does not cover semantics that not the author but the reader of a publication may think of, e.g. related work. Readers rarely have access to the authors' source documents but rather just to PDFs created from them. Where publishers ask for the sources, which most commercial publishers do, they use them internally, e.g. for typesetting, but do not usually make them available. Some open access publishers, such as *arXiv*, publish sources, whereas most sites for sharing publications, e.g. *ResearchGate* or *SlideShare*, do not support all common source formats;[3] as a result, most users upload PDF. Thanks to the wide adoption of Adobe Reader there is not such a diversity of PDF readers as of document editors; however, Adobe's dominance is decreasing, with recent versions of the Chrome and Firefox web browsers providing their own integrated PDF readers and the default PDF readers of Mac OS X and common Unix desktop environments catching up with Adobe Reader in functionality.

Posing a low entry barrier to users means that the user interface for annotation should "invade" the reader's preferred reading interface as seamlessly as possible. Providing an annotation plugin for a PDF reader is more challenging than developing an annotation plugin for a web browser. Adobe Reader offers scripting support similar to web browsers[4], but the problem is that the PDF format is designed for layouting pages. Well-behaved authoring tools can be configured to preserve some of the original structure of a text, e.g. words before hyphenation, but authors and publishers still rarely pay attention to such aspects. However, it is inherently impossible to fully preserve the original text in a PDF. When a paragraph crosses a page break, selecting that paragraph will always include the footer of the first page and the header of the second page, thus making it impossible to precisely annotate the paragraph.

We lack an architecture of participation for linking and contextualizing research articles. In order to realize such an architecture, we need to provide instant benefits for semantic annotations (e.g.: find related work, gain reputation on social networks, visualization, fun) as well as medium and long-term benefits for semantic annotations (e.g. being cited by more authors, or being more visible to funding bodies).

---

[3] ResearchGate and SlideShare only allow single-file uploads, which is suitable for office documents but hardly for LaTeX documents, which usually involve multiple source files.

[4] http://www.adobe.com/devnet/acrobat/javascript.html

2 Example and Prototype

The following example code in RDF/Turtle shows a possible annotation for a paper describing a novel link discovery approach as well as its implementation and evaluation.

```
limes-paper  describes    appr123 , impl123 , eval123 .
appr123      a            Approach ;
             for          Link_Discovery ;
             hasProp      lossless .

impl123      a            Implementation ;
             implements   appr123 ;
             language     Java .

eval123      a            Evaluation ;
             evaluates    impl123 ;
             uses         DBpedia .
```

Figure 2 shows the early prototype of a semantic annotation platform[5], where an article is shown on the left hand side and an annotation panel on the right. When a user selects a certain part of the article (e.g. a named entity, paragraph, table etc.) an annotation can be added on the right, describing what the selected element represents as well as its features. For example, the section describing the implementation can be annotated with features, such as the programming language chosen for the implementation. During the process of adding annotations, existing properties, concepts and entities are suggested to the user for reuse. As a result, annotations are not isolated but reuse existing vocabulary and establish semantic links between annotated papers. An instant benefit for the user is then, for example, the retrieval of similar articles as shown in the lower right corner of Fig. 2.

3 Related Work

Invasive editing in traditional authoring software has, for example, been realised for mathematical and rhetorical structures of knowledge, by semantic macro packages for *LaTeX* [2, 4], and by plugins for PowerPoint [5]. None of these solutions has been adopted widely. Of the three examples given, only sTeX is still being maintained. With HTML5 advancing, lightweight invasive editing solutions have more recently been realised in web interfaces, which have been extended to enrich the HTML document being authored with RDFa annotations. Examples include the RDFa Content Editor RDFaCE [6] and the One Click Annotator [7]. Both are based on Tiny-MCE, an HTML editing component widely used in web content management systems. A similar JavaScript-based architecture could be adopted by a browser plugin for annotating read-only HTML documents published on the Web.

---

[5] The prototype is based on the PDF.js plugin bundled with recent Firefox browsers (https://github.com/mozilla/pdf.js). Source code is available at https://github.com/AKSW/semann.

Fig. 2. Prototype of a semantic annotation platform, with document display (left) annotation panel (upper right) and semantic similarity search (lower right).

4   Conclusions

Exploring new ways of how scientific knowledge can be shared is a very promising area of research and technology. While a number of approaches for semantic annotations and representations of scholarly content exist, an architecture of participation, where researchers are instantly gratified for contributions in the form of small semantic annotations created while reading, is still missing. In this article we presented some requirements as well as an example and first prototype for a semantic annotation platform for research articles.

References

1. Lange, C.: Ontologies and languages for representing mathematical knowledge on the semantic web. Semant. Web J. **4**(2), 119–158 (2013). http://www.semantic-web-journal.net/content/ontologies-and-languages-representing-mathematical-knowledge-semantic-web
2. Groza, T., Möller, K., Handschuh, S., Trif, D., Decker, S.: SALT: weaving the claim web. In: Aberer, K., Choi, K.-S., Noy, N., Allemang, D., Lee, K-Il, Nixon, L., Golbeck, J., Mika, P., Maynard, D., Mizoguchi, R., Schreiber, G., Cudré-Mauroux, P. (eds.) ASWC 2007 and ISWC 2007. LNCS, vol. 4825, pp. 197–210. Springer, Heidelberg (2007)
3. Shotton, D., Peroni, S.: Libraries and linked data #5: using the SPAR ontologies to publish bibliographic records. Semantic Publishing Weblog (2013). http://semanticpublishing.wordpress.com/2013/03/01/lld5-using-spar-ontologies/
4. Kohlhase, A., Kohlhase, M., Lange, C.: sTeX – a system for flexible formalization of linked data. In: I-Semantics. ACM (2010). http://kwarc.info/kohlhase/papers/isem10.pdf
5. Kohlhase, A.: Semantic interaction design: composing knowledge with CPoint. Ph.D. thesis, University of Bremen (2008)
6. Khalili, A., Auer, S., Hladky, D.: The RDFa Content Editor – From WYSIWYG to WYSIWYM. In: Proceedings of COMPSAC 2012 – Trustworthy Software Systems for the Digital Society. IEEE (2012). http://svn.aksw.org/papers/2012/COMPSAC2012_RDFaCE/public.pdf
7. Heese, R., Luczak-Rösch, M., Oldakowski, R., Streibel, O., Paschke, A.: One click annotation. In: Proceedings of the Sixth Workshop on Scripting and Development for the Semantic Web (SFSW), CEUR-WS.org Workshop, vol. 699 (2010). http://ceur-ws.org/Vol-699/Paper4.pdf

Tagging Scientific Publications Using Wikipedia and Natural Language Processing Tools
Comparison on the ArXiv Dataset

Michał Lopuszyński[✉] and Łukasz Bolikowski

Interdisciplinary Centre for Mathematical and Computational Modelling,
University of Warsaw, Pawińskiego 5a, 02-106 Warsaw, Poland
{m.lopuszynski,l.bolikowski}@icm.edu.pl
http://www.icm.edu.pl

Abstract. In this work, we compare two simple methods of tagging scientific publications with labels reflecting their content. As a first source of labels Wikipedia is employed, second label set is constructed from the noun phrases occurring in the analyzed corpus. We examine the statistical properties and the effectiveness of both approaches on the dataset consisting of abstracts from 0.7 million of scientific documents deposited in the ArXiv preprint collection. We believe that obtained tags can be later on applied as useful document features in various machine learning tasks (document similarity, clustering, topic modelling, etc.).

Keywords: Tagging document collections · Natural language processing · Wikipedia

1 Introduction

In this work, we present a study of two methods for contextualizing scientific publications by tagging them with labels reflecting their content. First method is based on Wikipedia and second approach relies on the noun phrases detected by the natural language processing (NLP) tools. The motivation behind this study is threefold.

First, we would like to develop new meaningful features for document content representation, which will go beyond basic bag of words approach. The tags can serve as such features, which later on can be employed for various applications, e.g., determining document similarity, clustering, topic modelling, and other machine learning tasks. After the appropriate filtering and ranking, obtained tags can also be used as keyphrases, summarizing the document.

Our second goal is the comparison of the two approaches to tagging publications with labels reflecting their content. We employed two methods, abbreviated hereafter NP and WIKI. The NP approach relies on the tags' dictionary generated from *noun phrases* detected in analyzed corpus using NLP tools. Similar approaches based on NLP techniques were used, e.g., for keyphrase extraction [1,2]. Conversely, the WIKI method relies on readily available dictionary of

L. Bolikowski et al. (Eds.): TPDL 2013, CCIS 416, pp. 16–27, 2014.
DOI: 10.1007/978-3-319-08425-1_3, © Springer International Publishing Switzerland 2014

meaningful tags coming from filtered Wikipedia entries. Wikipedia was already applied in many studies on conceptualizing and contextualizing document collections. To name just a few recent examples, applications include clustering [3,4], assigning readable labels to the obtained document clusters [5,6], facilitating classification [7], or extracting keywords [8]. However, not much is known about the effectiveness of Wikipedia when it comes to processing scientific texts. Especially, in the case of collections covering broad range of disciplines, there is a lot of domain-specific vocabulary involved, usually beyond the scope of interest of the average Internet user, i.e., Wikipedia reader and author. Example of such a broad collection is the ArXiv preprint repository [9]. Manually creating the "gold standard" dictionary of meaningful tags is a difficult task, as it would require a large team of highly qualified experts from different disciplines. Therefore, we find that it is insightful to compare the results obtained using the WIKI method with the independent competitive NP approach. Interesting questions include the relative effectiveness of the WIKI/NP methods for different fields of science, the average number of tags per document in both methods, the typical tags missed by one of the methods and included in the other, etc. Such a comparison can also show if the methods are complementary or if one is superior than the other.

The third goal of this work is the analysis of statistical properties for obtained tags. We look at distributions of number of different tags per document. We also examine, if the Zipf's law is valid for the rank-frequency curves of labels detected by both methods. It is also interesting to check, if the aforementioned statistical properties are qualitatively similar for the NP and WIKI tags.

The paper is organized as follows. In Sect. 2, the employed datasets are described. Afterwards, in Sect. 3, we provide the details of both tagging procedures — the one based on Wikipedia (WIKI) and the complementary approach based on the noun phrases (NP). Comparison of both methods is the subject of Sect. 4. Statistical properties of the obtained tags are investigated in Sect. 5. The paper is summarized in Sect. 6.

2 Employed Datasets

The ArXiv repository [9] was started in 1991 by a physicist Paul Ginsparg. Originally, it was intended to host documents from the domain of physics. However, later on it gained popularity in other areas. Currently, it hosts entries from physics, mathematics, computer science, quantitative biology, quantitative finance, and statistics. The content is not peer-reviewed, however, many documents are simply preprints, published later on in scientific journals or presented on conferences. In this work, we analyze the ArXiv publications metadata harvested via OAI/PMH protocol up to the end of March 2012. This made up to over 0.7 million of documents. For our study, the distribution of the manuscripts across domains is of high interest. For this purpose, we used <setSpec> field of the ArXiv XML format, which gives a coarse-grained information about the field of document. All the ArXiv coarse-grained categories together with their full-names are presented in Table 1. The percentage of documents in each category

Table 1. The ArXiv categories and their abbreviations.

Abbreviation	Category full name
cs	Computer Science
math	Mathematics
nlin	Nonlinear Sciences
physics-astro-ph	Astrophysics
physics-cond-mat	Condensed Matter Physics
physics-gr-qc	Physics — General Relativity and Quantum Cosmology
physics-hep-ex	High energy Physics — Experiment
physics-hep-lat	High energy Physics — Lattice
physics-hep-ph	High energy Physics — Phenomenology
physics-hep-th	High energy Physics — Theory
physics-math-ph	Mathematical Physics
physics-nucl-ex	Nuclear Physics — Experiment
physics-nucl-th	Nuclear Physics — Theory
physics-quant-ph	Quantum Physics
physics-physics	Physics — Other Fields
q-bio	Quantitative Biology
q-fin	Quantitative Finance
stat	Statistics

is displayed in Fig. 1. The presented values do not add up to 100 % since multiple categories per document are allowed. In this study, we have also employed Wikipedia. We have used raw data available from the Wikipedia dump website, dated 2013.01.02.

3   Processing Methods

Our processing methods consisted of three phases — generating the preliminary dictionary, cleaning the dictionary and tagging. Only the first phase differentiated the two analyzed methods that is, the the approach employing Wikipedia (WIKI) and the procedure making use of the noun phrases (NP).

1. **Generating the preliminary dictionary.** During this stage the preliminary version of the dictionary used later on for labeling was obtained. For the WIKI case, simply all multi-word entries form Wikipedia dump were extracted. For the NP method all the abstract from ArXiv corpus were analyzed using general purpose natural language processing library OpenNLP [10], detecting all the noun phrases containing two or more words. Noun phrases occurring in fewer than 4 documents were excluded from the dictionary.
2. **Cleaning the dictionary.** Clearly, on this level both dictionaries contain a lot of non-informative entries. Therefore, we apply a cleaning procedure to both preliminary tag sets. For each tag we remove initial and final words, if they belong to the set of stopwords. The labels which contain only one word

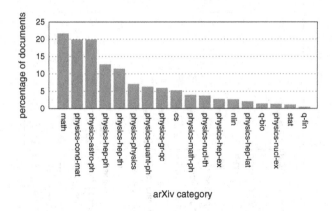

Fig. 1. The percentage of documents marked with various ArXiv categories. Note that, since multiple categories per paper are possible, the sum of the numbers above exceeds 100 %. The labels for categories are explained in Table 1.

after such filtering are removed. Then we use a simple heuristic observation that good label candidates usually do not contain stopword in the middle, see the study [11] for more details. One notable exception here is the word *of*. We drop all entries according to this heuristic rule. Naturally, many far more sophisticated algorithms can be employed here, e.g., matching grammatical pattern devised to select true keywords, which could be employed, when the knowledge about the part-of-speech classification is available [12,13]. However, the simple stopword method worked well enough for us, especially that we are mostly aiming at labels for further applications in machine learning and hence we can afford having certain fraction of "bogus labels". The generated dictionaries after the cleaning procedure contained around 5 million entries for the WIKI method and 0.3 million for the NP case.

3. **Tagging.** Finally we tag the analyzed corpus of ArXiv abstracts with the obtained filtered dictionaries. In the process of tagging, we make use of the Porter stemming [14], to alleviate the problem of different grammatical forms. All abstracts that contain sequence of words that stems to the same roots as label contained in the WIKI/NP dictionary are tagged with it.

4   Comparison of the WIKI and NP Tags Across Domains

As a first step in the comparison of the WIKI and NP methods we calculated the average number of tags per document. This quantity was examined across different disciplines, the results are presented in Fig. 2. The disciplines in Fig. 2 are sorted according to the average result for the WIKI method in ascending order. This allows us to observe that both methods are weakly correlated. In other words, if the WIKI method gives high number of tags for certain category, it does not imply that the NP approach yields high average as well. This observation can be quantified by calculating the correlation coefficient between the

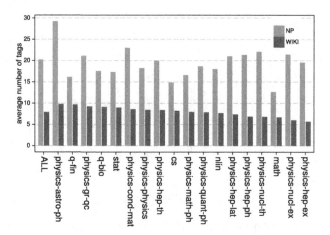

Fig. 2. Average number of tags per article for the WIKI and NP cases separated into ArXiv categories. Note that categories are sorted according to the average number of WIKI tags in the descending order.

average number of the WIKI and NP tags for each category, which indeed turns out to have very low value of $\rho = 0.13$. Another conclusion from Fig. 2 is that clearly the NP method yields higher number of tags across all the domains. The average number of WIKI tags is roughly in the range from 0.3 to 0.6 of the NP result. The exact ratios for all the domains are visualized in Fig. 3. The bar chart is sorted according to the descending ratios. The sequence of disciplines can be, to a certain extent, intuitively understood. The leading categories, such as computer science and quantitative finance, are probably more familiar to the average Internet user than experimental nuclear physics or high-energy physics. Thus the coverage of the WIKI labels is also better in these domains. This indicates that various methods, relying on the knowledge from Wikipedia and verified on the computer science texts (such as, e.g., keyphrases in [8]) can have considerably lower performance when applied to documents from different scientific field.

To further investigate the differences between the two methods we displayed the most frequent tags generated by both methods in Table 2. In addition, we also included the most frequent tags generated uniquely by each method, to be able to better judge the differences. We have performed this analysis for three different ArXiv categories. We have selected cs and math as they have high ratio of the WIKI/NP average number of tags (we have neglected here q-fin since there is very low number of documents from this field, see Fig. 1). We have also included physics-nucl-ex, as it is at the other end of the spectrum, having very low aforementioned ratio of the WIKI/NP average number of tags. There are a couple of interesting observations, which can be made from Table 2. Note that Top WIKI and Top NP categories are identical for cs and math categories, whereas for physics-nucl-ex there are much different. In the latter case, the top four WIKI tags occur also in the NP results, however, the NP adds a lot of additional labels. They are mostly related to various kinds of nuclei collision processes,

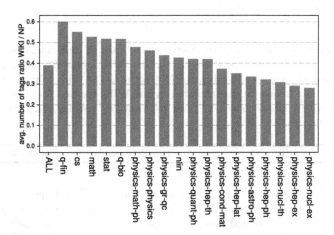

Fig. 3. The ratio of the average number of the WIKI tags to the number of the NP tags for different ArXiv categories. The categories are sorted in the order of ascending ratio.

which apparently are too specific to be described in Wikipedia. Interestingly, the *Au-Au* tag from the WIKI corresponds to the article about one of the on-line auction portals and has nothing to do with gold nuclei. Another interesting property is that the WIKI method is much better at detecting surnames related to various theories, equations, etc. In particular, this is visible for `math` and the WIKI-only category, where four out of ten tags are related to surnames. Clearly, not all of the above tags are perfect. It can be observed that noun-phrases detector sometimes yields the fragments of actual noun phrase, e.g., *hoc network* is a fragment of correct phrase *ad hoc network*, *time algorithm* comes from complexity statements, such as *polynomial time algorithm*, etc. There are also a few tags which do not yield any information, e.g., *et al*, *point of view*, *give rise*, *initial data*, etc. If there is a need, their impact can be reduced by improving the filtering procedure described in Sect. 3.

As a final stage of the analysis we decided to address a question, to what extent the tags generated by the WIKI and NP methods are different? Table 2 suggests that in many categories top rank labels might be similar. Larger deviations may get introduced for the less frequent tags. To examine this phenomenon, we propose the following measures that describes the percentage of unique tags detected by each method up to rank r

$$C_{\mathrm{WIKI}}(r) = \frac{\#(T_{\mathrm{WIKI}}(r) \setminus T_{\mathrm{NP}}(\infty))}{r}, \qquad C_{\mathrm{NP}}(r) = \frac{\#(T_{\mathrm{NP}}(r) \setminus T_{\mathrm{WIKI}}(\infty))}{r}, \qquad (1)$$

where $T_{\mathrm{WIKI}}(r)$ denotes the set of all tags up to rank r assigned by the WIKI method, $T_{\mathrm{WIKI}}(\infty)$ refers to the set of all tags assigned by the WIKI method. The meaning of $T_{\mathrm{NP}}(r)$ and $T_{\mathrm{NP}}(\infty)$ is analogous, but refers to the NP approach. The $C_{\mathrm{WIKI}}(r)$ function describes the percentage of tags up to rank r, obtained from the WIKI method that were not detected by the NP approach (independently of rank). The $C_{\mathrm{NP}}(r)$ has analogous meaning for the NP case. The plots

Table 2. Comparison of the top 10 most frequent tags in four categories. The first column (Top WIKI) denotes labels occurring in the WIKI method. The second column (Top NP) includes results produced by the NP method. The third column (Top WIKI-only) displays most frequent tags generated by the WIKI method, but not by the NP. Finally, the fourth column shows the most frequent NP results, not detected by the WIKI (Top NP-only).

Top WIKI	Top NP	Top WIKI-only	Top NP-only
cs			
lower bound	lower bound	state of art	large scale
upper bound	upper bound	degrees of freedom	interference channel
polynomial time	polynomial time	point of view	time algorithm
et al	et al	object oriented	proposed algorithm
sensor network	sensor network	quality of service	proposed method
logic programming	logic programming	order of magnitude	hoc network
wireless network	wireless network	game theory	considered problem
real time	real time	Reed Solomon	wireless sensor
network coding	network coding	multi agent system	channel state
ad hoc	ad hoc	multi user	capacity region
math			
Lie algebra	Lie algebra	Calabi Yau	give rise
differential equation	differential equation	Navier Stokes	higher order
moduli space	moduli space	point of view	initial data
lower bound	lower bound	non negative	infinitely many
field theory	field theory	Cohen Macaulay	new proof
finite dimensional	finite dimensional	algebraically closed	over field
sufficient condition	sufficient condition	degrees of freedom	value problem
upper bound	upper bound	self dual	large class
Lie group	Lie group	Gromov Witten	time dependence
two dimensional	two dimensional	answered question	mapping class
physics-nucl-ex			
cross section	cross section	equation of state	heavy ion
Au Au	heavy ion	center of mass	Au collisions
heavy ion collision	Au Au	order of magnitude	ion collision
form factor	Au collisions	degrees of freedom	Au Au collision
beta decay	ion collision	ultra relativistic	transversal momentum
elliptic flow	Au Au collision	Drell Yan	200 GeV
high energies	heavy ion collision	time of flight	relativistic heavy
experimental data	transversal momentum	presented first	relativistic heavy ions
charged particle	200 GeV	long lived	low energies
nuclear matter	form factor	national laboratory	Pb Pb

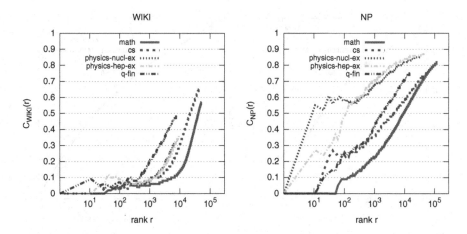

Fig. 4. The dependence of C_{WIKI} (left panel) and C_{NP} (right panel) on rank r, i.e., the percentage of tags up to rank r for the WIKI/NP method that were not detected by the other approach. Only a few sample categories were selected, including edge cases with the fastest and the slowest growing dependencies. See Eq. (1) and the main text for details.

of the above quantities for a few sample ArXiv categories are presented in Fig. 4. We have selected the categories in a way that the edge cases of the fastest and the slowest growing dependencies are included. The figures clearly show that for the WIKI case the percentage of the unique tags is low, i.e. around 10 %, up to relatively high ranks, mostly $\sim 10^3$–10^4. This confirms the intuition that the relevant WIKI tags are indeed in majority noun phrases. On the other hand, the curves for the NP case show a different behaviour, the percentage of the unique tags grows much faster in this case, indicating that they might yield much richer information. The 10 % level of unique tags is exceeded for the ranks lower than 10^2 for the most categories. However, to give the definitive statement about the quality of the above tags, the domain experts should be consulted.

5   Statistical Properties of the WIKI and NP Tags

Tags can be expected to have similar statistical properties as ordinary words. One of the universal properties observed for words is the so-called Zipf's law, which states that the word frequency f as a function of its rank r in the frequency table should exhibit power-law behaviour

$$f(r; A, N) = A\, r^{-N}, \tag{2}$$

where A and N are parameters. This type of simple dependency was observed not only for words, but also keyphrases, e.g., in the PNAS Journal bibliographic dataset [15]. However, the detailed investigation reveals that for large corpora, in particular when many different authors and hence different styles are involved,

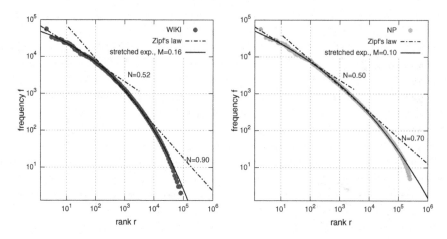

Fig. 5. Comparison of the frequency dependence on rank observed for tags obtained from both approaches — the WIKI (left panel) and the NP (right panel). The models fitted to the observed distributions are Zipf's law, see Eq. (2), and stretched exponential model, see Eq. (3).

the simple model (2) might be insufficient to describe the frequency-rank dependence throughout the whole r variability range [16]. Sometimes a few curves of the type (2) are necessary in order to accurately describe the observed distribution throughout the whole rank domain.

In the case of our tags, the observed rank-frequency dependencies are presented in Fig. 5. In both cases (WIKI and NP), the crude approximation for the observed data was obtained using a combination of two Zipf type curves for different rank regimes. It turned out that up to rank 100, the values of exponent N were very similar in both cases and approximately equal to 0.5. However, for larger values the WIKI case showed more rapid decay with $N = 0.95$, as opposed to $N = 0.73$ in the NP case. Nevertheless, it is easily observed that a simple combination of the Zipf type curves does not fit the data very well. It turns out that the observed rank-frequency dependencies are much better approximated by one of the alternatives to the power-law (2), namely the stretched exponential distribution. This type of distribution is used to describe large variety of phenomena from physics to finance [17]. It was observed, e.g., for rank distributions of radio/light emission intensities from galaxies, French and US agglomeration sizes, daily Forex US-Mark price variation, etc. The stretched exponential model yields the following dependence of frequency on rank

$$f(r; C, D, M) = C \exp\left(-D\, r^M\right),\tag{3}$$

with C, D, and M being parameters. As can be observed in Fig. 5, this model fits the data much better. Similarly to the Zipf's law, the value of the exponent for the NP case, which reads $M = 0.12$, is lower than for the WIKI, where $M = 0.19$. This indicates slower decay and "fatter tail" for the NP tags case.

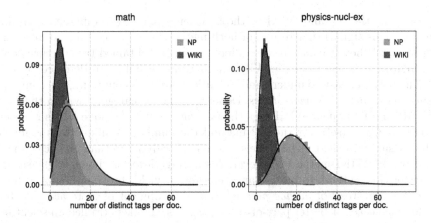

Fig. 6. Distribution for the number of tags per document within two sample ArXiv categories `math` (left panel) and `physics-nucl-ex` (right panel). The distribution can be well approximated by the negative binomial distribution, see Eq. (4). The black line represents the fits of this model to the observed data.

Another interesting statistical property of the generated tags is the distribution for number of distinct labels per document. It turns out that, even though the average tag counts per document are quite different for the WIKI and NP methods (see Sect. 4), the distributions in both cases come from the same family. Observed histograms can be approximated with the negative binomial distribution. According to this model, the probability of finding document with k tags reads

$$\text{Prob}(k; P, R) = \binom{k + R - 1}{k} P^R (1 - P)^k, \tag{4}$$

where $R > 0$ and $P \in (0, 1)$ are the parameters of the distribution. The comparison of the above model with the observed histograms can be found in Fig. 6.

6   Summary and Outlook

In this paper, we have compared two methods of tagging scientific publications. First, abbreviated WIKI, was based on the multi-word entries from Wikipedia. Second, referenced as NP, relied on the multi-word noun phrases detected by the NLP tools. We have focused on the effectiveness of each method across domains and on the statistical properties of the obtained labels.

When it comes to the effectiveness of the above methods, it turned out that the NP approach yields higher average number of tags per document. The difference is by a factor between two and three with respect to the WIKI case. This strongly depends on domain. The WIKI tags coverage is better in the areas more relevant to the Internet community, such as computer science or quantitative finance than in more exotic domains such as nuclear experimental physics. In addition, there is almost no correlation between the average number of labels generated by the NP and WIKI methods, when separated to different scientific domains. This signals that results of both methods are to a certain extent complementary. When it comes to the differences in the obtained tags, it turns out that high-rank labels from the WIKI method are usually also detected by the NP. The notable, easy to understand exceptions are tags containing the complex of surnames, such as *Navier-Stokes*. Depending on the category, within the first $10^3 - 10^4$ most frequent WIKI tags the percentage of the unique labels is lower than 10 %. Conversely, for the NP method the number of unique tags is much higher. Usually in the top 100 labels, there is already more than 10 % cases not found by the WIKI method. However, the average level of "bogus tags" seems higher for this method. In particular, sometimes it yields broken phrases such as *hoc network* instead of *ad hoc network*. The development of more accurate filters for such cases or better part-of-speech taggers/chunkers trained on scientific corpora could improve the method.

As far as the statistical properties are concerned, it turned out that both the WIKI and NP methods exhibit qualitatively very similar behaviour. The dependence of the tag frequency on the tag rank can be approximated by the Zipf's law, however, only in the limited rank range. To be able to cover the whole rank domain the so-called stretched exponential model has to be employed. It constitutes a good fit for both the WIKI and NP. Obtained curve parameters indicate much slower decay ("fatter tail") for the NP method. The investigation of the distribution for the number of tags per document revealed that in both the WIKI and NP cases it follows quite closely the negative-binomial model.

Overall, in our opinion, both the WIKI and NP methods seem useful, and to a certain extent complementary. In future we plan to apply the generated tags as features, extending the simple bag of words document representation, in various types of machine learning tasks (document similarity, clustering, etc.). Verifying the performance on such tasks will enable for more definite statement on the usefulness of both methods.

Acknowledgement. This research was carried out with the support of the "HPC Infrastructure for Grand Challenges of Science and Engineering (POWIEW)" Project, co-financed by the European Regional Development Fund under the Innovative Economy Operational Programme.

References

1. Barker, K., Cornacchia, N.: Using noun phrase heads to extract document keyphrases. In: Hamilton, H.J. (ed.) Canadian AI 2000. LNCS (LNAI), vol. 1822, pp. 40–52. Springer, Heidelberg (2000)
2. Hulth, A.: Improved automatic keyword extraction given more linguistic knowledge. In: Proceedings of the 2003 Conference on Empirical Methods in Natural Language Processing, EMNLP '03, p. 216. Association for Computational Linguistics, Stroudsburg (2003)

3. Spanakis, G., Siolas, G., Stafylopatis, A.: Exploiting Wikipedia knowledge for conceptual hierarchical clustering of documents. Comput. J. **55**(3), 299 (2012)
4. Spanakis, G., Siolas, G., Stafylopatis, A.: DoSO: a document self-organizer. J. Intell. Inf. Syst. **39**(3), 577 (2012)
5. Nomoto, T.: WikiLabel: an encyclopedic approach to labeling documents en masse. In: Proceedings of the 20th ACM International Conference on Information and Knowledge Management, CIKM '11, p. 2341. ACM, New York (2011)
6. Nomoto, T., Kando, N.: Conceptualizing documents with Wikipedia. In: Proceedings of the Fifth Workshop on Exploiting Semantic Annotations in Information Retrieval, ESAIR '12, p. 11. ACM, New York (2012)
7. Wang, P., Hu, J., Zeng, H.J., Chen, Z.: Using Wikipedia knowledge to improve text classification. Knowl. Inf. Syst. **19**(3), 265 (2009)
8. Joorabchi, A., Mahdi, A.E.: Automatic keyphrase annotation of scientific documents using Wikipedia and genetic algorithms. J. Inf. Sci. **39**(3), 410 (2013)
9. arXiv preprint server. http://arxiv.org
10. Apache OpenNLP. http://opennlp.apache.org
11. Rose, S., Engel, D., Cramer, N., Cowley, W.: Automatic Keyword Extraction from Individual Documents, p. 1. Wiley, New York (2010)
12. Justeson, J.S., Katz, S.M.: Technical terminology: some linguistic properties and an algorithm for identification in text. Nat. Lang. Eng. **1**(01), 9 (1995)
13. Agrawal, R., Gollapudi, S., Kannan, A., Kenthapadi, K.: Data mining for improving textbooks. SIGKDD Explor. Newsl. **13**(2), 7 (2012)
14. Porter, M.: An algorithm for suffix stripping. Program: Electron. Libr. Inf. Syst. **14**(3), 130 (1980)
15. Zhang, Z.K., Lü, L., Liu, J.G., Zhou, T.: Empirical analysis on a keyword-based semantic system. Eur. Phys. J. B **66**(4), 557 (2008)
16. Montemurro, M.A.: Beyond the Zipf-Mandelbrot law in quantitative linguistics. Physica A **300**(3–4), 567 (2001)
17. Laherrère, J., Sornette, D.: Stretched exponential distributions in nature and economy: "fat tails" with characteristic scales. Eur. Phys. J. B **2**(4), 525 (1998)

Understanding Climate Data Through Commentary Metadata: The CHARMe Project

Jon D. Blower[1,3]($\boxtimes$), Raquel Alegre[1,3], Victoria L. Bennett[2,3],
Debbie J. Clifford[1,3], Philip J. Kershaw[2,3], Bryan N. Lawrence[1,2,4],
Jane P. Lewis[1,3], Kevin Marsh[2,3,4], Maurizio Nagni[2], Alan O'Neill[1,3],
and Rhona A. Phipps[1,3]

[1] Department of Meteorology, University of Reading, Reading, UK
[2] STFC Centre for Environmental Data Archival,
Rutherford Appleton Laboratory, Didcot, UK
[3] National Centre for Earth Observation, Reading, UK
[4] National Centre for Atmospheric Science, Reading, UK
j.d.blower@reading.ac.uk

Abstract. We describe the CHARMe project, which aims to link climate datasets with publications, user feedback and other items of "commentary metadata". The system will help users learn from previous community experience and select datasets that best suit their needs, as well as providing direct traceability between conclusions and the data that supported them. The project applies the principles of Linked Data and adopts the Open Annotation standard to record and publish commentary information. CHARMe contributes to the emerging landscape of "climate services", which will provide climate data and information to influence policy and decision-making. Although the project focuses on climate science, the technologies and concepts are very general and could be applied to other fields.

Keywords: Climate data · Climate services · Open annotation · Linked data · Semantic web · Metadata

1 Introduction and Motivation

Accurate, long-term monitoring of the Earth is of vital importance for gathering information about our climate. This information, in turn, forms an important part of the evidence base for operational and policy decisions that have far-reaching effects on society. Climate data are used by both the public and private sectors for applications such as controlling greenhouse gas emissions, energy production, food security and flood prediction [1].

Climate data come from various sources and encompass many types of physical, chemical and biological variables. Networks of *in situ* sensors have been used in climate studies for over 75 years and provide (generally) highly-accurate measurements at a limited set of points in space and time. In the past few decades,

L. Bolikowski et al. (Eds.): TPDL 2013, CCIS 416, pp. 28–39, 2014.
DOI: 10.1007/978-3-319-08425-1_4, © Springer International Publishing Switzerland 2014

the importance of space-based measurements from satellites (i.e. *Earth Observation*) has increased. Satellites provide measurements of a highly diverse range of variables, with the key advantage that measurements can be produced at a range of spatial scales (local, regional and global). Further information about our climate comes from numerical simulations, which capture (as best we can) our knowledge of fundamental physical, chemical and biological processes in order to make predictions of the future. These different systems have complementary strengths and weaknesses, therefore many problems in modern environmental science (including weather forecasting for example) are tackled by combining multiple sources of information.

Users of climate data are highly diverse, ranging from research scientists (for example, searching for signals of long-term climate change) through government policy-makers (for example, setting caps on carbon dioxide emissions) to operational decision-makers (for example, planning construction of flood defences). All these users require access to expert knowledge to help them to decide which climate datasets to use in their studies and to understand the fitness for purpose of those datasets for their problem.

The climate science community has made great strides in the past decade in providing high-quality metadata to help users to discover and use climate data (e.g. [2]). Most of this metadata encompasses information about the *intrinsic* characteristics of datasets (e.g. spatial and temporal resolution and coverage), although increasingly information is being released also about dataset provenance (i.e. the processes that led to the production of the dataset). One important aspect that is currently very little addressed is the systematic publication of information about how a dataset has been used by the community. This information is useful for several reasons, including:

1. Usage information helps new users to select between apparently similar datasets to choose the best dataset for their purpose, in a similar manner to the use of reviews on a shopping or travel website.
2. It increases the probability that vital results and lessons concerning the strengths and weaknesses of datasets are retained by the community, helping to avoid reinvention and the loss of information that is caused when results are not formally published (or are published in locations that are obscure to the user in question).
3. It provides another view of *data quality* (in the sense of "fitness for purpose") to complement other quality information that should be reported by the data provider (such as accuracy, uncertainty and metrological traceability).
4. It increases the traceability of conclusions back to their source data and the reproducibility of results (e.g. the draft 3rd US National Climate Assessment [3], refers to the importance of the "line of sight between conclusions and data").
5. It provides a new route to data discovery, particularly where users record information about how datasets relate to each other.
6. It provides valuable feedback to data providers, as it helps them to improve their data and report back to their own funding agencies.

Publication of such usage information is currently difficult, primarily because the metadata/information paradigm around environmental data is mostly provider focused, and where third party (user) information exists, it is not easily discoverable alongside the original data. Here we describe the "CHARacterization of Metadata to enable high-quality climate applications and services"(CHARMe) project, which aims to provide mechanisms to address this problem, applied to some specific problems in earth observation.

In the remainder of the paper, we first introduce an information paradigm for discussing metadata and the concept of "commentary metadata". We then describe the CHARMe project itself, the expected users and their requirements in the context of our information paradigm, before introducing the CHARMe technical approach. The paper concludes with a summary and brief discussion of future work.

2   Commentary Metadata and CHARMe

2.1   A Short Introduction to Metadata

Lawrence et al. [4] provide a taxonomy of different kinds of metadata employed in data infrastructures:

- Archive (A) metadata encompasses precise descriptions of information such as spatial and temporal referencing at the level of individual samples. A-metadata is required to actually use the data in calculations.
- Browse (B) metadata supports understanding the context of data (including provenance) and choosing between similar datasets, and generally conforms to some community standard metadata semantics.
- Commentary (C) metadata includes citations of the data and post-fact assertions about quality. In their original taxonomy, Lawrence et al. use the term "Character" metadata in their paper, but we feel that the word "Commentary" is more helpful here, particularly since we expand the scope of C-metadata to go well beyond those envisaged in the original taxonomy.
- Discovery (D) metadata is typically harvested into catalogues, encompassing summary information about dataset contents and overal spatial-temporal extent.
- Extra (E) metadata is highly discipline-specific (e.g. highly structured descriptions of sensors or documents describing experimental protocols).

The boundaries between these types are not completely sharp, but, in general, Archive, Browse and Discovery and Extra metadata are intrinsic to the dataset and hence known to the data provider *a priori*. Commentary metadata (hereafter referred to as "C-metadata") are normally produced *after* the dataset has been published and reflects real use in the community. C-metadata will typically therefore be closely allied with the particular application to which the dataset has been put, and is therefore *extrinsic* to the dataset itself.

Examples of C-metadata include peer-reviewed publications, technical reports, third-party quality assessments and error characterizations, together with more informal material such as websites, blog entries and ad-hoc comments. These kinds of C-metadata are the focus of this paper. However, we know from interactions with users that other kinds of information, which might formally be thought of as B- or E-metadata (such as properties of data distribution or service interface descriptions), are often made available by third parties. So here we include within our definition of C-metadata, intrinsic data properties which typically have not yet been published by the data providers alongside their data. (Such metadata might even be published by third parties, but it might even initially be published using the C-metadata formalism by the data providers themselves, before formal ingestion into their B- or E-metadata systems). Additional important categories of information include relevant events such as large volcanic eruptions and instrument failure logs. Although many of these are not discussed in detail in this paper they will nevertheless be addressed in the CHARMe project (see Sect. 5).

One way of thinking about these metadata categories is that the intrinsic metadata (A, B and E) form part of a provider data infrastructure, and C-metadata effectively describes the wider extended information ecosystem around data objects. A, B and E are generally managed, C evolves.

The importance of all such metadata is well understood — being ranked as important as instrinsic data quality [5]. However, it's also known that acquiring quality metadata is difficult, for example: "It's fine to say that scientists should record and preserve all this information, but it is far too laborious and expensive to document everything. The scientist wants to do science, not be a clerk" [6]. One method of addressing this is to introduce systems which reward quality metadata production, such as data publication (e.g. [7]), another is to make it easier to establish and use an information ecosystem (e.g. [8]). We think that both approaches are important, but here we concentrate on supporting such an information ecosystem, built around the concept of commentary metadata. However, we note that from a user perspective these notions of distinguishability between data infrastructure, external ecosystems and data publication, should be lost in a broad spectrum of information tools with which they interact.

2.2 The CHARMe Project

Although the notion of C-metadata is quite general and could be applied in any scientific discipline, the purpose of the CHARMe project is to apply the concept specifically to the use of satellite-derived climate data. The CHARMe project aims to connect users, and prospective users, of climate datasets with the previous expertise that has accumulated in the community, and enable them to contribute back information on their own experiences (Fig. 1).

The main objectives are:

1. To develop an open-source system for recording "Commentary metadata" that links with climate datasets and other sources of information such as descriptions of sensors and instruments.
2. To provide interfaces for Commentary metadata to be entered, queried and displayed through existing community websites and machine-readable interfaces (Sect. 4).

3. To identify, and engage with, key strategic stakeholders (including climate data users, producers and high-level global initiatives) to ensure that the CHARMe concept is understood and supported by providers and users of climate data.
4. To develop tools that demonstrate other ways in which Commentary metadata can be produced and exploited in a variety of scenarios (Sect. 5).

The CHARMe project operates in a wider context of the development of "Climate Services". Climate Services are conceived to be activities that produce climate-related information for policy-makers and decision-makers, in order to benefit society. Satellite-derived information will form an important component of future climate services, and it is recognized that there is a need for satellite data to be curated and shared in a systematic manner [9]. Figure 2 sketches a logical view of the transformations from remote sensing measurements to decisions. Data will be processed and re-processed multiple times, leading to a complex landscape of interrelated datasets, which require strong expertise (and good quality metadata) to interpret correctly. The Global Climate Observing System (GCOS) has published guidelines for data producers [10], to ensure good quality documentation for climate records, including a recommendation for data providers to provide a user feedback facility (guideline 10).

In the context of global climate services, therefore, CHARMe aims to help record, retain and disseminate community experience with interpreting climate data, and provide a means for feeding back this experience to the data providers.

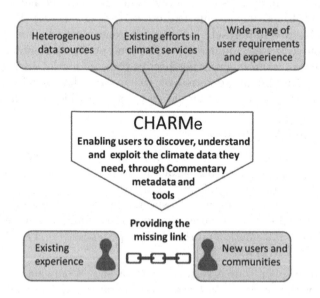

Fig. 1. Overview of the aims of the CHARMe project.

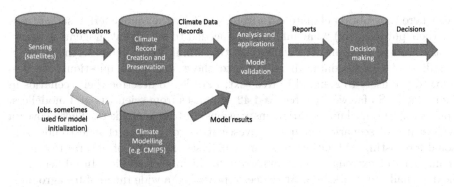

Fig. 2. The main components of a logical architecture for climate services, adapted from Dowell et al. (2013) [9]. We have added an extra activity to Dowell et al.'s diagram to encompass numerical modelling activities. Such models sometimes use satellite observations to set up their initial state. Analysts intercompare results from different models (e.g. in the Coupled Model Intercomparison Projects) and validate results, where possible, against observations. Both models and observations feed into reports (such as the IPCC Assessment Reports) that are used in decision-making and policy-making.

3   Users and Requirements

3.1   Who are the Users?

The CHARMe project has considered the needs of several kinds of end-user stakeholder, including scientists/researchers, commercial users and policy-makers. (In addition the project considers other kinds of stakeholder including data providers, auditors, quality assurance professionals and system administrators, although these are not discussed in detail in this paper.)

Although a key aim of CHARMe is to provide information that influences policy-making, Fig. 2 above shows that policy-makers will probably not usually be *direct* users of the CHARMe system. Instead, groups of analysts and scientists will use Climate Data Records directly, producing reports, digests and assessments for the policy-makers. CHARMe is therefore seeking to interact most closely with analysts (in academia, private consultancies, humanitarian institutions, government departments and elsewhere) who are tasked with the production of information for informing policy-making. The goal of CHARMe is to help these people select and use the best information available to them, and to provide guidance on interpreting the data correctly.

3.2   What do they Need?

CHARMe has performed an initial stage of requirements-gathering in order to inform the general technical approach described in Sect. 4 below. A full discussion of this process is beyond the scope of this paper, but a summary is presented here. We engaged a variety of users to assess (i) what they use climate data for,

(ii) where they obtain climate data from, (iii) how they judge a dataset's fitness for their purpose, (iv) what information needed to make that judgement is currently hard to find, and (v) what tools they think would increase their understanding of climate data. In addition to these structured questions, we also allowed the users to respond in free text, in order to describe their scenarios in more detail. So far we have received 42 responses from scientists and modellers, commercial users, humanitarian institutions and policy-makers. These cover a wide range of scenarios including investigations of climate change trends, seasonal forecasting, validation of ocean reanalyses, mapping of natural resources, monitoring of extreme events and agricultural impact studies. In addition, we held a small user workshop. Attendees represented a wide range of backgrounds, including academic researchers, Earth Observation consultants in industry, government agencies (including the UK Space Agency) and providers of meteorological services. These potential users and CHARMe consortium participants exchanged ideas through brainstorming sessions, resulting in some new ideas and requirements, discussed below. Additional user workshops will be held in future stages of the project to better assess CHARMe's focus.

The main findings from these interactions were:

1. C-metadata is important and a currently-unmet need. However, users require all the other kinds of metadata too (see Sect. 2.1) and so the metadata should be presented in an integrated fashion.
2. There was a great deal of commonality in the types of C-metadata that were requested. The most important of these were publications, including both peer-reviewed publications and other items such as technical reports (these can be currently hard to find because they are not usually systematically catalogued and lack a dedicated search engine). Other important items were user feedback, software support, assessments of errors and quality, maturity indices (e.g. [11]) and traceability information.
3. The need for high quality of the commentary itself, which includes such concerns as editing, de-duplication and, crucially, moderation. Users are concerned that other users could, maliciously or unintentionally, severely compromise the adoption of a dataset by making unfair or inaccurate comments. Thus, we have incorporated requirements on registration and authentication.
4. Other suggestions included a tool for "subscribing" to comments about a dataset (so that new information is automatically sent to the user) and supporting discussions (i.e. making comments on comments).

A feature that was frequently requested by users is to have a "quality stamp" that highlights the "best" dataset out of a choice of several. After careful consideration, we have rejected this requirement as out of scope for CHARMe as we believe that the choice of the "best" dataset is a highly subjective one that depends strongly on the application. Other groups have reached similar conclusions: for example, current developments to establish a "GEO Label" do not focus on the subjective quality of the dataset itself, but an objective summary of the presence or absence of key metadata items [12]. CHARMe may follow a similar path.

4   Technical Approach

4.1   Data Models for C-Metadata

As discussed in Sect. 2.1, C-metadata is different from other kinds of metadata. It is driven primarily by users of data (not producers), it can accumulate and change rapidly and it is highly diverse in nature, linking together information from many different sources. This presents several challenges when trying to apply traditional standards-based data models (e.g. ISO and OGC) and traditional model-driven development approaches, since the field is too immature and dynamic to enable the robust definition of a fixed data model *a priori* that can be sustained.

We plan to follow an iterative development methodology and we therefore sought a flexible, overarching data model that encompasses the general notion of commentary, permitting further sophistication to be added gradually as our developments and experiments progress. The recently-published Open Annotation (OA) standard from the World Wide Web Consortium (W3C) provides us with a very attractive solution, since the concept of an "annotation" is very similar to our notion of commentary metadata. OA is based on Linked Data principles and defines a simple and general data model, based on the Resource Description Framework (RDF) for recording annotations about objects. An annotation associates a piece of information (the *body*) with a subject (the *target*). This maps directly to CHARMe requirements: a target could be a dataset and an annotation body some user comment about that dataset, or a reference to a publication. OA supports the concept of a *motivation* for an annotation. This is a controlled list of terms, including *linking, describing, bookmarking* and *questioning*. These terms, together with terms from other vocabularies such as CiTO [13] can provide valuable semantic information that describes more precisely the relationship between publications and datasets (see Fig. 3).

Deliberately, no types are set for the target or body: users of OA can import terms from other vocabularies and ontologies to record types of interest. This enables the body of one annotation to be the target of another allowing for example, the creation of a chain of annotations in the manner of an online discussion forum. Annotations can contain multiple targets and bodies, enabling, for example, the linking of a publication to more than one dataset, a key CHARMe requirement.

As with all approaches based on Linked Data principles, the use of globally-unique and persistent identifiers is extremely important. A system for identifying formal peer-reviewed publications (using Digital Object Identifiers, DOIs) is now well-established, and the use of DOIs in identifying datasets is becoming more established. Web references (e.g. URLs to websites and blog entries) can be used, although they provide no guarantee of persistence.

We may compare this general and flexible approach with the more prescribed approach taken by the user feedback model of the GeoViQua system [14], which also aims to record information about dataset usage. In GeoViQua, the key class is a *FeedbackItem*, which defines a fixed set of fields that encompass user

```
@prefix oa:       <http://www.openannotation.org/spec/core/> .
@prefix dctypes: <http://purl.org/dc/dcmitype/> .
@prefix cito:     <http://purl.org/spar/cito/> .

<anno1> a oa:Annotation ;
    oa:hasBody      <citation> ;
    oa:hasTarget    <http://dataprovider.org/datasets/sst> ;
    oa:motivatedBy oa:linking .

<citation> a cito:CitationAct ;
    cito:hasCitingEntity  <http://dx.doi.org/12345.678910> ;
    cito:hasCitationEvent cito:citesAsDataSource ;
    cito:hasCitedEntity   <http://dataprovider.org/datasets/sst> .

<http://dx.doi.org/12345.678910> a dctypes:Document .
<http://dataprovider.org/datasets/sst> a dctypes:Dataset .
```

Fig. 3. Example of modelling the link between a publication and a dataset using the Open Annotation (OA) data model together with the CiTO ontology [13]. The citation records that the dataset was cited as a data source within the publication in question; other CiTO terms could be used to record different relationships, for example that the publication *describes* the dataset. The example could be extended to associate the publication with multiple datasets, perhaps with different types of relationship for each link.

comments, citations and the identity of the commenter. This approach has the advantage that feedback items have a consistent and structured form that can be entered and queried in a defined manner. However, if a user of the schema wishes to add new fields or employ different semantics (for example, to record a publication that references several datasets in different ways) this cannot easily be done without defining a new information class. By contrast, the OA approach allows users to express their intent however they wish, but querying and aggregating annotations becomes more difficult, unless there is wide agreement upon the use of particular structures and terms (this is a general challenge of Linked Data and the Semantic Web). Therefore, although OA provides a useful "top level" data model, CHARMe will need to develop more structured data models to encode the bodies of annotations, to enable querying and comparison.

The two approaches are not mutually exclusive and can be at least partly compatible and complementary. It is possible to express a GeoViQua Feedback-Item using the OA model, although the converse is more difficult because the OA model is more general. Practical experience will yield more information about their relative strengths and weaknesses.

4.2   Architecture of a CHARMe Node

A conventional client-server architectural pattern is envisaged for CHARMe with C-metadata stored in a repository served over web service interfaces to expose it to various client applications enabling them to search, add to, modify and delete metadata entries. Access control will need to be implemented for the latter three operations in order for comments to be attributable to their creators, and to ensure that modification and moderation are controlled.

Support for multiple "CHARMe nodes" (i.e. instances of the repository and services) is envisaged. This will enable individual organisations to host their own service instances. These could be linked in a federated model such that metadata can be shared or replicated between a number of trusted nodes. Alternatively some organisations may wish to host their own private node within an intranet.

The web service interfaces are envisaged to expose both SPARQL and RESTful query models (Fig. 4). Setting a standard interface to clients will make it possible to easily interchange the implementation of the persistence layer. Apache Jena has been used for initial tests. This uses the combination of a triple store for storing RDF together with Apache Lucene or Solr to create an index for free text search.

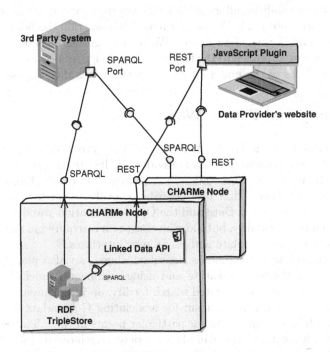

Fig. 4. Outline architecture of a CHARMe node. Annotations are stored in a triple-store, exposed through a SPARQL interface for querying. Using a translation layer (e.g. the Linked Data API, https://code.google.com/p/linked-data-api/) a RESTful interface is also provided, which provides a more convenient querying interface for many types of client.

4.3 User Interface

A strong user requirement is the need to draw the various pieces of metadata about a given dataset together into one place, whether they come from the original data provider or the CHARMe system. We also wish to ensure that C-metadata is available in the locations from which users already obtain climate data. Therefore, instead of creating a new web portal, we plan to develop plugins for existing data-access portals (see Fig. 4). This follows the approach of the Metafor project's metadata viewer (http://metaforclimate.eu), which uses a JavaScript plugin to inject new metadata into existing websites that serve data from climate simulations. There are some practical concerns with this approach (including security), which are beyond the scope of this paper but will be carefully considered in the CHARMe project.

Irrespective of the technology approach, the design of the user interface presents a strong challenge. The Open Annotation data model allows flexibility at the level of the database of C-metadata, but the user interfaces must collapse all the abstract possibilities afforded by RDF into particular concrete structures (menu items, forms etc.). This is another reason to constrain the bodies of annotations into a more formal data model. We plan to mitigate these concerns by adopting a modular approach to the user interface design and by closely coupling individual interfaces to the underlying C-metadata types they expose.

5 Summary and Future Work

We have described the motivation behind, and early progress of, the CHARMe project, which aims to assist users and providers of climate data by sharing experience through "commentary metadata". A primary use case is linking climate datasets with publications that use, describe or evaluate them. Our proposed approach, centred on Linked Data and the Open Annotation standard, will give flexibility and interoperability, but more investigation is required in certain areas, chiefly the design of appropriate and useful user interfaces.

In addition to the developments described above, we also plan to explore more advanced methods for creating and using commentary metadata. These include the development of a faceted search facility, an intercomparison tool for data and metadata and a mechanism for associating C-metadata with *subsets* of datasets, such as spatial regions or particular points in time. This will enable "fine-grained commentary" and will allow users to correlate "significant events" (such as volcanic eruptions or satellite instrument failures) with features in the datasets.

Although the CHARMe project focuses on climate science, the approach is very general and could be applied readily to other fields.

Acknowledgements. This research has received funding from the European Union Seventh Framework Programme (FP7/2007–2013) under grant agreement number 312641. The authors are very grateful to all the other members of the CHARMe consortium (http://www.charme.org.uk), and the project's advisory board, for all input and discussions. We thank two anonymous reviewers for helpful comments.

References

1. Core Writing Team, Pachauri, R.K., Reisinger, A.: IPCC, 2007: Climate change 2007: Synthesis report. Contribution of working groups I, II and III to the fourth assessment report of the intergovernmental panel on climate change. Technical report, Geneva, Switzerland (2008)
2. Lawrence, B.N., Balaji, V., Bentley, P., Callaghan, S., DeLuca, C., Denvil, S., Devine, G., Elkington, M., Ford, R.W., Guilyardi, E.: Describing earth system simulations with the metafor CIM. Geoscientific Model Dev. **5**, 1669–1689 (2012). doi:10.5194/gmdd-5-1669-2012
3. National Climate Assessment and Development Advisory Committee: 3rd national climate assessment (draft) (2013). http://ncadac.globalchange.gov/
4. Lawrence, B., Lowry, R., Miller, P., Snaith, H., Woolf, A.: Information in environmental data grids. Philos. Trans. R. Soci. A: Math., Phys. Eng. Sci. **367**, 1003–1014 (2009). doi:10.1098/rsta.2008.0237
5. Wang, R.Y., Strong, D.M.: Beyond accuracy: what data quality means to data consumers. J. Manage. Inf. Syst. **12**(4), 5–33 (1996)
6. Gray, J., Szalay, A.S., Thakar, A.R., Stoughton, C.: Online scientific data curation, publication, and archiving. In: Astronomical Telescopes and Instrumentation, pp. 103–107 (2002)
7. Lawrence, B., Pepler, S., Jones, C., Matthews, B., Callaghan, S.: Citation and peer review of data: moving towards formal data publication. Int. J. Digit. Curation **6**(2), 4–37 (2011). doi:10.2218/ijdc.v6i2.205
8. Parsons, M.A., Fox, P.A.: Is data publication the right metaphor? Data Sci. J. **12**, WDS32–WDS46 (2013). doi:10.2481/dsj.wds-042
9. Dowell, M., Lecomte, P., Husband, R., Schulz, J., Mohr, T., Tahara, Y., Eckman, R., Lindstrom, E., Wooldridge, C., Hilding, S., Bates, J., Ryan, B., Lafeuille, J., Bojinski, S.: Strategy towards an architecture for climate monitoring from space (2013). http://www.wmo.int/pages/prog/sat/documents/ARCHstrategy-climate-architecture-space.pdf
10. World Meteorological Organization: Guideline for the generation of datasets and products meeting GCOS requirements (GCOS-143) (2010). https://www.wmo.int/pages/prog/gcos/Publications/gcos-143.pdf
11. Bates, J.J., Barkstrom, B.: A maturity model for satellite-derived climate data records. In: 14th Conference on Satellite Meteorology and Oceanography, Atlanta, USA (2006)
12. Lush, V., Bastin, L., Lumsden, J.: Developing a GEO label: providing the GIS community with quality metadata visualisation tools. In: Proceedings of the 21st GIS Research UK (GISRUK 3013), Liverpool, UK, 3–5 April 2013
13. Shotton, D., Peroni, S.: CiTO, the Citation Typing Ontology. http://purl.org/spar/cito/
14. Yang, X., Blower, J.D., Bastin, L., Lush, V., Zabala, A., Masó, J., Cornford, D., Díaz, P., Lumsden, J.: An integrated view of data quality in earth observation. Philos. Trans. R. Soci. A: Math., Phys. Eng. Sci. **371**(1983) (2013). doi:10.1098/rsta.2012.0072

Trismegistos: An Interdisciplinary Platform for Ancient World Texts and Related Information

Mark Depauw[✉] and Tom Gheldof

Research Group Ancient History, KU Leuven, Leuven, Belgium
{mark.depauw,tom.gheldof}@arts.kuleuven.be

Abstract. Trismegistos (TM) is a KU Leuven coordinated metadata platform for the study of texts from the Ancient World. This article provides a survey of its development, from the roots in a prosopography of Ptolemaic Egypt to an all-encompassing database with information about texts from Egypt for the period from 800 BC to AD 800. The current technical setup is detailed in a next section, with special attention for the structure of the many interconnected relational databases. A final section presents the current expansion to include material from outside Egypt, particularly Latin (and to some extent also Greek) inscriptions, in the framework of the CIP-Europeana EAGLE project. It also discusses some potential technological innovations to facilitate data exchange in a linked Open Data environment.

Keywords: Trismegistos · Ancient history texts · Relational database · Linked open data

1 Introduction

Trismegistos (http://www.trismegistos.org/; TM) is a KU Leuven coordinated metadata platform for the study of all texts from the Ancient World. Its aim is to surmount barriers of language and discipline in the study of texts from the ancient world, roughly 800 BC – AD 800. Traditionally scholars often exclude ancient sources written in languages they are less familiar with, even though they may be very relevant to the subject they study; historically grown chronological periodizations may also make long-term evolutions difficult to study. TM wants to facilitate access to all written sources, not necessarily by providing the actual text or even less by making images accessible, but by collecting basic metadata about all texts, by providing stable identifiers for texts and related information such as (modern) text collections, (ancient) archives, places and people, and by pointing out to other databases where more information can be found.

Epigraphy and papyrology of the ancient world are exceptional in the sense that there is a tradition of making sources (individual textual "items" written on an ancient writing surface) accessible to the wide scholarly community by publishing them, i.e. providing comprehensive information (such as physical

L. Bolikowski et al. (Eds.): TPDL 2013, CCIS 416, pp. 40–52, 2014.
DOI: 10.1007/978-3-319-08425-1_5, © Springer International Publishing Switzerland 2014

description, image, reading, and translation) in a public place, traditionally a scholarly journal or monograph. As a result of the digital revolution, "unpublished" texts are also progressively entering the public domain, which increases the need for a universal identifier of the kind Trismegistos hopes to offer.

1.1 History

Trismegistos is the result of intense collaboration between the universities of Leuven and Cologne, but would never have been possible without the support of many other projects.

Leuven pre-history. The database structure, technical setup and multilingual and interdisciplinary approach are ultimately derived from the Prosopographia Ptolemaica (PP), a long-term project set up by Willy Peremans in 1937 as a spin-off of his book "Vreemdelingen en Egyptenaren in Ptolemeïsch Egypte" [1]. The original idea was to create a prosopography of all people living in Ptolemaic Egypt, i.e. from 332 until 30 BC. These were collected, on index cards, from several thousands of papyrus documents, preserved in Egypt because of specific climatological circumstances, but also from inscriptions on stone and other writing surfaces. Not only evidence in Greek, the main language of the new foreign rulers, was gathered, but also sources written in the indigenous languages and script of Egypt, hieroglyphic, hieratic, and mostly Demotic, were used. This inclusive approach was quite revolutionary at the time.

The PP resulted in a series of volumes published in the series Studia Hellenistica between 1950 and 1981 [2–10]. For this purpose, Ptolemaic society was structured in domains such as "administration", "army", "clergy", etc. and within each domain people with the same title were listed alphabetically and assigned consecutive numbers. A purely alphabetical list in a separate volume facilitated access, and two volumes of *addenda et corrigenda* appeared. These already illustrated the problems with the combination of alphabetic order and consecutive numbering, leading to additions such as "a" and "b" or even "α", "β", or "bis".

This all changed in the early eighties, when the computer made its entry [11]. All information was gradually transferred from index cards to a database. After some experimentation, the PP opted for Filemaker on a Macintosh computer, and set up a relational structure with separate but interconnected databases for texts, individuals, attestations of individuals, family relations, names and functions. Fonts remained a major problem in this new digital environment. Lack of funding was another obstacle, but work was continued in the margin of fellowships, e.g. the work on ethnics by Láda [12], and during projects coordinated by Willy Clarysse and Katelijn Vandorpe, on the Fayum oasis (1998–2002) [13] and on papyrus archives (2002–2006) [14].

Meanwhile, Willy Clarysse had set up two other databases which would turn out to be very important for Trismegistos, but which were originally separate. The Leuven Database of Ancient Books (LDAB) was a collection of Greek and Latin literary manuscripts written before AD 800, and the Leuven Homepage of Papyrus Collections provided information about the main modern collections of papyri all over the world [15].

Cologne: Setting up Trismegistos. In 2004 Mark Depauw was then granted a Sofja Kovalevskaja Award of the Alexander von Humboldt-Stiftung to set up his own research team at a German university, in this case Cologne. The project "Multilingualism and Multiculturalism in Graeco-Roman Egypt" wanted to investigate language shifts in relation to cultural identity, by setting up an online database of Graeco-Roman papyrological material in Egyptian scripts. This database would be parallel to the existing tools of Greek papyrology: the Heidelberger Gesamtverzeichnis griechischer Urkunden aus gypten (HGV) for documentary texts, and its literary counterpart, the LDAB. On the basis of this new platform, factors influencing language preferences would then be analyzed.

The new project relied on the existing Leuven technical infrastructure, although this was of course adapted and fine-tuned. The data present in the PP database of texts were supplemented with a database of Demotic papyri provided at the start by the Cologne professor of Egyptology Heinz-Josef Thissen, the Gastgeber. The latter formed the core of the database Demotic and Abnormal Hieratic Texts (DAHT), which was soon integrated with an electronic version of the Demotistische Literaturbersicht, again on the basis of a database by Heinz-Josef Thissen. In addition, the Cologne team set up another egyptological metadata database, called Hieroglyphic and Hieratic Papyri (HHP).

Building these databases raised a number of questions:

- *Why include only papyrological texts?* The evidence of inscriptions is equally valuable for the study of shifting language preferences, and in egyptology there is no strict disciplinary boundary between epigraphy and papyrology.
- *Why separate Egyptian language and scripts from Greek and Latin?* The two languages were spoken in the same region at the same time, and occur together on a sizeable amount of texts. Mapping this overlap would be easier if everything was in a single database.
- *Why limit the database to the Graeco-Roman period?* Demotic starts in the 7th century BC and the hiatus in the documentation of the 3rd Intermediate Period, around 800 BC, seemed a better terminus post quem. Greek also continues to be used in the Byzantine period, and AD 800 seemed more suitable here.

In view of these considerations, the project decided to set up partnerships with HGV and LDAB, and merge everything into a single text database, which was called Trismegistos after the famous epithet of Hermes-Thoth, the Egyptian god of wisdom and writing who also played a major role in Greek religion and philosophy. The overlap between Greek papyrological and Egyptological databases was mapped; everything was assigned a unique numeric id (the TM number); and criteria were established for what made out a record in the database and was given a separate number. The large scale of the database with multiple collaborators increasingly also necessitated strict metadata standards, which were also facilitated by an ever more complex relational structure with separate databases for information such as publications, modern collections, places and dates.

After HGV and LDAB, many other projects were kind enough to put some of their information to our disposal. Some of these already existed before, e.g. the

Brussels Coptic Database (BCD) of Alain Delattre, while others were set up in collaboration, e.g. Aramaic Texts from Egypt (ATE) of Alexander Schütze. Some of the smaller gaps for minor languages such as Meroitic, Carian or Nabataean were filled up by integrating existing corpora, awaiting formal collaboration with specialist partners.

2   Current Structure

In its current setup, Trismegistos consists of multiple interconnected databases, mostly linked by the Trismegistos number. The online version of TM works with MySQL and PHP, but for data entry a single server is used in a mixed Filemaker 7–11 environment, soon to be updated to Filemaker 12 (Fig. 1).

2.1   Trismegistos Texts: The Trismegistos Number

The core component of TM is Trismegistos Texts, a database providing metadata about texts or documents. Each individual record is identified by a unique Trismegistos number, which can be used to form a stable URL, e.g. http://www. trismegistos.org/text/12345. This number does not change when the text is re-edited or interpreted in a different way (e.g. as a magical text rather than as a document). The only way in which it can disappear is if the database turns out to contain a double entry or if two fragments are joined because they can be shown to belong together physically. Even in those cases, however, track is kept of the number in the so-called old number database, and the user is redirected towards the currently valid number (e.g. http://www.trismegistos.org/text/107).

In principle a Trismegistos number (TM_id) that identifies records in the database corresponds to a single document or book. In the majority of cases no distinction has to be made between a document or book (which is identified by the number), the physical object (e.g. a papyrus) and the text (e.g. a Demotic letter). Frequently, however, several (sub)texts are found together on a single writing surface and then it must be decided whether these all should become individual records with their own TM_id or not.

To determine what constitutes a document or book or inscription (and thus should become a separate record), priority is given to material aspects: **in principle all texts written on what was in antiquity a single writing surface belong together and form one document receiving a single Trismegistos number, unless there are good reasons to believe that the only (and unintended) relation between the two texts is the writing surface itself.**

This means that related texts on the same surface are considered a single document, even if the relation is merely that they were written by the same scribe consecutively, but also that related texts which were in antiquity written on separate surfaces are considered separate documents. Even if a single text written by the same scribe and in a single action does not fit on a single papyrus

Trismegistos: database structure

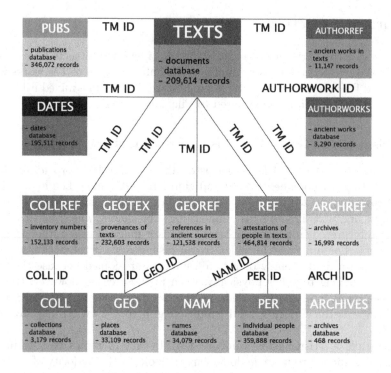

Legend Trismegistos website:

Fig. 1. Overview of the Trismegistos database structure (October 10, 2013)

sheet or ostracon but is continued on another for pure material reasons, two writing surfaces which were physically separate in antiquity cannot be considered a single document. Exceptions to this rule are rare and have explicitly been marked as such.

In other words the burden of proof rests with the scholar who wants to argue that two texts on the same writing surface belong to different documents because in the scribe's intention they have nothing to do with each other. Of course there are borderline cases and the crucial clause "unless there are good reasons to believe that the only (and unintended) relation between the two texts is the writing surface itself" is subjective. For inscriptions on rock surfaces, for instance, topological proximity should be combined with subject matter.

This newly developed paradigm has the advantage that it follows the current practice of most publications, although the issue has received remarkably little attention in the pre-digital era [16]. This may be related to the fact that quantification has long been a marginal issue. Other pioneering databases have taken a different approach, often related to their specific focus of interest: HGV concentrated on dates, and as a result texts were entered three times if necessary to deal with three possible interpretations of regnal dates; the Advanced Papyrological Information System (APIS) did not standardize across the participating partners, but many just followed the practical approach of creating a single record for each inventory number in their collection.

2.2 Trismegistos Texts: Traditional Text Identifiers

Although the TM number is increasingly used as an identifier, its use in a nondigital or human-readable environment is not yet very widespread. According to the discipline, scholars traditionally rely on three types of identifiers: publications, inventory numbers, and names. In Trismegistos, each of these is dealt with differently.

Text publications. Publications of texts are stored in a separate related table, connected to the main table by means of the TM number. Because of the great diversity of standards between the different disciplines and even within each discipline, this table follows a very eclectic set of rules.

Very often these publication references take the form of *sigla*, short abbreviations for publication series, followed by numbers identifying volume (optional) and text, e.g. P. Oxy. 19 2232 bis or SEG 8 664 a. In many cases Trismegistos has opted to provide the full title followed by the most common abbreviation, e.g. Rix, Etruskische Texte [ET] pp. 149–168 no. AS 1.336 or Monumenta Linguae Messapicae [MLM] 1 Ad. A tool has been developed trying to cope with the variation of publication sigla used in Greek and Latin papyrology and epigraphy.

Other publications, not taking the form of *sigla*, normally take the form JHS 57 (1937), pp. 30–32 no. 6 or Studies Quaegebeur 1 (OLA 84) pp. 441–454, although exceptions and idiosyncrasies no doubt remain.

TM also has separate fields in the publications database for the date of publication and the editor (i.e. the person responsible for reading the text), but these are not always shown in the online version.

Because the bibliographic abbreviations do not follow strict rules, it would be ideal if each reference would point to a bibliographic database with the non-abbreviated form. TM has only done this systematically for Demotic, with links to the Demotistische Literaturübersicht, and to some extent for Aramaic and Hieratic (in the TM Bibliography). For other scripts and languages, TM looks forward to linking to other digital bibliographies in the future, such as the Bibliographie Papyrologique or Arachne.

Text collections. The numbers assigned to objects with texts in museums or collections are stored in a separated database, connected on the one hand to the main table by means of the TM number, and on the other hand to Trismegistos Collections.

Examples of collection information are Vienna, Kunsthistorisches Museum dem. 6052, Berlin, gyptisches Museum S. 85 Abth. VIII Nr. 8, or Oxford, Private collection Crum number unknown. This information has three components: the collection, a specification of the numbering system (optional), and the number itself.

The first part of the information, with normally the (English) name of the city or town, and the (local) name of the collection, is pulled in from TM Collections. In this database of collections of ancient texts, each collection has its own numeric id, e.g. 357 for the Kunsthistorisches Museum (http://www.trismegistos.org/collection/357).

TM encourages the use of its full list of collections by partner databases and would be happy to add missing collections at simple request. Both public and private collections are included, provided there is sufficient information for their identification. Preservation information about texts that are not in collections (e.g. those *in situ* or "lost") is given in a separate field ("inventory_temp"), which is joined with the compound field for the online edition.

The second (optional) part specifies which numbering system is used. Some large collections are split up in subcollections for the different areas and culture they cover, and in some museum a wide variety of numbering systems is in use (or has been used in the past). TM tries to cover most of these, but obviously there is scope for improvement. For each museum the information on number systems is listed also in a separate field.

The third element is the number itself. Although almost invariably a number (or numbers) constitute the core, there are many possible alternatives including full stops, commas, "a", "bis", etc., which may make searching and sorting problematic.

Text names. Although names such as "the Rosetta stone" or "the Book of Armagh" are very common in everyday use, they are not always easy to process in a database. TM has opted to include information of this kind in the non-standardized field for collection and inventory ("inventory_temp"), which makes names searchable online.

2.3   Trismegistos Texts: Information About the Writing Process

Trismegistos contains information about some material aspects of the text and the surface on which it was written. A distinction is made between the material itself, the form of the material, the tool used, and the possible reuse for another text.

Material. Since Trismegistos is not limited to texts on a specific writing surface, it contains very diverse writing materials, from paper to stone and from eggshell to camel bone. At this stage, Trismegistos uses its own system with entries such as "leather" or "stone: limestone". Trismegistos is aware that standards to describe material are developing and is contemplating their use in a future consolidation period.

Form. There is no real standardized vocabulary to describe the form a writing material takes, and developing one would imply consultation of all disciplines and fields involved. This seems a daunting task, which may explain why Trismegistos is not currently attempting to actually standardize this information, although attempts have been made in the past, leading to compound entries such as "architecture: door" or "statue: naophoros".

Tool. The tool with which the text was written is not systematically specified in Trismegistos. The field was originally created to provide information about whether an Egyptian "rush" was used or a Greek "reed", but with the expansion to epigraphy "chisel" became a third possibility and the occasional inclusion of numismatic and sigillographic sources led to "mint" and "mould".

Reuse. In principle, a single Trismegistos number (TM_id) is assigned to "multiple (sub)texts written on what was in antiquity a single writing surface, unless there are good reasons to believe that the only (and unintended) relation between the texts is the writing surface itself". This implies that if a writing surface was reused as "old paper" or otherwise recycled for an unrelated text, two TM_id's are assigned, and Trismegistos then connects these two (or more) records in the "reuse" section.

The connection between the texts is normally specified by expressions such as "blank side reused, new text is:" or "reuse of blank side, old text is:". In many cases, however, TM uses a generic "another text on papyrus is:" or in cases of complicated reuse the procedure is explained in a free-form text field.

2.4   Trismegistos Texts: Information About the Contents

Apart from language and script, Trismegistos also contains general information about the type of text with occasionally more details, including attestations of ancient authors.

Language and script. Although language and script are two separate aspects of a text, they are currently not systematically split up. For the time being, Trismegistos for most languages and scripts assumes that they form an organic whole, in the sense that Greek language is normally written in the "Greek" (alphabetical) script, while "Demotic" is the script which is normally combined with the stage of the Egyptian language commonly called Demotic. Only for languages with are not more or less stably associated with a script is the script itself normally indicated, e.g. for Italic languages.

When more than one language or script are used in a single TM-record, the text is "multilingual" and the various languages or scripts used are enumerated separated by slashes, e.g. "multilingual: Greek/Coptic" If an entire text or a longer passage in a text is written in a non-standard combination of script and language, this is indicated by the prefix "anomalous:" followed by a description of the combination, e.g. "anomalous: Greek written in Latin characters".

Type. The field "type" describes the genre the text belongs to and its contents. This is without doubt the least standardized field in the database, and it is normally currently not shown in the online version. An exception is the DAHT database, where the information is somewhat more standardized. Nevertheless much work remains to be done, and this will require intense interdisciplinary cooperation.

Author and work. A specific case of "type" is when a text is an attestation of a "classical" author and one of his works. These authors are mainly attested through mediaeval manuscripts, which fall outside the chronological scope of TM. There are, however, over 10,000 instances from before AD 800 in our partner database LDAB. To facilitate links with existing full-text repositories such as Perseus or the Thesaurus Linguae Graecae (TLG) we have recently created the related Authorworks database.

2.5   Trismegistos Texts: Chronological and Geographical Information

Date. In Trismegistos, a separate database stores the dates on which the text was written (not the date of the original in the case of copies!). Each date is linked to the main database by means of the TM_id, and this relational system allows us to have e.g. multiple possible precise dates attached to a single text (e.g. when a year 4 can refer to multiple kings or emperors), or multiple dates attached to sections of the document (e.g. one for the manuscript itself and the other the glosses dating to two centuries later). As a rule, TM does not currently use this system to implement different dates suggested by different authors, e.g. AD 100–199 by X and AD 300–399 by Y.

For database-historic reasons, Trismegistos converts "second century AD" to AD 100–199 rather than the more correct AD 101–200. For "middle second century" AD 125–175 is used, for "early" AD 100–125 and for "late" AD 175–199. Of course other projects use 30 years for early, and others still 33. Trismegistos will be happy to adapt to any standards that develop, but there are no clear signs that any are forthcoming.

The dates are based on multiple, mostly numeric fields, which are converted to something more humanly readable. The use of figures is potentially confusing, since some of the analogue vagueness is lost, but it has many advantages for searching and sorting. For BC dates negative numbers are used, e.g. −99 to −1 for the first century BC (note that this century because of the nature of our system is one year shorter than the other centuries). The fields are the following:

y1 the earliest year of the range
y2 the latest year of the range
m1 & m2 id. but month
d1 & d2 id. but day
uncertain 0 or 1, to express uncertainty
extra precisions such as "before", "after", "shortly before", "not earlier than", etc.

If there is an exact date, the same figure is used in **y1** and **y2** (and if necessary also in **m1** and **m2** and **d1** and **d2**): e.g. 25 January 435 BC = −435 in **y1** and **y2**, 1 in **m1** and **m2**, and 25 in **d1** and **d2**; between 25 Jan 435 BC and 27 February 434 BC is **y1** = −435, **m1** = 1, **d1** = 25; **y2** = −434, **m2** = 2, **d2** = 27.

Trismegistos always tends to date texts, e.g. when a Demotic text is undated and no indication whatsoever is provided by the editor, −699 is filled out in **y1** and 499 in **y2**.

Place. Information about where a text was written or found is also stored in a separate database, with records that are on the one hand linked to the text database by the TM number, and on the other hand with the Trismegistos Places database. The latter is a geographical database designed to be used for ancient texts, and is currently being mapped with databases such as Pleiades and Geonames. Each site has its own numeric id, e.g. 332 for Egypt, 00 – Arsinoites (Fayum) (http://www.trismegistos.org/place/332). Again this was originally limited to Egypt, but is now being expanded.

The related database structure allows easy differentiation between where a text was found or written, and sometimes also its destination is added. Trismegistos is currently also exploring to include the current whereabouts in this database, provided the text is not kept in a collection (for which see above).

3 Current Work and Perspectives

3.1 The Expansion of Trismegistos

When Trismegistos was created in 2005, it focused on providing information (metadata) on published papyrological documents from Graeco-Roman Egypt. Chronological boundaries are always artificial, and the nature of the sources soon suggested that BC 800 and AD 800 were more suited. Since egyptology does not know a disciplinary boundary between papyri and inscriptions, TM almost from its inception also decided to expand by adding all epigraphic material as well. Two other expansions are more recent, however.

Since 2011 Trismegistos no longer exclusively deals with published texts only, but also includes unpublished texts for which information is available in online repositories. The distinction between published and unpublished had become increasingly less productive in a digital environment, and cooperation with collections such as Ghent and consortia such as APIS are now possible.

Already in 2010, the idea also grew to expand Trismegistos further to include texts from outside Egypt. In a first step the Epigraphische Datenbank Heidelberg (EDH) was contacted, later followed by the Epigraphic Database Rome (EDR). After pilot projects for Macedonia and Regio X Venetia et Histria, Trismegistos became a partner in a CIP Europeana project, which started on 1 April 2013. Trismegistos is currently integrating all the Latin (and to a lesser extent Greek) inscriptions present in the EAGLE partner databases.

The integration of new, often overlapping datasets is achieved through strict adaption to the Trismegistos standards, especially of the traditional text identifiers mentioned above (Sect. 2.2). The different systems used and the lack of accepted standards for abbreviations of e.g. publications have often made it problematic to identify automatically which text is meant in partner databases and whether this same text is also present in other datasets. By structuring the data in the related databases of Trismegistos, the text for which information is provided can be identified unambiguously, and a TM number can be assigned. This unique ID is then implemented in the background by the partner databases, enabling to link without imposing changes. To facilitate linking further, Trismegistos has recently also set up a "text relations" database in which all one-to-one, one-to-many, and many-to-one relationships are stored, with clarifications for the difficult cases. This will enable linking without implementing the TM number.

3.2 Trismegistos People and Places

Since 2008, Trismegistos has also returned to its original focus on personal names (as in the Prosopographia Ptolemaica) and place names (as in the Fayum project). A KU Leuven project set up Trismegistos People for all attestations of personal names in texts from Egypt [17]. For this a complex structure with separate databases for attestations of people, people, declined name variants, name variants and names has been developed, which cannot be discussed here. For places a similar structure is currently being set up.

Also for this aspect of the database, Trismegistos is currently discussing a possible expansion of its scope to include the Ancient World in general, but talks are still at a very early stage here.

3.3 Technological Innovations

Participating in the EAGLE project has brought us into closer contact with other technological partners. As a result, Trismegistos is exploring a conversion of some of its data to new models, which would make them more accessible in an Open Data environment. This should not be too difficult, as the relational structure itself already implies the RDF structure with subject (e.g. http://www.trismegistos.org/text/12345), attribute (e.g. "is written in"), and object (in this case http://www.trismegistos.org/place/2287). Some of the information about the links is currently in specific fields in the related records (e.g. "default" or "outdated" for the publications linked to the text), and their controlled vocabularies used there could be adapted to create ontologies for attributes in the RDF structure.

Other improvements would be the use of existing controlled vocabularies for aspects Trismegistos does not aim to cover exhaustively, e.g. the Simplified Petrography of Ubi Erat Lupa for the description of the material aspects of the writing surface. Or the implementation of links to related datasets such as Pleiades (ancient places) and Geonames (modern place names) for the different types of geographical information.

References

1. Peremans, W.: Vreemdelingen en Egyptenaren in Ptolemaeïsch Egypte. Paleis der Academiën, Brussel (1987)
2. Peremans, W., Van't Dack, E.: Prosopographia Ptolemaica 1: L'administration civile et financière, nos 1–1824 (Studia Hellenistica 6). Bibliotheca Universitatis Lovanii, Louvain (1950)
3. Peremans, W., Van't Dack, E.: Prosopographia Ptolemaica 2: L'armée de terre et la police, nos 1825–4983 (Studia Hellenistica 8). Bibliotheca Universitatis Lovanii, Louvain (1952)
4. Peremans, W., De Meulenaere, H., IJsewijn, J., Van't Dack, E.: Prosopographia Ptolemaica 3: Le clergé, le notariat, les tribunaux, nos 4984–8040 (Studia Hellenistica 11). Bibliotheca Universitatis Lovanii, Louvain (1956)
5. Peremans, W., Van't Dack, E.: Prosopographia Ptolemaica 4: L'agriculture et l'élevage, nos 8041–12459 (Studia Hellenistica 12). Bibliotheca Universitatis Lovanii, Louvain (1959)
6. Peremans, W., Van't Dack, E.: Prosopographia Ptolemaica 5: Le commerce et l'industrie, le transport sur terre et la flotte, la domesticité, nos 12460–14478 (Studia Hellenistica 13). Bibliotheca Universitatis Lovanii, Louvain (1963)
7. Peremans, W., Van't Dack, E., Mooren, L., Swinnen, W.: Prosopographia Ptolemaica 6: La cour, les relations internationales et les possessions extérieures, la vie culturelle, nos 14479–17250 (Studia Hellenistica 17). Bibliotheca Universitatis Lovanii, Louvain (1968)
8. Peremans, W., De Meulemeester-Swinne, L., Hauben, H., Van't Dack, E.: Prosopographia Ptolemaica 7: Index Nominum (Studia Hellenistica 20). Lovanii, Louvain (1975)
9. Peremans, W., Van't Dack, E., Mooren, L., Swinnen, W.: Prosopographia Ptolemaica 8: Addenda et corrigenda aux volumes 1(1950) et 2(1952) (Studia Hellenistica 21) Lovanii, Louvain (1975)
10. Peremans, W., Van't Dack, E., Clarysse, W.: Prosopographia Ptolemaica 9: Addenda et corrigenda au volume 3(1956) (Studia Hellenistica 25). Lovanii, Louvain (1981)
11. Mooren, L.: The automatization of the prosopographia ptolemaica. In: Atti del XXII Congresso Internazionale di Papirologia Firenze 23–29 agosto 1998, pp. 995–1007. Istituto papirologico G. Vitelli, Firenze (2001)
12. Láda, C.A.: Prosopographia Ptolemaica 10: Foreign ethnics in Hellenistic Egypt. (Studia Hellenistica 38). Peeters Leuven, Louvain (2002)

13. The Fayum Project. http://www.trismegistos.org/fayum/
14. Papyrus Archives in Graeco-Roman Egypt. http://www.trismegistos.org/arch/biblio.php
15. Clarysse, W.: The leuven database of ancient books (LDAB). In: Atti del XXII congresso internazionale di Papirologia. Firenze 23–29 agosto 1998, pp. 237–249. Istituto papirologico G. Vitelli, Firenze (2001)
16. Van Minnen, P.: The future of papyrology. In: Bagnall, R.S. (ed.) Oxford Handbook of Papyrology, pp. 644–660. Oxford University Press, Oxford (2009). doi:10.1093/oxfordhb/9780199843695.013.0027
17. Van Beek, B., Depauw, M.: People in Greek documentary papyri: first results of a research project. JJP (The Journal of Juristic Papyrology) **39**, 31–47 (2009)

Preliminary Analysis
of Data Sources Interlinking
Data Searchery: A Case Study

Andrea Mannocci$^{(\boxtimes)}$ and Paolo Manghi$^{(\boxtimes)}$

Consiglio Nazionale delle Ricerche,
Istituto di Scienza e Tecnologie dell'Informazione "A. Faedo", Pisa, Italy
{andrea.mannocci,paolo.manghi}@isti.cnr.it

Abstract. The novel e-Science's data-centric paradigm has proved that interlinking publications and research data objects coming from different realms and data sources (e.g. publication repositories, data repositories) makes dissemination, re-use, and validation of research activities more effective. Scholarly Communication Infrastructures (SCIs) are advocated for bridging such data sources by offering an overlay of services for identification, creation, and navigation of relationships among objects of different nature. Since realization and maintenance of such infrastructures is in general very cost-consuming, in this paper we propose a lightweight approach for "preliminary analysis of data source interlinking" to help practitioners at evaluating whether and to what extent realizing them can be effective. We present Data Searchery, a configurable tool delivering a service for relating objects across data sources, be them publications or research data, by identifying relationships between their metadata descriptions in real-time.

Keywords: Interoperability · Interlinking · Research data · Publications · Metadata · Inference

1 Introduction

The Research Digital Libraries (RDLs) ecosystem is ever growing since creating and publishing a proprietary *publication repository* is essentially mandatory for any institution striving to gain a modicum of visibility and relevance. However, despite printed papers and their digital shadows still are and will remain the principal carriers for research outcome dissemination, they will never be *per se* adequate to embed huge datasets, software, code listings, workflows, media files and any other sidecar-information which simply cannot fit into the traditional publishing model [1,2]. This drawback is worsened by the advent of e-Science and data-intensive research [3] which turned research data into a first class citizen in research processes and output [4,5]. *Data repositories* for publishing, curating

L. Bolikowski et al. (Eds.): TPDL 2013, CCIS 416, pp. 53–64, 2014.
DOI: 10.1007/978-3-319-08425-1_6, © Springer International Publishing Switzerland 2014

and persisting research data are becoming more and more common in many scientific communities [5] as well as *data papers*, peer-reviewed articles which are intended as a thorough description of a dataset (or a group of datasets) and the way they have been produced [6].

For such reasons, the availability of overlay services capable of bridging the data and publication worlds is getting more and more appealing for research communities [4]. In particular, inferring relationships among objects belonging to different domains, i.e. publication-publication, publication-data and data-data interlinking, becomes crucial in order to: (*i*) foster multi-disciplinary research by looking at adherences among distinct disciplines [7]; (*ii*) enable a better review, reproduction and re-use of research activities [1,4,8]. However, identifying which domains are worth bridging in such a plethora of publication and data repositories is not an easy task. In addition, understanding which kind of relationships can be inferred across objects of different domains is yet another challenge. Finally, interoperability issues generally arise, since access protocols, metadata formats and object models are likely to differ for different repositories, due to technological and scientific domain peculiarities.

In order to solve such issues, scientific communities lately started realizing *Scholarly Communication Infrastructures* (SCIs) [9], providing tools and services to aggregate object files and metadata coming from different data sources (e.g. repositories or other SCIs) and scientific realms and enable both humans and machinery to interlink such objects by identifying relationships via user-interfaces or advanced inference-by-mining algorithms (e.g. OpenAIRE and OpenAIREplus [10,11], Mendeley[1], ORCID[2], Utopia Documents [12]).

Since requirements differ both from case to case and over time, SCIs have to specifically address ever changing requirements and therefore must be planned and designed very carefully. Additionally, once deployed they have to undergo a continuous and expensive process of extension, optimization and maintenance. Thus, their cost in terms of time and skills tends to be generally high and sometime prohibitive for the smallest communities. In particular, the majority of the total costs are due to data source aggregation efforts. For such reasons, planning the realization of a SCI would benefit from tools assessing metadata interlinking capabilities among data sources in a preliminary lightweight fashion without the need of any prior object file and/or metadata collection and processing.

In this paper we present Data Searchery, a tool conceived and developed within the efforts of the two FP7 projects OpenAIREplus [10,11] and iCORDI[3]. Data Searchery is intended to help practitioners willing to realize new SCIs or extend existing SCIs with functionalities to interlink objects across data sources by evaluating whether and to what extent such an investment would be effective for the community. To this aim, the tool offers an intuitive interface enabling end-users to identify meaningful relationships between objects of given data sources

---

[1] Mendeley, http://www.mendeley.com/.
[2] ORCID, http://orcid.org/.
[3] The Research Data Alliance, http://europe.rd-alliance.org/.

via advanced cross-search mechanisms over their metadata descriptions. Data Searchery is designed to facilitate the integration of new data sources into the framework as well as flexibly integrate keyword extraction filters to specialize cross-metadata search to given scientific fields.

Outline. The remainder of the paper is organized as follows. Section 2 provides functional requirements and an high-level overview of Data Searchery architecture and design. Section 3 describes our real-life experience gathered through the use of Data Searchery within the OpenAIREplus project efforts. Section 4 describes related work. Finally Sect. 5 makes final remarks and paves the way for future enhancements of the method.

2   Data Searchery Overview

Because of the dramatic impact the aggregation phase has on global cost of SCIs development, we advocate here the convenience of a tool able to preliminary assess the feasibility and effectiveness of efforts in the aggregation phase. Given the high availability of repositories over the Internet, we want to let the user search for and play with metadata there exposed and be able to surf and (best-effort) *relate on-the-fly* metadata present in two different *data sources*, here referenced as *origin* and *target* data sources, which may contain both publications and research data objects. For the sake of flexibility and effectiveness, such a tool should also offer some mechanism to leverage in order to *filter and extract* relevant information from metadata records for driving new searches and inferring relationships.

Such features are traditionally offered by the service overlay exposed by SCIs, alas available only at the end of all design and implementation efforts. When not available, the user has to face with the discovery of repositories, the individual querying process for each one of them and the manual comparison of returned results scattered across multiple search portals. By taking advantage of a lightweight mechanisms for preliminary exploration of interlinking capabilities among data sources, the advantage is twofold. On one side it would cut unneeded costs by preventing ineffective tasks to take place during SCIs development, on the other side traditional users usually performing multiple queries juggling between several search pages would benefit of a single-paged UI providing all the tools needed for running guided and meaningful cross-queries.

2.1   Scenario and Functional Requirements

In the following, we refer to a *data source* as an entry-point publicly queryable from the Internet able to offer objects (i.e. *metadata records*) optionally organized into sets, hereafter mentioned as *collections*, against whom it is possible to narrow queries down. A data source can be either a publication repository, or a dataset repository, or a repository aggregator (e.g. DataCite[4], NARCIS[5]),

---

[4] The DataCite Initiative, http://datacite.org.

[5] NARCIS, http://www.narcis.nl/.

or a SCI (e.g. OpenAIRE[6], DRIVER[7], Google Scholar[8]). Each data source adopts its own metadata schema (either proprietary or standardized), but in general we assume a metadata format can be considered as a flat list of $< field, type >$ pairs.

Given two data sources, common sense and experience would suggest the user to feed the same query to both (possibly via web portals) and optionally refine the second query with additional information coming from a record of interest out of the results of the first query. This *refinement process* has been modeled in Data Searchery with the concept of the *extraction filter*. Hereafter, we refer to extraction filter as an abstraction capable of automatic extraction of textual and semantic features given one metadata record of preference; this additional information can be used in subsequent queries in order to refine results and infer more precise relationships among objects. For example, semantically relevant keywords can be extracted from the title of the selected metadata record and can be used for running a second query on the target data source.

The Data Searchery approach relies entirely on metadata descriptions of objects provided by data sources, hence the more metadata are accurate and thorough, the more the recall of the tool tends to be accurate. However in general, poor or incomplete metadata content does not necessarily invalidate the generic reasoning behind the approach. More on metadata quality definition, issues and frameworks for metadata quality assessment can be found in [13,14].

Data Searchery is a tool aiming to satisfy the following typical use-cases. The former describes what has been anticipated so far and reflects the point of view of the final user enjoying a service for cross-searching data sources in couples availing of a set of configurable extraction filters in order to gather contextual information out of metadata. The latter describes the developer perspective in customizing a Data Searchery instance by adding additional data sources and extraction filters in a flexible and easy way.

Data Searchery Final User. As shown in Fig. 1, the prototype guides the user in a two-step process: (*i*) querying an origin data source of preference; (*ii*) given one record of interest returned by the first query, crafting a second query on a target data source of preference. The user drafts the first query by typing keywords and (optionally) by narrowing down to one or more collections made available by the origin data source. The second query is tool-crafted by automatically extracting keywords from one metadata record of interest, chosen among the ones returned by the first query. Keywords are extracted by applying one or more extraction filters selected by the user from a list; as in the first step, the user can narrow the query down to one or more collections present on the target data source.

The solution has to be as generic and flexible as possible and make the user able to navigate metadata starting either from research data or scientific

---

[6] The OpenAIRE project, http://www.openaire.eu/en.

[7] The DRIVER repository, http://www.driver-repository.eu/.

[8] Google Scholar, http://scholar.google.com.

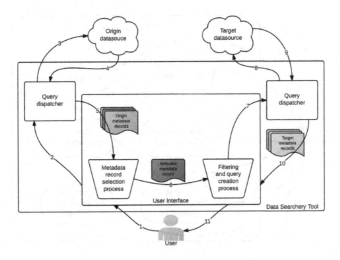

Fig. 1. Data Searchery interlinking session

publications indifferently. Furthermore, it should be possible to "promote" a target data source into an origin data source for subsequent queries; in this way, the aforementioned scenario can be re-iterated and lead to a new interlinking session targeting a third different data source and so on.

Data Searchery Developer. A programmer in charge of developing a customized instance of Data Searchery needs to plug-in both data sources and extraction filters in an easy and flexible way through minimal changes (hopefully only adding new implementation rather than modifying pre-existing one). Finally, Data Searchery user interface should be to some extent oblivious to the addition and modification of such abstractions and adapts itself seamlessly to such changes. Developer's use cases are summarized in Fig. 2.

2.2   Architectural and Design Overview

Data Searchery is open source and developed in Java; it interfaces real-world data source via the abstraction named `DsDatasource` which is in charge of fetching and mapping native metadata records to Data Searchery format. Similarly, the refinement process extracting context information out of metadata records is performed via functions called `DsExtractionFilter`. Developers can easily plug-in new instances of data sources and extraction filters as new implementations of the corresponding Java classes briefly described below.

DS Data Source. The `DsDatasource` abstraction requires implementing two API methods capable of (*i*) responding to *keyword-based queries* and returning a page of metadata records (i.e. `getMetadataPage()::List<DsMetadataRecord>`)

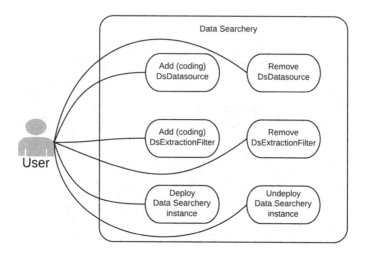

Fig. 2. Developer's use cases

and (*ii*) *collection queries* returning a list of collections available at the data source (i.e. `getCollections()::List<DsCollection>`).

The first API method is responsible for (*i*) querying a data source and wait for results, and (*ii*) mapping returned native metadata records into Data Searchery metadata records (i.e. `DsMetadataRecord`). We assume the minimal requirement for a data source to be compliant with Data Searchery is the availability of a search API (e.g. Solr[9] or Elasticsearch[10] APIs) accepting textual queries and returning paginated *XML-formatted results* (i.e. metadata records). It must be noticed that harvesting, storing and cleaning metadata fall out the scope of Data Searchery which on the contrary relies solely on "live-queries" over remote data sources; no standard protocol such as OAI-PMH or OAI-ORE is thus involved. Since each data source generally adopts a different metadata schema, for the sake of simplicity we designed a simple model class `DsMetadataRecord` onto which mirroring relevant information for interlinking purposes contained inside original metadata fields. For each native metadata record returned by a queried data source, a `DsMetadataRecord` instance is created (stored in memory with no caching mechanism) and populated with information from the original metadata. A `DsDatasource` maps native records as the search API provides them (e.g. ordered by field relevance in the case of Solr index) without applying any additional re-ordering or scoring policy. More precisely, for each native metadata record it is possible to map authors, title, abstract/description, keywords/subject, publisher and native repository in our model. Since some metadata format might carry a list of *related DOIs* (both within the same data source and external), saving this identifiers is useful too as it already solves partially the problem statement by providing a set of simply related items. When

---

[9] Apache Solr, http://lucene.apache.org/solr/.
[10] Elasticsearch, http://www.elasticsearch.org/.

available, publication date is mapped too for the sake of completeness, so that time-aware interlinking queries can be performed. The simple model described here can be extended as needed with due modifications to `DsMetadataRecord` class; the changes introduced are reflected seamlessly onto the web UI without any additional coding effort.

The second API method provides a list of collections optionally exposed by a data source. Such list of available collections could be either hard-coded (hence statically loaded), or dynamically retrieved from the Internet by several means (e.g. from a web resource or from the filesystem). According to the data sources examined so far, the idea of collection has been implemented by indexing (for each record) a special field containing to the name of the collection of provenance. Narrowing queries against this field gives the impression of querying a logical index reserved to the collection.

An example, regarding the DataCite data source, in our prototype we created a new `DataciteDS.java` class deriving `DsDatasource.java` which maps native records from Datacite metadata format into `DsMetadataRecord`, and retrieves the collection list by parsing a plain text web page hosted at DataCite facilities. Similarly, for the Driver project [15,16], we implemented another class (`DriverDS.java`) derived from `DsDatasource.java` which maps from Driver metadata format and fetches the collection list by parsing an XML-formatted page returned by a query performed over D-Net[11] Information Service, the data infrastructure on top of which the project has been realized.

DS Extraction Filter. Extraction filters are instantiated by extending `DsExtractionFilter` abstraction which requires implementing the function `processMetadataRecord()::List<String>` and returns a set of inferred keywords given an input metadata record. In particular, an extraction filter operates over a set of fields of a `DsMetadataRecord` object trying to identify and extract given ontology terms or semantically meaningful keywords. The logic for such extraction function can be implemented "in-house" as local implementation or can be demanded to an external service. For example, in our prototype the two text taggers invoke an external service made available by EBI[12]. On the contrary, all the other extraction filters implemented in the prototype rely on local implementation. Extraction filters can be selectively associated to the data sources for which they are needed. For example, a "keyword finder" extraction filter which is looking for keywords semantically related to the world of biodiversity should not be available for data sources offering technical science metadata, or at least it would not make sense in principle.

A running instance of the Data Searchery prototype, in Fig. 3, with sample built-in data sources (DataCite, DRIVER, OpenAIREplus) and extraction filters (author extractor, keyword extractor, EBI text taggers) can be found online at: http://goo.gl/pI3VR.

---

[11] D-Net Software Toolkit, http://www.d-net.research-infrastructures.eu.

[12] WhatIzIt - EBI, http://www.ebi.ac.uk/webservices/whatizit/.

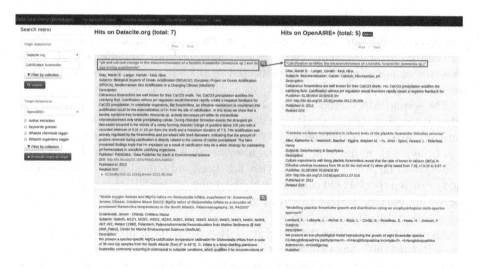

Fig. 3. Screenshot of Data Searchery web app

3   OpenAIREplus: An Use Case

The OpenAIREplus project (2nd generation of the former project OpenAIRE) [10,11] deals with the delivery and operation of the OpenAIRE scholarly communication infrastructure, currently integrating about 400 OpenAIRE-validated repositories across Europe (from a total of 2,500 OpenDOAR publication repositories and 250 re3data.org data repositories). The SCI also offers inference-by-mining algorithms and search mechanisms over 8,000,000 publications and 1,500,000 datasets.

Being more accurate, in OpenAIREplus inference is performed over harmonized metadata present in the information space (i.e. right after aggregation and cleaning phases) and mainly focuses on (*i*) identifying project-publication relationships (funding sources), (*ii*) publication-dataset linking, and (*iii*) publication-publication inference w.r.t. citation, similarity, duplicates [10].

Data Searchery has been tested in a few use cases within the efforts of the OpenAIREplus project in order to preliminary explore adherences between couples of selected data sources and examine metadata prior to aggregation phase. For example, through the use of Data Searchery, we were able to perform several positive interlinking sessions confirming that all the premises for an effective interlinking among dataset objects from DataCite repositories and publication objects from OpenDOAR repositories were righteous in the first place.

A demonstrative interlinking session is briefly summarized below.

Step 1. A first query is launched using the keywords *"Calcification foraminifer"* on the DataCite repository as origin data source. The query returns 7 metadata records, the first of which describes a dataset titled *"pH and calcium change in the microenvironment of a benthic foraminifer (Ammonia sp.)*

and its size during experiments" by Glas *et al.*, published by PANGAEA[13] repository, one of the partner joining the DataCite initiative.

Step 2. Next the interlinking session is performed (*i*) having selected OpenAIREplus as target data source and (*ii*) having activated keywords and authors extraction filters. This second (tool-crafted) query returns a publication by the same authors titled *"Calcification acidifies the microenvironment of a benthic foraminifer (Ammonia sp.)"* which refers the same dataset found at the previous step. The publication is stored at "Web of Science" repository which joins OpenAIREplus infrastructure.

As a result of further positive sessions, the analysis suggested that publications in WoS and PANGAEA are likely related by discipline bindings, hence that investigation on more advanced infrastructure interlinking services capable of identifying and persisting such links is likely worth the effort.

4 Related Work

To the best our knowledge, literature on cross metadata search of web data sources with the purpose of interlinking data and publication is lacking. On the contrary, literature on Linked Open Data [17] (LOD) and RDF interlinking is copious. In [18], Wölger *et al.* draw some indicators for the classification of methods and frameworks for Linked Open Data and RDF datasets interlinking. As the classification seems reasonable and sufficiently generic to contextualize inference mechanisms for metadata interlinking, we refer to their work which is focused on the following key indicators:

degree of automation whether the tool needs human intervention or not and to which extent;

human contribution the type of interaction an user has to provide in order to be able to use effectively the tool;

domain whether the method is bound to a specific domain or domain independent;

matching techniques the mechanisms leveraged in order to match data;

ontologies whether ontologies are taken into account or not;

input what and in which format has to be fed to the tool;

output what and in which format the tool returns;

post-processing post-processing capabilities offered by the tool;

data access protocol or method used for accessing data.

Let us extend this classification by adding a couple of novel indicators to the list: *real-timeliness* and *volatility*. A tool is classified as a *real-time* tool if it tries to infer links on-the-fly and does not require any *a priori* knowledge or processing of datasets; a tool is classified as *deferred* otherwise, since it fetches required metadata and then processes it looking for inference (e.g. the majority of the

---

[13] PANGAEA - Data Publisher for Earth & Environmental Science, http://www.pangaea.de.

methods analyzed in [18] belong to this category). A tool is declared *volatile* if persisting inferred relationships falls out the scope of the approach (i.e. the tool is only exploratory); the tool is said to be *persistent* otherwise, since links are someway persisted for future navigation.

According to the proposed extension, the Data Searchery prototype can be classified as follows:

real-timeliness fully real-time. No pre-processing needed;
degree of automation manual (semi-automatic mode is a work in progress);
human contribution selected data sources, keywords and search parameters;
domain domain independent;
matching techniques string matching, word relation matching (synonyms, taxonomic similarities);
ontologies pluggable as extraction filters;
input one XML-formatted metadata (out of results returned from the query performed on the origin data source) plus an extraction filters configuration;
volatility volatile;
output a page of XML-formatted metadata returned from the target data source;
post-processing n/a;
data access searchable API (e.g. SOLR index API, elasticsearch API).

In [19], Nikolaidou *et al.* describe a meta-search service for gathering knowledge about music genres, bands and discographies by combining metadata results coming from three different data sources (MusicBrainz, Last.fm, and Discogs). In their approach, the three data sources are queried separately and results retrieved by one become a possible input for a more specialized search in the other two; results are combined at real-time as the user proceeds with his/her interrogation and nothing is persisted on disk.

Another recent work describes a service, namely Linkitup [20], which helps authors to enrich metadata of their own items shared on Figshare[14] platform. Given a metadata record, Linkitup extracts information from metadata fields and looks for possible matches over five other web services (at the time of writing). Results are returned to the user, which is able to check and manually confirm the discovered suggestions, thus combing such an extra-information with original metadata. The resulting "enhanced metadata" can be fed back to the original record on Figshare and its RDF representation can be either downloaded separately or published as research output on Figshare. According to the classification proposed, Linkitup works with partial user interaction, provides results in real-time and gives the chance to persist the output.

5   Conclusions and Future Work

The ability to relate either data or publications hosted in different data sources and realms is becoming a key aspect in modern scholarly communication as

---

[14] Figshare.com, http://figshare.com/.

it fosters findability, review and reuse of previous work and promotes multidisciplinary research and idea dissemination across communities. SCIs address this new trend by offering a service overlay and tools tackling this need, however their realization and maintenance raise serious sustainability issues and makes them seldom viable for the smallest communities.

Being able to infer on-the-fly relationships between objects of different nature and belonging to different contexts without any prior metadata harvesting and processing would be an appealing perspective. Data Searchery is a configurable tool allowing for lightweight and preliminary evaluation of the existence of meaningful links between objects from different data sources. The tool offers an intuitive web interface allowing users to surf and relate on-the-fly metadata across two different data sources by leveraging advanced mining tools manipulating and extracting context information out of selected metadata records.

Currently Data Searchery is being extended with functionalities to elaborate extensive statistical reports on the overall degree of correlation between two data sources w.r.t. a set of user queries (e.g. a pool of authors and/or keywords). Another planned extension deals with the possibility to plug-in additional data sources and extraction filter by editing simple property files instead of writing new Java classes.

Data Searchery will be released to the OpenAIREplus community as an experimental real-time mining tool for end-users, as an addition to the preprocessing based inference services already implemented in the platform. The tool will automatically integrate repositories aggregated by the OpenAIRE infrastructure as DS data sources, hence make it possible for end-users to cross-search OpenAIRE repositories to discover relationships.

References

1. Bourne, P.E., Clark, T.W., Dale, R., de Waard, A., Herman, I., Hovy, E.H., Shotton, D.: Improving the future of research communications and e-scholarship (Dagstuhl perspectives workshop 11331). Dagstuhl Manifestos 1(1), 41–60 (2012)
2. Hogenaar, A.: What is an enhanced publication? http://www.openaire.eu/en/component/content/article/76-highlights/344-a-short-introduction-to-enhanced-publications
3. Gray, J.: A transformed scientific method. In: Hey, T., Tansley, S., Tolle, K. (eds.) The Fourth Paradigm: Data-Intensive Scientific Discovery. Microsoft Research, Redmond (2009)
4. Reilly, S., Schallier, W., Schrimpf, S., Smit, E., Wilkinson, M.: Report on integration of data and publications. ODE Opportunities for Data Exchange
5. Callaghan, S., Donegan, S.: Making data a first class scientific output: data citation and publication by NERC's environmental data centres. Int. J. Digit. Curation 7(1), 107–113 (2012)
6. Chavan, V., Penev, L.: The data paper: a mechanism to incentivize data publishing in biodiversity science. BMC Bioinform. 12(Suppl 15), S2 (2011)
7. Hoogerwerf, M., Lösch, M., Schirrwagen, J., Callaghan, S., Manghi, P., Iatropoulou, K., Keramida, D., Rettberg, N.: Linking data and publications: towards a cross-disciplinary approach. Int. J. Digit. Curation 8(1), 244–254 (2013)

8. Wallis, J.C., Rolando, E., Borgman, C.L.: If we share data, will anyone use them? data sharing and reuse in the long tail of science and technology. PLoS ONE **8**(7), e67332 (2013)

9. Castelli, D., Manghi, P., Thanos, C.: A vision towards scientific communication infrastructures - on bridging the realms of research digital libraries and scientific data centers. J. Digit. Libr. **13**(3/4), 155–169 (2013)

10. Manghi, P., Bolikowski, L., Manola, N., Shirrwagen, J., Smith, T.: Openaireplus: the European scholarly communication data infrastructure. D-Lib Mag. **18**(9–10) (2012). http://www.bibsonomy.org/bibtex/23435c839e8f925c6ca94a4c2972015b1/dblp

11. Manghi, P., Manola, N., Horstmann, W., Peters, D.: An infrastructure for managing EC funded research output - the openaire project. Grey J. (TGJ): Int. J. Grey Lit. **6**(1), 31–40 (2010)

12. Attwood, T.K., Kell, D.B., McDermott, P., Marsh, J., Pettifer, S.R., Thorne, D.: Utopia documents: linking scholarly literature with research data. Bioinformatics **26**(18), 568–574 (2010)

13. Bruce, T.R., Hillmann, D.: The Continuum of Metadata Quality: Defining, Expressing, Exploiting. American Library Association, Chicago (2004)

14. Tani, A., Candela, L., Castelli, D.: Dealing with metadata quality: the legacy of digital library efforts. Inf. Process. Manag. **49**(6), 1194–1205 (2013)

15. Feijen, M., Horstmann, W., Manghi, P., Robinson, M., Russell, R.: DRIVER: Building the Network for Accessing Digital Repositories across Europe. In: Ariadne Magazine, vol. 53, pp. 1–4, Ariadne (2007). http://puma.isti.cnr.it/dfdownload.php?ident=/cnr.isti/2007-A0-047

16. Manghi, P., Mikulicic, M., Candela, L., Castelli, D., Pagano, P.: Realizing and maintaining aggregative digital library systems: D-net software toolkit and oaister system. D-Lib Mag. **16**(3/4) (2010). http://www.bibsonomy.org/bib/bibtex/2d5fb59f6245dc730c4d86882d7bfb18d/dblp

17. Berners-Lee, T.: Linked data. http://www.w3.org/DesignIssues/LinkedData.html

18. Wölger, S., Siorpaes, K., Bürger, T., Simperl, E., Thaler, S., Hofer, C.: A survey on data interlinking methods. Technical report, Semantic Technology Institute (STI), University of Insbruck (March 2011)

19. Nikolaidou, P.T., Shaeles, S.N., Karakos, A.S.: MusicPedia: retrieving and merging-interlinking music metadata. Int. J. Comput. **3**(8) (2011)

20. Rinke Hoekstra, P.G.: Linkitup: Link discovery for research data. In: Proceedings of the AAAI Fall Symposium on Discovery Informatics (2013)

Linked Logainm: Enhancing Library Metadata Using Linked Data of Irish Place Names

Nuno Lopes[1,2], Rebecca Grant[2]([✉]),
Brian Ó Raghallaigh[3], Eoghan Ó Carragáin[4],
Sandra Collins[2], and Stefan Decker[1]

[1] Digital Enterprise Research Institute, National University of Ireland,
Galway, Ireland
{nuno.lopes,stefan.decker}@deri.org
[2] Digital Repository of Ireland, Dublin, Ireland
{r.grant,s.collins}@ria.ie
[3] Dublin City University, Dublin, Ireland
brian.oraghallaigh@dcu.ie
[4] National Library of Ireland, Dublin, Ireland
eocarragain@nli.ie

Abstract. Linked Logainm is the newly created Linked Data version of Logainm.ie, an online database holding the authoritative hierarchical list of Irish and English language place names in Ireland. As a use case to demonstrate the benefit of Linked Data to the library community, the Linked Logainm dataset was used to enhance the Longfield Map collection, a set of digitised 18th–19th century maps held by the National Library of Ireland. This paper describes the process of creating Linked Logainm, including the transformation of the data from XML to RDF, the generation of links to external geographic datasets like DBpedia and the Faceted Application of Subject Terminology, and the enhancement of the Library's metadata records.

1 Introduction

Linked Logainm is a collaborative project that aims to create a Linked Data version of Irish place name data held by Logainm.[1] Logainm includes a list of Irish place names, their validated translations between the English and Irish languages, and administrative hierarchy information (stating in which other place names they are included).

Our example collection, the Longfield Maps, are a collection of 1570 map surveys carried out in Ireland between 1770 and 1840. Derived from the maps themselves, the existing metadata records include subject headings for counties, baronies, and occasionally parishes. The emphasis on baronies and parishes in this metadata, as well as the presence of minor geographical features in the surveys, make this collection particularly suitable for linking to the geographical

---

[1] http://logainm.ie/

L. Bolikowski et al. (Eds.): TPDL 2013, CCIS 416, pp. 65–76, 2014.
DOI: 10.1007/978-3-319-08425-1_7, © Springer International Publishing Switzerland 2014

entities found uniquely in the Logainm dataset. The place names stored in the metadata about the maps are in English, preventing any searches for place names represented in the maps to be specified in Irish. We describe ways in which this problem may be overcome by relying on Linked Data from the Linked Logainm project. Our initial approach is to enhance the existing metadata by recording the corresponding identifier in the Linked Data version of Logainm.

Linked Data [2] refers to data published on the Web following a set of principles designed to promote linking between entities on the Web. An essential requirement to enable this linking is that each entity (for example a place name or personal name) is given a unique identifier, generally in the form of a Uniform Resource Identifier (URI). Having determined these URI identifiers, Linked Data reuses other data models such as the Resource Description Framework (RDF) [9] to represent the data about each entity and specify the links, and their type, between two URIs.

The structured data published on the Web enables developers to reuse Logainm's data to build applications, taking advantage of query languages like SPARQL [7] that allow the user to go beyond string matching for searching for place names. For example by using SPARQL one can retrieve only entities of a specified type, with specific values for any property, or simply count the number of entities in a dataset.

We briefly present the project's demonstrator website, which gives an accessible introduction to other potential applications of linked place name data, drawing in digitised content from a range of sources via a Google maps interface.

Related Work. Geographical data forms a substantial portion of the Linked Data landscape. Some of the most relevant data providers and related approaches are LinkedGeoData, GeoLinkedData, Geonames, and DBpedia.

LinkedGeoData [12] consists of a mapping from OpenStreetMap (OSM) data to RDF. The OSM data model contains three types of place names: *nodes*, *ways*, and *relations*. It includes links to DBpedia and GeoNames that are created based on geographical location, the name, and type of place name. GeoLinkedData [4] contains information specific to the Spanish national scenario and mostly relates information about coastal areas with other Spanish national statistics. The UK Ordnance Survey is mapping agency for Great Britain and exposes some of its data as Linked Data [6]. While originally exposing only simple indexes of place names (*gazetteers*), they have now defined custom ontologies to describe the relationships between place names such as topological relations (e.g. *borders*, *spatially contains*).

GeoNames[2] is a worldwide geographical database, freely available and also exposes its data as Linked Data. DBpedia [3] publishes information extracted from Wikipedia as Linked Data. Although not specifically targeted at geographical data, it includes geospatial entities along with point representations for their locations.

---

[2] http://geonames.org

The following section (Sect. 2) presents the Logainm Placenames database of Ireland. Section 3 details the Linked Logainm project, while Sect. 4 introduces the project results in the form of the enhanced Longfield Maps metadata and the demonstrator website. Finally, we present the conclusions and future work in Sect. 5.

2 The Logainm Placenames Database of Ireland

Logainm is an online database containing just over 100,000 Irish geographical names, including authoritative Irish language translations and historical variants. Furthermore approximately 50,000 place names include geographical coordinates. This dataset is generated by the Placenames Branch of the Department of Arts, Heritage and the Gaeltacht, and the database was created and is maintained in collaboration with Fiontar, DCU. The Logainm data is intended as a resource for researchers including educators, students and genealogists. As a bilingual authoritative list of place names, it is also used as the basis for cataloguing and key wording collections from heritage institutions including museums, archives and libraries nationally and internationally. While Logainm's complete dataset has been made available by Fiontar on a request basis, the inclusion of Linked Data in their website allows immediate access to structured data which can be used by cataloguers, as well as computer scientists and application developers.

We next present a set of requirements for the dataset, based on the Linked Data principles and other requirements specific to Logainm:

Place name identifiers: Each place name is identified by a URI under the new sub-domain http://data.logainm.ie/. URI identifiers for place names follow the pattern http://data.logainm.ie/place/{LogainmID}, where {LogainmID} is the place name identifier from the Logainm dataset.

Names in Irish and English: Data representing the Irish and English names is retrievable from the respective URI. To represent the different languages, we use XML "language tags" associated with values of the same property (e.g. foaf:name). Another approach would be to use different properties for English and Irish names, as done by the UK Ordnance Survey: "hasOfficialName" and "hasOfficialWelshName" for Wales [6]. Furthermore, place names include the concept of a validated place name to enable the administrative process of translation, and also include alternate spellings for the place name in Irish.

Types for Place Names: Each place name has a Category, e.g. Barony, Town, County. Each type is identified by a URI http://data.logainm.ie/category/{categoryID}, where {categoryID} is the category identifier from the Logainm dataset.

Place names are contained in (possibly multiple) other place names: The Logainm dataset contains information regarding hierarchical inclusion of place names. This information represents the administrative structure of the place names.

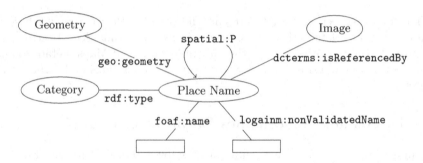

Fig. 1. Initial schema for representing Logainm place names in RDF

Geographical Coordinates: Place names are generally represented by one coordinate according to the Irish Grid Format [10]. In some cases, place names can have multiple coordinates: e.g. for Rivers. For town lands and other types the coordinate approximates the geographical centre, while for rivers the two coordinates are used represent the source and mouth.

A depiction of the Linked Logainm schema is presented in Fig. 1. The generated RDF follows the NeoGeo vocabulary [11], where each place typed as "Feature". The NeoGeo vocabulary also defines several spatial relations between entities, for our data we are relying on the is_part_of relation (spatial:P).

3   Linked Logainm

In this section we describe the process for transforming Logainm's dataset into RDF and determining equivalence links to entities in other datasets. The contents of Logainm's database were provided as an XML dump that included all English and Irish place names along with their type, and if available, the geolocation of the place in Irish Grid Reference format. The approach of using an XML dump rather than other techniques, for example RDB2RDF [5], is due to Fiontar's plans to migrate Logainm's database from a relational database to an XML database.

3.1   Creating RDF Data

The translation of Logainm's database dump (in XML) into RDF was performed using XSPARQL [1], by developing a query that transforms the input XML into the target RDF schema. A partial example of this query is presented in Fig. 2. The presented example creates a subset of the RDF data from the input XML, that contains:

(i) the place name identifiers (generated in line 3 with the help of an auxiliary function);
(ii) the connection to the original page in Logainm's website (line 5); and
(iii) the (possibly multiple) types of the place name (lines 6–8).

```
1  for $place in places/place
2  let $id := fn:data($place/@id)
3  let $URI := local:createURI($id, "place")
4  construct { <{$URI}> a spatial:Feature ;
5                    foaf:isPrimaryTopicOf <{fn:concat("http://
                        logainm.ie/",$id,".aspx")}> .
6          { for $type in $place/type
7             construct { <{$URI}> a <{ local:createURI(fn:data(
                  $type/@id), "category") }> } }
8          }.
9          }
```

Fig. 2. XSPARQL transformation

The target RDF representation contains the information in the original Logainm dataset and also includes the geo-location of the place following the World Geodetic System (WGS) coordinates, the reference coordinate system used by the Global Positioning System (GPS). These coordinates were translated from the provided Irish Grid Format coordinates and used to aid the determination of links between the Logainm dataset and other Linked Data sources on the Web.

The Logainm RDF dataset has been deployed in the Logainm website and the SPARQL endpoint is available at http://data.logainm.ie/sparql/. The resulting RDF dataset contains approximately 1.3 million triples.

3.2   Linking the Datasets

From the relevant sources of Geographical Linked Data (briefly presented in Sect. 1), we elected to generate links to DBpedia, LinkedGeoData, and Geonames.[3] We used the Silk Link Discovery Framework [8] to generate the links between the Logainm RDF dataset and the other target datasets. The Silk framework compares entities from the different datasets according to a pre-defined set of rules and assigns a normalised value (in the interval $[0, 1]$) to the similarity between entities. The entities with highest similarity value are considered to be equivalent.

Next we present the set of comparison rules that we devised for establishing the links between the datasets. The final rule was based on the following similarity values:

- place name (n);
- type of the place name (t);
- name of the parent place (p); and
- geographical coordinates (g) (if available).

---

[3] Since we are interested in matching Irish names we did not consider the GeoLinkedData dataset.

For defining the different similarity values we used the functions and aggregation operations provided by the Silk framework. For example for comparing the place names we used the provided string comparison function based on the *jaro* distance metric[4] or for comparing the geographical coordinates we used the provided spatial comparison function *wgs84*.[5] Both p and g allow us to distinguish between place names that have a similar name but are located in different parts of Ireland, e.g. Newcastle in Dublin, Newcastle in Cork, and Newcastle in Galway.

To calculate the aggregated comparison value, we used a weighted comparison, according to the following formula:

$$\frac{1}{2}n + \frac{3}{8}p + \frac{1}{8}g \ . \tag{1}$$

This formula places a higher weight on the string comparison values, both of the place name and the place name it is included in, rather than the geographical location. This meant that we were not overly penalised by any errors in the geographical coordinates of the place names and could still detect links for the place names that do not have any geographical information. This formula can still be iterated, for example a more fine-tuned approach, as presented in [12], can be investigated. However the initial link evaluation (presented in the next section) is positive. Also noteworthy is that for determining the links to GeoNames, we omit p from the formula, since hierarchical information in GeoNames is not freely available. We also generated the GeoNames RDF from the provided data dumps (in tabular separated format) since RDF dumps are another premium feature.

We also take into account the type of the place name, as such this weighted comparison is only performed between entities of types that have been considered similar. This matching of types was a manual process, performed by the domain experts. The results of this matching (for the most relevant types) is presented in Table 1.[6] The most problematic types to match were "townland" and "population centre", as these can be mapped to different types in the target datasets. We have taken the approach of matching against a more general type (as in the case of DBpedia) or matching against several types (as in LinkedGeoData and GeoNames).

Linking to the FAST Dataset. Given our interest in enhancing library metadata, we investigated the possibility of linking to existing library subject heading schema available as Linked Data. The Online Computer Library Centre (OCLC) has released the Faceted Application of Subject Terminology (FAST) dataset as Linked Data. FAST is a subject heading vocabulary which is derived from the

---

[4] Further details regarding the comparison functions are provided at https://www.assembla.com/spaces/silk/wiki/Comparison.

[5] This function allows to define an approximation value to account for offsets in the geographical locations. We have currently set this value to 1 kilometre.

[6] A description of the GeoNames feature codes can be found at http://www.geonames.org/export/codes.html.

Table 1. Mapping of types between the different datasets

Type	DBpedia	LinkedGeoData	GeoNames
townland	Populated place	Locality	LCTY, PPLF
population centre	Populated place	Town, village, suburb, locality	PPLS, PPL, PPLL
town	Town	Town, village	PPL, PPLS
mountain or mountain range	Mountain, Mountain range	Mountain pass, peak	MT, MTS, PASS, PKU, PKSU
village	Village	Village, Hamlet	PPL
island or archipelago	Island	Island	ISL, ISLET
river	River	River	STM
monument	Monument	Monument	MNMT
city	City	City	PPL
valley	Valley	NaturalValley	VAL

Library of Congress Subject Headings (LCSH), the most widely used subject vocabulary in the library domain. Although the full LCSH dataset has also been published as Linked Data, the simplified FAST syntax and, in particular, the presence of GeoNames references in the FAST data made it an easier target for matching with Linked Logainm. However, since FAST in turn contains links to the Library of Congress Linked Data Service,[7] Linked Logainm will be related to LCSH in the wider Linked Open Data cloud. We looked at reusing the previously described rules and similar process to determine the links, however the FAST data is not structured in such a way that would make this possible. As an alternative, we have decided to leverage the links to GeoNames present in FAST and, combined with our own links to GeoNames, establish an initial set of links from Logainm to FAST.[8] Using this approach we matched approximately one third of the Irish geographical entities present in FAST (500 out of 1,400). In order to obtain a complete matching from Logainm to FAST, the datasets were manually linked along with the link evaluation process (described in the next section). From this manual linking we determined approximately 1,000 links to FAST, and for the remaining entities no adequate match was found.

3.3 Link Evaluation

From the similarity value that the Silk framework assigns to each link we consider only those above 0.95, i.e. the result of Eq. (1) is above 0.95. The evaluation of the rules presented in the previous section generated a set of approximately 16,000 links to the different datasets. A breakdown of the number of links by types and to the different datasets is presented in Table 2. It is noteworthy that the vast majority of links was established for "townlands", which was also the

---

[7] http://id.loc.gov/
[8] This matching was determined using a SPARQL query.

Table 2. Number of links between the different datasets

Logainm		# Links			
Type	# Entities	DBpedia	LinkedGeoData	GeoNames	Total
townland	61,104	747	4,970	7,024	12,741
population centre	2,226	505	1,151	970	2,626
town	849	560	688	605	1,853
mountain or mountain range	372	63	115	111	289
village	142	79	90	10	179
island or archipelago	1,087	20	26	120	166
river	930	12	4	82	98
monument	245	22	36	39	97
city	8	8	7	5	20
valley	111	1	6	9	16

type that was matched to an higher-level type in the target ontologies, and such an approach may introduce errors in the generated links.

In order to determine the precision of the links generated between Logainm and the other datasets we manually checked a subset of these links. The task was to examine the information provided by each pair of URIs (via accessing the URI with a web browser) and deciding if the suggested matching was correct or incorrect. Since Logainm is a manually curated database, our mains focus was to ensure the correctness of the generated links, thus maintaining the dataset's reputation of trusted quality data. As such, we are aiming at a higher precision of the generated links rather than covering all the place names (higher recall). From this manual checking of the links we estimate that the precision of the generated set of links is 97 %.

Below is a breakdown of the link evaluation per dataset and some of the problems in the matching:

DBpedia: For DBpedia we manually checked all the generated links, and determined a precision of 98 %. Some common issues that were encountered in the generated matching were:

(i) Since Logainm contains more fine-grained information, it can contain different entries for "towns", "population centre", and "townland" with the same name. However DBpedia contains only an entry for "town" or "population centre". For example, Adrigole is a "population centre" and a "townland" in Logainm (with two distinct identifiers, http://data.logainm. ie/place/1412693 and http://data.logainm.ie/place/8649), while in DBpedia Adrigole is only a "village" and both Logainm entities are matched to the same DBpedia entitiy: http://dbpedia.org/resource/Adrigole.

(ii) Another issue, although less common, is the discrepancy between types in Logainm and DBpedia. For example, Kentstown is a "townland" in Logainm (http://data.logainm.ie/place/38671), while in DBpedia classifies it as a "village" (http://dbpedia.org/resource/Kentstown).

LinkedGeodata: For LinkedGeoData we have checked a random set of 500 links from all the generated links. Within this subset the precision was of 96 %. Also for LinkedGeoData a common source of errors were "townlands", often matching other types in LinkedGeoData. Also the geographical coordinates in between Logainm and LinkedGeoData are often above the defined offset in our rules (1km), especially for "townlands". This suggests that increasing the value of the offset in our rules may provide further links to LinkedGeoData but may also increase the number of incorrect links.

GeoNames: The links to GeoNames provided very accurate results, from the subset of 500 links we checked, the precision was 99.6 %.

FAST: The links to the FAST dataset were manually generated, based on an initial set of approximately 500 links with GeoNames. In this initial set of links, 1.2 % were found incorrect, possibly due to errors in the links established between Logainm and GeoNames. Overall it was not possible to determine links for approximately 12 % of the entities in the FAST dataset to Logainm entities, frequently because no hierarchy nor geographical coordinates are provided and is thus impossible to distinguish between place names with the same name across Ireland. Also the FAST database frequently conflates "town", "townland", "parish", and other types. We followed the approach of matching to "town" in Logainm.

A workflow for editing incorrect links was put in place so that any incorrect links that may be discovered can be fixed.

4   Applying Linked Logainm to Library Metadata

As previously stated, a key use case which motivated the Linked Logainm project was the potential re-use of Logainm data by cultural heritage organisations and information professionals such as achivists and librarians. Some of the potential benefits identified at the start of the Linked Logainm project were:

– The potential to link to other digital objects or information from other Open Datasets. For example, by relating objects from other projects (e.g. the Royal Irish Academy's Historic Towns Atlas Project) to Logainm entities they could be presented alongside the Longfield maps. Furthermore, by linking Logainm entities to international Open Datasets like GeoNames and DBpedia, contextual information about those locations could also be imported into the library catalogue.
– The potential to enhance discovery by drawing on Irish-language and historical forms of place names found in Logainm. For example, a user searching for "Ceara" or "Cera" could be directed to maps for the barony of Carra.
– The potential to enhance discovery by drawing the hierarchical information in the Logainm dataset. For example, a user searching for a townland name not found in the existing records could be directed to maps for the related barony.

– The potential use Linked Logainm, along with the linking techniques described above, as a source against which to clean and normalise legacy metadata during conversion to a standard schema.

Having established the Linked Data URIs for the Logainm dataset, place names in the National Library's MARCXML metadata records of the Longfield Maps collection were compared and linked to place names in the Logainm dataset. The MARCXML records contained place names as subdivisions of Topical Subject Headings (i.e. the MARC *650* field); however, we decided to use information from the Geographic Coverage Note field (i.e. MARC *522* field). Although, this field normally contains free-text, uncontrolled values, in the case of the Longfield Map records the information had been entered with sufficient consistency to allow predictable parsing. Most importantly, the information in this field not only included a place name (n), but also hierarchical information such that the name of the parent place (p) could also be taken into account as per the linking methods described above. We manually checked approximately 300 of the linked records to determine that the URIs were correct and no errors were found.

In order to show the potential to link to other sources, we have created a demonstrator website that combines information about Irish places from various sources such as DBpedia (via the established links) and the Longfield Maps but also other content from Europeana, the Placenames Branch's digitised archival records, and the Irish Historical Towns Atlas' Dublin volumes. This demonstrator is ongoing work and is available at http://logainm.deri.ie/demo/.

In terms of enhancing the National Library's metadata and catalogue, our initial approach is to record the corresponding identifier in the Linked Data version of Logainm in the bibliographic record. An excerpt of an enhanced record is presented in Fig. 3. The URIs was stored in the MARCXML record by adding a new Geographic Name Subject Heading (a MARC *651* field). Standard MARC linking practices were followed as closely as possible: for example the prove-

```
1  <marc:datafield tag="522" ind1=" " ind2=" ">
2    <marc:subfield code="a">
3      Barony of Coshma, County Limerick, Province of Munster,
         Ireland.
4    </marc:subfield>
5  </marc:datafield>
6  <marc:datafield tag="651" ind2="7" ind1="">
7    <marc:subfield code="2">logainm.ie</marc:subfield>
8    <marc:subfield code="a">Coshma</marc:subfield>
9    <marc:subfield code="0">
10     http://data.logainm.ie/place/145
11   </marc:subfield>
12 </marc:datafield>
```

Fig. 3. Enhanced MARCXML catalogue record

nance of the heading was encoded using the *subfield "2"* with a second indicator value of 7, while the URI itself was encoded in the Authority Record Control Number subfield (*subfield "0"*). This approach is adequate for maintaining the relationship between the MARCXML record and Linked Logainm; however, it is hoped that as new library encoding standards such as the BIBFRAME initiative emerge, more standard techniques for relating bibliographic data to Linked Data resources will be agreed.

5   Conclusions and Future Work

In this paper we presented our approach to enhance library records, specifically the National Library of Ireland's Longfield Map Collection, with extra information about the places that are contained in these maps. By using Irish specific Geographical Linked Data, based on Logainm's data, we presented possible options to also extend the library's catalogue to enable searching for place names in Irish.

We also detailed the process of transforming the Logainm dataset into RDF and how to establish the links to other external datasets, namely DBpedia, LinkedGeoData, GeoNames, and the OCLC FAST subject heading schema, along with an initial evaluation of the determined links. Although some issues presented in this paper are specific to the datasets and the Irish language, for example the alternate spellings of place names in Irish or the matching of categories between Logainm and the external datasets, the presented methodology, also similar to [12], can be used in other countries with place name translations in multiple languages.

We are in the process of writing guidelines and use cases that demonstrate the value of Linked Data — along with other available tools — for heritage professionals, aiming to encourage reuse of Linked Logainm in Ireland.

Future Work. Along with the promotion of the Linked Logainm project, further work can be done in the Silk rules to attempt to obtain a larger number of links. However it should be taken into consideration that the precision of these links should remain high. Another type of entities whose links can be improved are streets, currently a large number of entities in Logainm refers to street names. Even though streets are present in some of the datasets we are linking to — DBpedia includes information about the most important streets in Dublin and other cities; LinkedGeoData contains streets exported from OpenStreetMap — our current linking rules to not provide adequate links for streets. Further work is planned to enhance discovery of the Longfield Maps with the National Library's online catalogue. Rather than add to or modify Authority Data stored at the Library Management System level at this stage, the planned approach is to index Irish and variant forms of place names found in Linked Logainm into VuFind,[9]

---

[9] http://www.vufind.org/

the Library's discovery interface. This system has existing functionality to provide serach suggestions based on cross- references found in traditional library authority records (i.e. MARC *4XX* authority fields); this functionality will also work for the Linked Logainm forms once correctly indexed. Furthermore, the National Library is currently evaluating the use of the Linked Logainm dataset to help with vocabulary standardisation as part of a conversion of a legacy metadata set which contains approximately 18,000 distinct, uncontrolled Irish place names.

Acknowledgements. The work presented in this paper has been funded in part by Science Foundation Ireland under Grant No. SFI/08/CE/I1380 (Líon-2). DRI gratefully acknowledges its core funding from HEA PRTLI cycle 5 (NAVR).

References

1. Bischof, S., Decker, S., Krennwallner, T., Lopes, N., Polleres, A.: Mapping between RDF and XML with XSPARQL. J. Data Sem. **1**, 147–185 (2012)
2. Bizer, C., Heath, T., Berners-Lee, T.: Linked data - the story so far. Int. J. Sem. Web Inf. Syst. **5**(3), 1–22 (2009a)
3. Bizer, C., Lehmann, J., Kobilarov, G., Auer, S., Becker, C., Cyganiak, R., Hellmann, S.: DBpedia - a crystallization point for the web of data. J. Web Sem. **7**(3), 154–165 (2009b)
4. Vilches Blázquez, L.M., Villazón-Terrazas, B., Saquicela, V., de León, A., Corcho, Ó., Gómez-Pérez, A.: GeoLinked data and INSPIRE through an application case. In: Agrawal, D., Zhang, P., El Abbadi, A., Mokbel, M.F. (eds.) GIS, pp. 446–449. ACM (2010)
5. Das, S., Sundara, S., Cyganiak, R.: R2RML: RDB to RDF Mapping Language. W3C Recommendation, W3C, September 2012. http://www.w3.org/TR/2012/REC-r2rml-20120927/
6. Goodwin, J., Dolbear, C., Hart, G.: Geographical linked data: the administrative geography of great britain on the semantic web. Trans. GIS **12**, 19–30 (2008)
7. Harris, S., Seaborne, A.: SPARQL 1.1 Query Language. W3C recommendation, W3C, March 2013. http://www.w3.org/TR/sparql11-query/
8. Isele, R., Jentzsch, A., Bizer, C.: Silk server - adding missing links while consuming linked data. In: Hartig, O., Harth, A., Sequeda, J., (eds.) COLD. CEUR Workshop Proceedings, vol. 665. CEUR-WS.org (2010)
9. Manola, F., Miller, E.: RDF Primer. W3C Recommendation, W3C, February 2004. http://www.w3.org/TR/2004/REC-rdf-primer-20040210/
10. Ordnance Survey of Ireland. The Irish Grid - A Description of the Co-ordinate Reference System used in Ireland. Technical report, Ordnance Survey of Ireland (1996). http://osi.ie/OSI/media/OSI/Content/Publications/The-Irish-Grid-A-Description-of-the-Coordinate-Reference-System-Used-in-Ireland_1.pdf
11. Salas, J.M., Harth, A.: NeoGeo Vocabulary Specification - Madrid Edition. Public draft, February 2012. http://geovocab.org/doc/neogeo/
12. Stadler, C., Lehmann, J., Höffner, K., Auer, S.: Linkedgeodata: a core for a web of spatial open data. Sem. Web **3**(4), 333–354 (2012)

From Linked Data to Concept Networks

Marcin Skulimowski[✉]

Faculty of Physics and Applied Informatics, University of Lodz,
Pomorska 149/153, 90-236 Lodz, Poland
mskulim@uni.lodz.pl

Abstract. Semantic enhancements of scientific papers have been gaining broader use in scientific journal publishing. They facilitate automated discovery and integration of published information. In this paper we consider Linked Data for scientific publications. In particular, we introduce and discuss the notion of a *concept network* containing RDF links between entities from such publications. We show an example of the concept network for publications on quantum mechanics. Moreover, we shortly present a web tool supporting creation of concept networks.

Keywords: Semantic publishing · Semantic web · Linked science

1 Introduction

Semantic Web technologies attract widespread interest in scientific journal publishing. Increasingly, human-readable content of electronic publications is enhanced by machine-readable semantic content [1]. These semantic enhancements make extraction of understanding and knowledge from published articles easier. Thus they facilitate automated discovery and integration of published information. Various enhancements have already been proposed. They can be limited only to bibliographic metadata. However, article metadata can be extended, for example, by adding taxonomic names, identifiers for cited material and geographical coordinates [2]. Semantic enhancements may also include live DOIs, semantic markup of textual terms, tag clouds, interactive figures, "Citations in Context" and machine-readable RDF metadata about the article [3]. Taking into account the diversity and rapid development of semantic enhancements, one can imagine that in the future the machine-readable content will be expanded to encompass all human-readable content of the publication. This way all published knowledge, theories and data will become machine understandable. According to the idea of *semantic science*, in the future, scientific theories and data will be described using vocabulary formally specified by ontologies [4]. Thanks to that machines will understand all scientific knowledge. This will allow semantic interoperability. The idea of semantic science is very tempting but its realization seems difficult, at least in the near future. In order to realize the idea we need ontologies corresponding to various scientific disciplines. Indeed for many disciplines (e.g. medicine, biology, chemistry) such ontologies have

L. Bolikowski et al. (Eds.): TPDL 2013, CCIS 416, pp. 77–88, 2014.
DOI: 10.1007/978-3-319-08425-1_8, © Springer International Publishing Switzerland 2014

already been successfully developed. However, there are disciplines employing complicated mathematical formalism (e.g. physics) for which development of ontologies seems to be a technically difficult task. In fact, current languages for ontology representation are not able to express complicated mathematical concepts and relations. In these cases an ontology can be used to represent a particular domain only "approximately", omitting complicated mathematical details (see e.g. [5]). A more fundamental problem (even for disciplines without advanced mathematical formalisms) is that a transformation of the whole research paper into machine-readable form seems to be difficult to perform. However, it is possible to transform only some part of the paper. Transformations of this kind have already been considered. For example, in a series of papers Gerstein et al. [6,7] proposed the adoption of Structured Digital Abstracts (SDAs), which facilitate access to articles for text-mining engines. A similar idea was developed by Shotton [1]. They published machine-readable RDF metadata for the case of a biomedical research paper. An RDF representation is also used in so called nanopublications which are small units of scientific results [8]. What is very important, a nanopublication can be treated as an independent publication (which can be cited by others) with or without accompanying a research article. Finally, we should also mention about the Linked Data principles which have gained popularity in many fields, including science [9,10]. Applying the principles to scientific data makes it more accessible and easier to reuse [11].

In this study we address the problem of obtaining RDF links for scientific publications in the context of citation networks. It is well known that citation networks do not describe relations between publications in a precise way [13]. In his seminal paper of 2009 Shotton proposed to publish citations in machine-readable form as RDF [14]. Representing citations in RDF will make them machine understandable and processable. Moreover, Shotton proposed to describe the nature of citations using terms from CiTO, the Citation Typing ontology [15]. The benefits of these proposals are obvious. In this paper, we go further and propose to describe in RDF not only links between scientific publications but also links between concepts discussed in them[1]. With this in mind, we introduce the notion of a *concept network* which can be treated, in some sense, as an "extension" of a *citation network* [13]. We discuss the notion and explain precisely the relationship between these two networks (Sect. 2). As an example we show a concept network for a set of publications on quantum mechanics (Sect. 3). Finally, a prototype web tool supporting creation of concept networks is shortly presented (Sect. 4). The paper ends with discussion and the future directions of the present work (Sect. 5).

2   Concept Networks

2.1   Idea

In our previous paper we proposed a procedure to obtain, for a given scientific article, RDF links (for details see [12]). We have focused there on papers on

---

[1] Throughout this paper we use the terms *concept* and *entity* interchangeably.

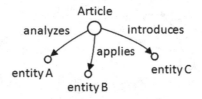

Fig. 1. The graph of relations between an article and some entities.

physics but it seems that the procedure can be applied to other disciplines. Assume now that we want to create RDF links for some paper. The procedure consists of the following six steps.

1. In the first step, the entities from the article (which we want to link with other entities) are selected. We assume that the entities have some names e.g. *concept D, definition 5, plot 7, formula (12)* etc.
2. The entities selected in Step 1 are named with URIs (Uniform Resource Identifiers) using a URL of the article (`artURI`) and the names of the entities selected in the first step. Each URI can be obtained by adding to this URL the hash symbol (#) and some fragment identifier related to the name of the entity e.g. `artURI#concept_D`, `artURI#definition_5`, `artURI#plot7`, `artURI#12`.
3. In this step, relations between the article and the selected entities (see Fig. 1) are described. To this end terms from ontologies can be used. For example, terms from the SACO ontology (*Scientific Article Content Ontology*) [16]. The ontology contains a set of object properties enabling characterization of what is done (used, applied, considered etc.) within a scientific article. Some entities (e.g. elements of the theory, concepts) can be *considered, described, used, derived etc.* in the article. Equivalently, it can be said that the article *considers, describes, presents, derives* something. The ontology also enables to describe relations between the entities considered in a scientific paper.
4. In this step, the types of the selected entities are described using appropriate ontologies. In this way *vocabulary links* are created.
5. *Identity links* (using e.g. `owl:sameAs`) pointing at URIs used in other articles to identify the same entities are described.
6. Using terms from ontologies, *relationship links* between the entities from the considered article and entities from other articles are created.

RDF links obtained according to the above procedure can be divided in two groups:

– *Internal links* - links representing relations between a paper and entities within it (see Fig. 1). They also represent relations between entities considered in a paper.

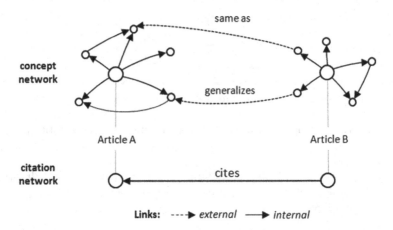

Fig. 2. A *concept network* and the *citation network* for two articles (for the sake of readability, some labels are omitted).

– *External links* - links between entities from a considered paper and terms from ontologies and entities from other articles. These links are particularly important because they describe relationships among entities from various papers.

Internal and external links obtained according to the presented procedure form a network, which we will call a *concept network* (see Fig. 2). The structure of a concept network is more complex than that of a citation network [13]. If we model them as graphs in the latter nodes are publications which are linked by relation *cites*. In concept networks there are two kind of nodes: publications and entities from publications. The nodes can be linked by various relations defined in ontologies. Notice, however, that in concept networks (in contrast to citation networks) nodes corresponding to publications are not directly linked (see Fig. 2). Let us now examine the relationship between these two networks more carefully.

2.2   From a Concept Network to the Citation Network

It follows from the definition that a *concept network* can be represented as a directed graph. Let us now consider the nodes $p_1, p_2, \ldots$ of this graph corresponding to publications. For each node p_k ($k = 1, 2, \ldots$) we consider the set $R(p_k)$ of all nodes e_i corresponding to entities from the publications which are reachable from p_k. In $R(p_k)$ we introduce the following an equivalence relation $\cong$:

$$e_i \cong e_j \Leftrightarrow base_{URI}(e_i) = base_{URI}(e_j)$$

where $e_i, e_j \in R(p_k)$ and $base_{URI}$ is a function assigning the *base part* of a URI to each e_i (e_i is named with a URI containing a *base part*, hash symbol (#) and a *fragment identifier*). Then one particular equivalence class consists of all concepts with the same base part of URI (which is the URL of a publication). The quotient set $R(p_k)/\cong$ can be naturally identified with the set of publications. We can add directed arcs (with labels *cites*) between the node p_k and each publication $p_i = [e_i] \in R(p_k)/\cong$ (where $p_i \neq p_k$). In this way we obtain a directed graph representing citations which is a *subgraph* of the *citation network* [13]. The citations contained in this subgraph are only part of citations which can be found in the publication p_k. This is because *there are many reasons why authors cite the works of others* [13]. It often happens that some article cites to an earlier article without any reference to any entity from this article. For example, the following (or similar) expression can be found in scientific publications: "*...much attention has been devoted to this problem [1–10]*". The expression can be interpreted as providing background reading or giving credit to related works. Citations of this kind do not need to be associated with any reference to entities from earlier publications. Consequently, they are omitted in the fragment of citation network obtained from the concept network according to the presented construction. We may say that a concept network describes relations between articles *more precisely* than a citation network. However, such precise description of citations is not always possible.

2.3   From a Concept Network to the SameAs Network

According to the definition of a concept network it may contain *identity links* created using `owl:sameAs` predicate. If we take into account only identity links in a concept network then we obtain its subnetwork called a *SameAs network* [17]. This (sub)network is very important because it formally describes reuse of entities among scientific publications. We may say that the larger *SameAs network* contained in a concept network, the larger reuse of entities among publications from the concept network.

Although the predicate `owl:sameAs` is very useful it has to be used in concept networks with caution. There are at least two reasons for it.

First, it is well known within the Linked Data community that this predicate has no precise meaning [18]. However, for the case of scientific publications using advanced mathematical formalism the matter seems to be simplified. In those cases the precision of mathematics may influence the precision of *owl:sameAs* relation. This is because entities from such publications are very often *mathematical objects and relations* which are strictly defined. Consequently, in those cases the relation *owl:sameAs* is symmetric and transitive (see e.g. [17]). However, not in all disciplines terms have well defined, accepted and shared meaning. These disciplines may require alternative identity links [18].

The second reason is that, if we forget about some identity link between entities from various publications then it may be drawn the wrong conclusion about the publication in which some entity was introduced the first time.

3 Example

Let us now consider an example of a concept network for real scientific publications. To this end we limit ourselves to a scientific domain called quantum mechanics. There are at least two reasons for this limitation. The first reason is that in this discipline linking concepts does not seem to be very difficult. Thanks to mathematical formalism entities and relations between them are precisely defined. The second reason is that the creation of concept networks requires knowledge of the considered domain and special vocabularies used to link entities. The author of this article is an expert in quantum mechanics and has been developing such vocabularies (see below).

In order to create a concept network we take into account two articles on related problems: *the time operator problem* and *the time of arrival problem*. These articles are available online at the following URLs:
http://link.aps.org/doi/10.1103/PhysRevA.54.4676
http://link.aps.org/doi/10.1103/PhysRevA.59.1804

In the concept network created for these articles we use terms from the SACO ontology mentioned previously and the following two draft ontologies:

1. quONTOm [19] - an OWL ontology describing the main concepts (e.g. *state, observable*) and relations (e.g. *commutator, orthogonality*) of quantum mechanics (for more information see [5]).
2. PHYSO *Physical Sciences Ontology* [20] - an OWL ontology describing general concepts (e.g. *problem, observation*) and relationships (e.g. *problem with, observation of*) of physical sciences.

For convenience, in our example we use Turtle notation and the following prefixes:

```
@prefix phys: <http://purl.org/lyr/physo/> .
@prefix sac: <http://purl.org/lyr/saco/> .
@prefix quo: <http://purl.org/quONTOm/> .
@prefix rdf: <http://www.w3.org/1999/02/22-rdf-syntax-ns#> .
@prefix rdfs: <http://www.w3.org/TR/rdf-schema/#> .
@prefix owl: <http://www.w3.org/2002/07/owl#> .
```

The base URIs for our examples are respectively the URLs of the papers. According to the procedure described in Sect. 2.1 we obtain the following RDF links for the first article[2]:

```
#Internal links
<> sac:introduces <#37>, <#63>.
<> sac:determines <#73>, <#56>.
<#56> phys:obtainedFrom <#37>.
```

---

[2] It is worth to mention that for both articles it is possible to create more a larger number of links. In particular, the links describing types of entities. For simplicity they are omitted.

```
<#73> phys:relatedTo <#37>.
<#63> rdfs:comment "time representation".

#External links
<> phys:problem quo:TimeOfArrivalProblem, quo:TimeOperatorProblem.
<#37> rdf:type quo:SelfAdjointOperator, quo:TimeOfArrivalOperator.
<#56> rdf:type quo:ProbabilityDensity.
<#63> rdf:type quo:Representation.
<#73> rdf:type quo:UncertaintyRelation.
<#37> phys:forSystem quo:FreeParticle.
<#56> quo:probabilityDensityFor quo:ArrivalTime.
```

For the second article we obtain the following RDF links:

```
#Internal links
<> sac:introduces <#problem>.
<> sac:analyzes <#5>.
<#problem> phys:problemWith <#6>.
<#problem> phys:problemDescription "In an eigenstate of the modified time-of-arrival
operator, the particle, at the predicted time of arrival, is found far away
from the point of arrival with probability 1/2".
<#6> quo:eigenStatesOf <#5>.

#External links
<> phys:problem quo:TimeOfArrival,quo:TimeOperatorProblem .
<#problem> rdf:type phys:Problem.
<#6> rdf:type quo:EigenStates.
<#5> rdf:type quo:SelfAdjointOperator.
<#5> owl:sameAs <http://link.aps.org/doi/10.1103/PhysRevA.54.4676#37>.
<#6> owl:sameAs <http://link.aps.org/doi/10.1103/PhysRevA.54.4676#41>.
```

Notice that in both examples we indicate the problems which are considered (relation `phys:problem`). In the case when a problem is already named with a URI we simply create the following link:

```
<> phys:problem <problemURI> .
```

A new problem (without a URI) can be described in the following way:

```
<> phys:problem <#problem> .
<#problem> phys:problemDescription "..." ;
           phys:problemRelatedTo <entityURI> .
```

The concept network obtained for these two papers is presented in Fig. 3 (labels are omitted for simplicity)[3]. First, notice that both articles refer to the same problems (the nodes P_1 and P_2). Moreover, both articles are related to the same entity (E). It can be also seen that the second article indicates some problem (the node P_3) with the entity E introduced in the first article. Notice also that each entity in this concept network is linked to some class from the ontologies. Figure 4 shows the *concept network* obtained for ten articles related to the same problems as previous two articles. The URLs of these articles are presented in

---

[3] The graphs on Figs. 3, 4, 5 and 6 are generated using Gephi (http://gephi.org) and SemanticWebImport plugin (https://gephi.org/plugins/semanticwebimport).

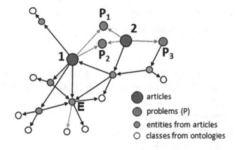

Fig. 3. The concept network for two articles (nodes 1 and 2) referring to the same problems (nodes P1 and P2). The article 2 considers the problem P3 with the entity E from the article 1 (for the sake of readability, some labels are omitted).

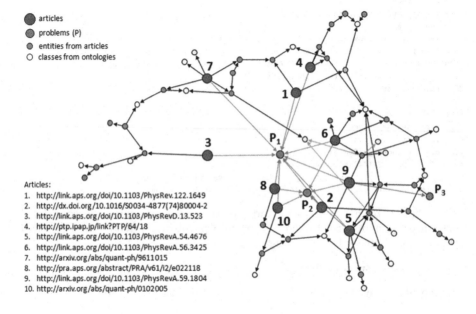

Articles:
1. http://link.aps.org/doi/10.1103/PhysRev.122.1649
2. http://dx.doi.org/10.1016/S0034-4877(74)80004-2
3. http://link.aps.org/doi/10.1103/PhysRevD.13.523
4. http://ptp.ipap.jp/link?PTP/64/18
5. http://link.aps.org/doi/10.1103/PhysRevA.54.4676
6. http://link.aps.org/doi/10.1103/PhysRevA.56.3425
7. http://arxiv.org/abs/quant-ph/9611015
8. http://pra.aps.org/abstract/PRA/v61/i2/e022118
9. http://link.aps.org/doi/10.1103/PhysRevA.59.1804
10. http://arxiv.org/abs/quant-ph/0102005

Fig. 4. The concept network for ten articles referring to problems P1 and P2.

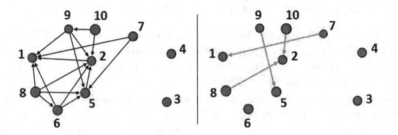

Fig. 5. The graph to the left shows the standard citation network for ten articles from Fig. 4. The graph to the right shows the citations obtained from the concept network (shown in Fig. 4) according to the construction presented in Sect. 2.2.

Fig. 4 where the numbers correspond to the order of publishing. Figure 5 (left side) illustrates the standard citation network for these articles. It is easy to note from the figure that there are two articles which do not refer to other articles. As was mentioned in the previous section a citation does not necessarily mean any reference to any entity from the cited article. We observe this in the case of Fig. 5 (right side) which shows the citations obtained from the concept network according to the construction described in previous section. It follows from the figure that there are only three entities (the nodes 1, 2 and 5) referenced from other articles.

4   Link Your Research: A Tool for Linking Scientific Publications

Applying Linked Data principles to scientific data makes it more accessible and easier to reuse [11]. However, it is not very popular among scientists to create Linked Data and share data. There are many reasons for this. The most important is probably lack of motivation [10]. Scientists simply do not know the benefits of using Linked Data. Another reason is that the creation of Linked Data requires time and additional complex knowledge. Moreover, even if it is possible, in general, to create Linked Data for experimental data it is obviously more complicated to represent as Linked Data knowledge contained in (non experimental) scientific publications. Consider for example a typical theoretical article on quantum mechanics (as considered in the previous section). In such cases, to the best knowledge of the author, automatic creation of RDF links is a difficult task, if not impossible. It turns out, however, that even for disciplines without advanced mathematical formalism (e.g. biology) automatic extraction of relationships is not easy and has to be verified and completed by human experts [21].

In order to facilitate the creation of concept networks we have been developing a prototype web tool called LYR (Link Your Research)[4]. The main aims of the tool are the following:

- to facilitate the <u>creation</u> of concept networks for scientific publications. The process of linking concepts should be simple and does not require much time and knowledge of the RDF syntax.
- to enable <u>storing</u> RDF links belonging to concept networks. Thanks to that, it will be possible to link concepts from publications regardless of its accessibility on the web.
- to enable easy <u>search</u> of the stored RDF links using SPARQL endpoint. Thanks to that the data from the LYR tool will be available to the public.
- to enable graphical <u>visualization</u> of stored concept networks for easy viewing and analysis of the RDF links. This functionality is particularly important to the future success of the LYR project.

---

[4] Additional information can be found online at `http://www.linkyourresearch.org`. The platform will be available soon for tests.

Let us now describe in more details the functionalities of the LYR tool implemented so far.

Within the LYR framework a publication is called a *context*. Each context is named with a URI and contains RDF links created for the publication. The creation of RDF links for a given context is carried out according to the procedure presented in Sect. 2. RDF links can be created only by registered users. The registration is needed in order to name each user with URI. The tool supports *registered users* to carry out the following activities:

- creation of new contexts
- addition/removal of links for any context
- commenting on entities and links

A *non-registered user* has only access to the search functionality (see below). The process of creating of RDF links consists of a few steps (presented in Sect. 2) and involves filling out a simple form available on the website (see Fig. 6). Thanks to that, only very elementary knowledge of RDF is needed. The links are created using terms from appropriate ontologies. The ontologies and the terms are selected from drop-down lists. What is very useful, a user can select ontologies he want to use from the list in his accounts settings. At present, there are ten ontologies available. New ontologies will be successively added. If necessary, a registered user can suggest adding new ontology.

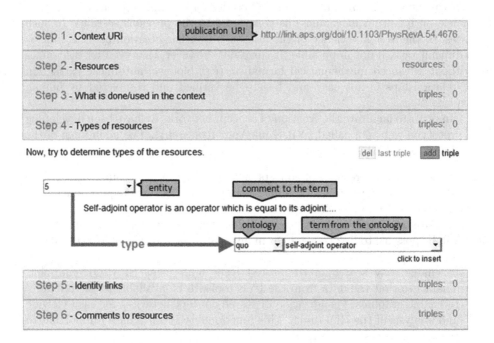

Fig. 6. LYR - creation of a link.

In order to facilitate the handling of URIs the tool offers the ability to assign local names to selected URIs. Thanks to that, instead of using the URI of a paper its local name can be used e.g. *myPaper2013*.

All RDF links generated using the tool are stored in Virtuoso Triple Store. Thanks to that it is possible to explore the dataset. The tool offers three searching options:

- *context* - search for all links created for a given publication (context).
- *entity* - search for links containing some entity identified by a URI.
- *term* - search for all entities (resources) corresponding to the term and not publications containing the term.

In the first two cases search results can be visualized using graphs of links (similarly as in Fig. 4). It is also possible to retrieve links between resources using SPARQL query language.

The test dataset obtained so far is rather small and consists of a few hundred of links generated for real scientific papers. However, new links are successively added.

5 Conclusions and Future Work

In this paper we consider RDF links between entities from scientific publications. In particular, we introduce the notion of a *concept network* containing such links and analyze the notion in the context of *citation networks* and *SameAs networks*. We also present an example of *the concept network* for publications on quantum mechanics. Moreover, we shortly describe a web tool supporting the creation of concept networks.

Our preliminary results are encouraging and provide the basis for further studies. In particular, we intend to create *concept networks* for larger sets of papers in various disciplines. We hope, that analysis of such "test" concept networks will allow to define precise guidelines of how to create them. In particular, an important issue is the selection of appropriate ontologies. We also plan to develop the presented draft ontologies to more complete forms.

Future work should also concentrate on the development of the presented LYR tool. In particular, we are going to work with the scientific community to identify additional requirements from scientists working in various disciplines. We also plan to increase the visualization capabilities of the tool. We believe that this is the main factor affecting the eventual popularity of the tool. Moreover, further work needs to be done to determine whether it is possible to create concept networks semi-automatically using texts of scientific papers.

Perhaps one day, in addition to putting references in scientific publications authors will create *concept networks*. That will bring us closer to *semantic science*.

References

1. Shotton, D.: Semantic publishing: the coming revolution in scientific journal publishing. Learn. Publ. **22**, 85–94 (2009). doi:10.1087/2009202
2. Page, R.D.M.: Enhanced display of scientifc articles using extended metadata. Web Semant. Sci. Serv. Agents World Wide Web **8**, 190–195 (2010)
3. Shotton, D., Portwin, K., Klyne, G., Miles, A.: Adventures in semantic publishing: exemplar semantic enhancement of a research article. PLoS Comput. Biol. **5**, 1–17 (2009). doi:10.1371/journal.pcbi.1000361
4. Poole, D.: Semantic science: machine understandable scientific theories and data (2007). www.cs.ubc.ca/spider/poole/Semantic-Science/SemanticScience.pdf
5. Skulimowski, M.: An OWL ontology for quantum mechanics. In: Proceedings of the 7th International Workshop on OWL: Experiences and Directions (OWLED 2010), San Francisco, California, USA (2010)
6. Gerstein, M., Seringhaus, M., Fields, S.: Structured digital abstract makes text mining easy. Nature **447**, 142 (2007)
7. Seringhaus, M.R., Gerstein, M.B.: Publishing perishing? Towards tomorrow's information architecture. BMC Bioinf. **8**, 17 (2007)
8. Mons, B., Velterop, J.: Nano-Publication in the Science Era, Workshop on Semantic Web Applications in Scientific Discourse (SWASD 2009), Washington, USA (2009)
9. Heath, T., Bizer, C., Hendler, J.: Linked Data (Synthesis Lectures on the Semantic Web: Theory and Technology). Morgan & Claypool Publishers, San Rafael (2011)
10. Wiljes, C., Cimiano, P.: Linked data for the natural sciences: two use cases in chemistry and biology. In: Proceedings of the Workshop on the Semantic Publishing (SePublica) (2012)
11. Kauppinen, T., Baglatzi, A., Keler, C.: Linked science: interconnecting scientific assets. In: Critchlow, T., Kleese-Van Dam, K. (eds.) Data Intensive Science. CRC Press, USA (2011)
12. Skulimowski, M.: Towards linked data in physics. In: Proceedings of the 5th International Conference on Computer Supported Education (CSEDU 2013), Aachen, 6–8 May 2013
13. Egghe, L., Rousseau, R.: Introduction to Informetrics: Quantitative Methods in Library, Documentation and Information Science. Elsevier, Amsterdam (1990)
14. Shotton, D.: CiTO, the citation typing ontology. J. Biomed. Semant. **1**(Suppl 1), 1–18 (2010)
15. CiTO. http://purl.org/spar/cito/
16. SACO. http://purl.org/lyr/saco/
17. Ding, L., Shinavier, J., Shangguan, Z., McGuinness, D.L.: SameAs networks and beyond: analyzing deployment status and implications of owl:sameAs in linked data. In: Proceedings of the 9th International Semantic Web Conference on the Semantic Web, Shanghai, China, 7–11 November 2010
18. Halpin, H., Hayes, P.J., Thompson, H.S.: When owl: sameAs isn't the same redux: a preliminary theory of identity and inference on the semantic web. In: LDH 2011, pp. 25–30 (2011)
19. quONTOm. http://purl.org/quONTOm/
20. PHYSO. http://purl.org/lyr/physo/
21. Leitner, F., Valencia, A.: A text-mining perspective on the requirements for electronically annotated abstracts. FEBS Lett. **582**, 1178–1181 (2008)

LODmilla: Shared Visualization of Linked Open Data

András Micsik[✉], Zoltán Tóth, and Sándor Turbucz

MTA SZTAKI, Budapest, Hungary
{andras.micsik,zoltan.toth,
sandor.turbucz}@sztaki.mta.hu

Abstract. Most current visualizations for Linked Open Data are created for a single purpose or a single dataset. These ad hoc approaches can hardly exploit the linkedness of LOD, and we miss the tools for comfortable and enjoyable LOD browsing. On the other hand WWW has mature generic visualization: the web browsers. With the LODmilla browser we try to find the basic commodity features for generic LOD browsing including views, graph manipulation, searching, etc. With our browser users can navigate and explore multiple LOD datasets and they can also save LOD views and share them with other users. This feature set enables the visualization of provenance and context for LOD entities as well as to navigate on the links between entities such as documents or datasets.

Keywords: Linked open data · Semantic web · Graph visualization · Graph exploration · Javascript · HTML5 · SPARQL · RDF

1 Introduction

The Semantic Web initiative provided the framework and the tools for sharing machine-understandable data on the Web. A lot of semantic data appeared since then on the Web, but most of these data were segmented and there were no uniform method for connecting facts and resources from different data sets. In 2006 Tim Berners-Lee outlined a set of best practices for publishing and connecting structured data on the Web: the Linked Data principles [1]. This bases the identification and linking of semantic entities on so-called dereferenceable URIs, which can be used to retrieve more and meaningful information on the referenced object. On the other hand, Open Data refers to the open access to data in open (non-proprietary) formats. The merge of the two concepts became very popular in last years and was named as Linked Open Data (LOD) [2]. The LOD cloud diagram [3] recorded the growth of available LOD data, and counted 295 datasets containing more than 31,000 million triples.

Usually, these LOD datasets are built using RDF, which is a general method for conceptual description or modeling of information for web resources. The basic piece of RDF is a triple (or statement) which consists of three elements: a subject, a predicate, and an object. With this approach, we are able to store not only data, but statements about the resources. All the three parts of a statement are resources themselves as well.

Ł. Bolikowski et al. (Eds.): TPDL 2013, CCIS 416, pp. 89–100, 2014.
DOI: 10.1007/978-3-319-08425-1_9, © Springer International Publishing Switzerland 2014

Although the Semantic Web and LOD are meant for machine processable data, their use by humans cannot be avoided. Semantic data is often the only available place for the information sought, and furthermore it is usually more accurate and richer than any human-readable representation. Therefore, it is the task of the IT to provide nice and useful visualizations of Semantic Data for humans. The problem with these visualizations is that they are not generic, but ad-hoc; they are capable of presenting limited types of datasets only. While the World Wide Web had its generic visualization method, the web browser since the very beginning, the LOD cloud is still missing a generic visual browser. In this paper we investigate previous generic LOD visualization approaches and present our own ideas in this respect which were implemented in the LODmilla prototype.

2 Related Work

There are quite a lot of approaches for presenting LOD data for humans. Most of these however are dedicated to specific purpose and specific datasets (see for example [4]). The obvious solution for all-purpose LOD browsing is a pure text-based approach (e.g. Virtuoso faceted browser or Graphity [5]). In this case, we usually see a single resource with all its referring triples listed. In this case we can read all data properties such as names, birthdate, etc., and we see all connected resources as links. Clicking on a connected resource brings up the tabular or list view of the selected new resource.

The disadvantage of the pure textual approach is that we see one resource only and the graph structure of connections cannot be seen. In case of hypertext, this is not a problem, but in RDF the connections carry much more information, for which users should have an overview. Therefore, the combination of graphical and textual browsers is a more popular approach, and in the rest of the section we provide an overview of these.

One thing that differentiates the applications using the semantic web is the level where it handles the data. As [6] points out, the grouping by the granularity of information can be the following:

- Collection level.
- Resource level.
- Intra-resource level.

While the collection level approach focuses on providing a general overview of a set of data, and mostly used for predictions, the resource level shows the attributes of the individual resources, and visualizes the connections between them, hence it provides more details on individual resources. Intra-resource level approaches show the distribution of the topics and attributes in a single resource, and they are used mostly for deeper analysis. In this work we aim at the resource level and try to point out the strong and weak points of related other work.

LodLive [7] represents the LOD resources and their connections in a graph structure. The visual design here is plain and simple, so it is relatively easy to understand the whole concept. Even so, the resources, represented by circles, do not contain enough information for the first sight. We only see a circle, with the resource's labels listed in different languages, plus some other circles around it. If we would like to know more about a resource, we have to open its detail box on the right. Here we can see the data properties attached to the selected node in a pre-processed format, for example image URLs are detected and shown, geographical location is extracted and put on map, etc. The major drawback of LodLive is the pure navigation on connections. Connections are grouped by property, and visualized as expanding small circles around the resource circle. This gives a limitation on the number of connections that can be shown, and in fact, LodLive truncates the shown connections to the first 30–40 for each connection type which results in information loss. It is also hard to see where the connection points, as only the resource URIs are shown as a hover for each small circle. Resource URIs can be quite cryptic for humans when they contain numeric identifiers. Therefore, in LODmilla we aim at showing the labels or titles of connection endpoint resources. LodLive has a nice design, but quite often the usability is sacrificed on the design. As an advantage, it is made as a pure HTML5 browser, which can be run in any modern browser.

OOBIAN [8] is a feature-rich, well-designed and useful LOD browser implemented in Silverlight. Technically this is a drawback as Silverlight is not available in all browsers. OOBIAN consists of several views: a graph view, a textual reader, a file explorer and a map. This application combines the visual and text based approaches, but it can't be used for advanced purposes. It is a good LOD browser to jump from one node to another or to filter properties. The main drawback is that we can see only a single resource and its connections in the graph view.

Microsoft Academic Search is a special tool for finding researchers, their publications, and the relations between these. It includes a Silverlight-based graph module named Visual Explorer [9] where we can visualize the connections between people, show the links between co-authors, and see the citations graph of a person. The main problem with this approach is that it is limited to a given scenario and requires the internal database of Microsoft which is not open for any other organizations.

The VisualDataWeb project produced a set of very interesting graphical user interfaces for the Semantic Web [10]. The RelFinder helps to find connection paths between selected resources. This is a very useful function if we want to know how two objects are related to each other. In LODmilla, we implemented a similar function, but with a different solution we are able to find longer paths and paths can also include nodes from different RDF stores.

gFacet and tFacet [10] are the graph-based and textual implementation of faceted browsing of RDF data. SemLens [10] provides tables and plots to analyse trends and correlations in RDF data. These tools cover specific needs for RDF data consumers, and may be applied as add-ons in future generic LOD browsers.

3 A Generic LOD Browser

Browsing the web is a commodity today with a number of web browsers on the market. These browsers share some default, fundamental controls and functions, which provide the basic browsing experience, as a result of crystallization during the last two decades. The basic functions are:

- Opening documents,
- Following links in documents,
- Going back to the previously seen document in the history,
- Searching for text in a document,
- Saving a local copy of the document.

Although the LOD has a much shorter existence than WWW, we cannot find a tool that provides comfortable and visual browsing of semantic data and LOD resources. The tools we examined are either built for specific datasets or they are difficult to use and lack important visualization features. We believe that there is a need for generic LOD browsers, with a set of common basic features the users can learn and get used to. This would greatly increase the impact and usefulness of LOD.

The following basic actions for generic LOD browsers have been identified:

- Visual representation of multiple resources and properties (most probably as a graph),
- Opening resources, viewing object and data properties,
- Searching in the resources,
- Searching in the graph,
- Manipulating a set of documents,
- Saving current LOD view,
- Sharing LOD views with others,
- Undoing previous actions (replacement of web browser history).

We implemented LODmilla as our prototype solution for the above listed goals of generic LOD browsing. LODmilla is a graph based browser, running in conventional web browsers, developed using HTML, CSS and Javascript. While it is primarily visual, it also contains textual representations of resource properties in order to combine the best of both worlds. Its goal is to provide a simple, yet feature-rich application for the interactive exploration of LOD content residing in multiple knowledge bases.

By its design, LODmilla does not hide any information available in RDF from the users, but it tries to organize and pre-process presented data. For example, incoming and outgoing properties are grouped by property type, and for the data properties URLs are made clickable, image URLs are shown inline and geographic locations are shown on a map. The work in the field of user experience is still in progress, but our long-term approach is to extend the interface with more advanced operations in a palette-like fashion, which work similarly to usual image manipulation software (e.g. Gimp).

3.1   Frontend

As the goal was to implement a solution for a wide set of browsers, first we had to choose from available drawing options (Flash, Java and Silverlight were excluded because they need separate plug-ins): SVG (Scalable Vector Graphics), HTML5 canvas, or plain HTML+CSS based graphics. Each of these have their own advantages and disadvantages regarding printing, zooming and other features; so finally we found that a mixed approach fits our needs the best. We used jsPlumb [11] as the visual engine, along with jQuery [12] as the most popular Javascript library. JsPlumb uses pure HTML+CSS for visualizing the graph nodes, and SVG for the links between them. With this approach we lost the ability to use built-in zooming and panning, but we could substitute these with our own implementation in Javascript. On the other hand, handling buttons, text and events got much easier with the HTML and CSS basis of the implementation.

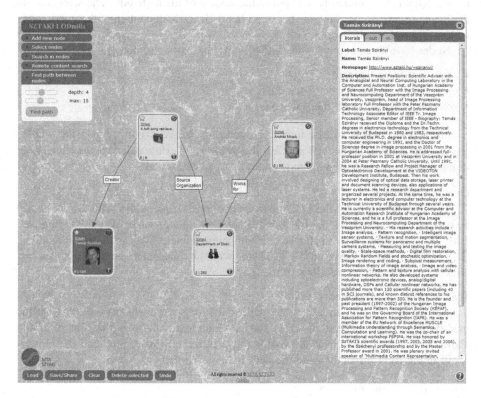

Fig. 1. LODmilla user interface

Figure 1 shows the four main parts of the web application:

- canvas
- palettes (top left)
- toolbar (bottom left)
- inspector (right).

The canvas is the background, on which the graph structure is drawn. The palettes contain various actions, grouped into "accordion" styled menu items. We have a toolbar at the bottom, with the standard operations like load, save, etc. Every node (LOD resource) has a lot of information; these can be viewed in the inspector window on the right, which opens by clicking the "I" (information) button in any node. The inspector window - unlike the other three main elements - can be moved, resized, and closed.

Complex operations can be started from the palettes, while simple ones can be found in every node. Each node has the following basic information in it: the source of the resource, its title or label, and the number of data properties and object properties associated with the resource. Additionally, an image representation (if found) or an icon based on the resource type is put in the middle of the node box. The selection of the image or icon to be shown is based on heuristics, which contain both generic and ad-hoc (dataset-specific) rules.

Nodes have three actions, which affect only the particular node:

- remove it from the canvas
- open details in the inspector window
- select/highlight it (with the star icon).

Furthermore nodes can be moved around, and we can zoom or pan the whole graph view. Actions in the toolbar affect the whole view, while palette actions are used to manipulate a set of (highlighted) nodes or to add new nodes.

Opening resources

The first step in using the LOD browser is to open some nodes. This can be done by pasting a resource URI, but for some datasets we offer an easier way: by typing the label of the resource, we can choose one with autocomplete. We can then start reading the content of the resource in the inspector window, and open some new nodes by clicking on selected connections in the list.

Searching in open resources

Resources may contain a lot of properties and long texts, which we don't want to read through. One palette item serves for searching text patterns in the content of all shown graph nodes. Figure 2 shows this menu in the left menu box, and the search result in the right inspector window, with red colored text.

Searching for new resources

When we don't find the requested information in open nodes, we can try to expand our graph view with new nodes. This is a different search function; it finds the resources which contain the given query word(s), and are connected to a selected resource. Figure 3 shows the use case of searching of the word "KOPI" (a plagiarism search service), from the starting document named "Máté Pataki", shown in the middle. All the resources surrounding are the search results containing the word "KOPI" in their content.

Saving/Sharing/Loading

The graph of currently open resources may demonstrate a new finding, or record a certain state of knowledge, which may be useful in the future for the user who created it. We offer the ability to fully save a graph state under user-given title, and load it later into the browser. Saved graphs can be shared via a unique URL (similarly to Google documents).

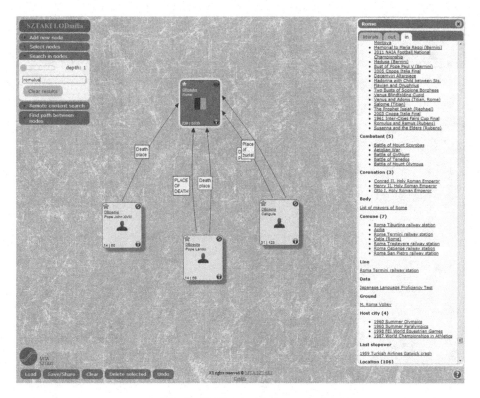

Fig. 2. Finding text in resources

Undo

As some actions may unexpectedly cover the canvas with many new nodes, an Undo function has also been implemented, which reverts the last action the user made.

Marking/highlighting (selection)

All resources on the canvas can be marked one-by-one or in groups. One method to achieve this is clicking on the star in the top-left corner of the nodes. Another method is using the "Select nodes" palette on the left, which can mark all nodes or nodes of the same type. Marking nodes provide the starting points for operations on node groups such as search. For example, we can select the person type resources, and perform a search with the word "KOPI" in those nodes, this way finding the people in a department, who are somehow related to "KOPI", which is the name of a project running in our department.

3.2   Backend

Most of the browsing functionality does not rely on a server, and thus our tool could have been run standalone in a browser without a dedicated server. In order to support saving and sharing users' views, we had to implement a server side component as well. The backend has an additional benefit for performance as it can load information

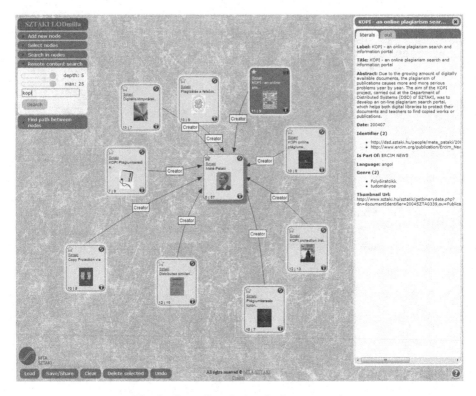

Fig. 3. Expanding the graph via text search

faster and cache visited nodes. Finally, we moved most of the search operations to the backend because of these reasons. Search operations use both graph traversal and SPARQL querying, as we cannot always rely on a SPARQL endpoint for datasets.

We put a requirement that our solution should work on as many datasets as possible, and it should use the latest information available, so harvesting and pre-processing datasets was not an option unlike in approaches such as [13]. These presumptions lead us to a graph traversal which can use either a SPARQL query (DESCRIBE for example), or HTTP GET method and dereferenceable URI mechanism to fetch the connections of resources. By using the Jena toolkit, we can parse incoming RDF as Turtle, RDF/XML, JSON, etc.

Three variations of LOD graph search have been implemented:

• Content search: we are searching neighbour nodes with data properties containing the given search pattern,
• Connection search: the nodes are expanded via object properties with names matching the search patterns,
• Path finder: paths are sought between selected nodes.

In all cases we wanted to avoid solutions that work in single datasets only and solutions which use pre-processing of whole datasets. These requirements lead to several problems: first, the quality of the RDF stores is quite different in capabilities, availability and speed, which has big impact on the performance and quality of the graph traversing and building process. Some of the RDF nodes might not be available during the search process, or they can be slowly harvested. The second problem is that the world-wide LOD graph is huge: nodes may have 500 or 1000 connections, and a 2-step path may cover 3 different RDF stores. The third problem also comes from the heterogeneity of our data sources: links between graph nodes sitting at different RDF stores are known only by one of the nodes (i.e. incoming links are not stored).

Because of these limitations, we chose to generate our graphs dynamically. When a user explores a part of the LOD graph, several search operations may be started in a sequence. These queries may be slow at first due to dynamic loading of nodes, but will get faster and faster after the graph area is cached.

As we only see a part of the whole graph at search time, most of the well-known fast graph search algorithms are not applicable in our case. We have to go back to A* style traversal and adapt it to our needs. It is hardly possible to estimate the distance to the goal node, but we can use some heuristics based on connection types. As a specificity of this task, there are paths we are simply not interested in, for example Book resources are all connected to the Book RDF type. Therefore, we simply not follow a set of trivial links denoting type, language or format of nodes. The traversal of the remaining links may be ordered heuristically based on learning, this remains as future work in the project.

In the case of remote content search our task is to answer the question: does a node containing a given string in a data property exists in the neighbourhood of a given node? To answer this question breadth-first traversal in the RDF graph structure is applied. We have to limit this algorithm in several ways. We specified a maximum depth until the algorithm tries to find results. As the result set may easily grow to hundreds of nodes, which is incomprehensible for the user, we limit the number of result nodes as well. The result of the search is shown as highlighted nodes in the graph for which the shortest paths from the start node are also displayed.

In the case of connection search only those connection types are followed which are matching with the given search text(s). Multiple search items might be added divided by a separator. The traversal of links is also breadth-first. The result of the query is a set of nodes which are accessible via the matching connections. The relevant incoming connections, just like in the case of the content search algorithm, might not be discovered, as these can only be retrieved using SPARQL endpoints, and even so, we cannot ask each SPARQL endpoint in the world for the existence of such connections.

For path finding the question is if a path exists between two RDF resources (Fig. 4). Our implementation is similar to Dijkstra's algorithm where all edges have the same weight and where the graph is produced on the fly. The starting parameters of our implementation are the two starting nodes, the maximum depth of the search, and the maximum number of nodes we can handle as a response. In the first iteration a breadth-first traversing starts from both endpoints. Their connections are checked and if common nodes can be found, they will be accepted as results and the algorithm finishes. In each further iteration the nodes accessible from the already found nodes are checked. One such iteration means two steps in depth increment since we are

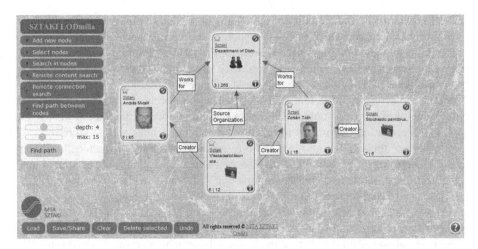

Fig. 4. Finding a path between two resources

growing our graph from both ends. The local target is to find nodes which have parents to both of the source nodes. When such node has been found, the resulting graph must be simplified. All nodes not on the common path are eliminated. In this case it still might happen that we have more nodes in the path than the number we can comfortably handle on the user interface.

Our department operates a LOD server (lod.sztaki.hu) with the contents of Hungarian archives based on the National Digital Data Archive of Hungary. The dataset (11 million triples) contains information about books, movies, articles published in Hungary with links to other datasets such as DBpedia or VIAF. Furthermore, publication data of SZTAKI are also converted to triples. These two datasets serve as the initial testbed for LODmilla, but it was also tested with DBpedia, DBLP and other servers.

Currently LODmilla is available internally in our institute to browse the lodified publication data of colleagues.

3.3   Example Use Case

In the following we briefly illustrate a use-case for the exploration of LOD space using LODmilla. The numbers in boxes represent the order of appearance for the nodes in Fig. 5. Let's assume that we found an interesting paper, so we enter its keywords into the "Add new node" box, and open the listed semantic description for the paper (1). We can now expand all the Creator type links of this node to see all authors (2). Next, we may check if the authors have created more papers together, and we find two more papers (3). Then we display all authors for the 3 papers, and we get 3 other authors (4). We see that Grid is a common topic in the papers found so far, so we issue a content search on connected nodes for the new authors containing the word Grid, and 2 more papers are shown (5). One of the papers is not linked to anybody from SZTAKI,

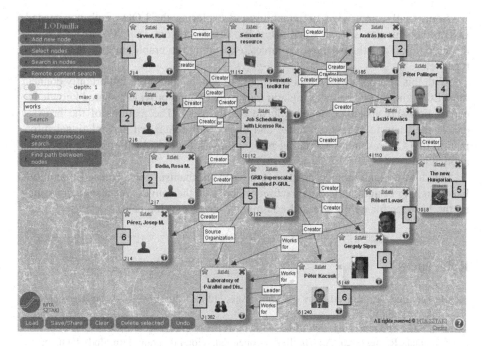

Fig. 5. A sample session of LODmilla demonstrating a use case

so we instruct to display all co-authors (6), and get 3 colleagues from a different department (7). As a result, we explored the neighborhood of a selected paper discovering 3 authors groups (one from Spain and two departments from SZTAKI), and found some more papers related to the topic of Grids and the Semantic Web. The graph can now be saved and shared with other colleagues.

4   Conclusion

In this paper we argue that generic tools for exploring and navigating the LOD cloud are necessary not only for computers but for humans as well. The example of Web browsers show that functionality for using a similar technology converges to a common visualization and a common set of functions. With the LODmilla browser we experiment and test these common functions for generic LOD browsing, based on some key features:

- The link structure of LOD is visualized as a graph,
- Browsing works on several datasets in the same time, connections are also shown between separate datasets,
- Either dereferenceable URIs or a SPARQL endpoint is required,
- Zooming and panning in the graph are supported,
- It is possible to save and share graph views among users.

Additionally, new ways of searching and exploring the LOD graph are needed. LODmilla supports several candidates for these: content search starting from a resource, finding paths between resources, expanding the graph via given connection types, etc.

With this approach LODmilla is capable to handle, and more importantly connect most LOD knowledge bases easily and transparently, and provide a shared knowledge exploration and visualization experience for its users. The features of the browser enable the users to access, visualize and explore all contextual and relational information of LOD resources including research datasets or publications as a particular application area.

Our future plans include creating a plug-in mechanism for advanced operations like searching or automatic organization of nodes on the canvas. We also plan to open up the browser for public use and community-based development.

References

1. Berners-Lee, T.: Linked data - design issues, (2006). http://www.w3.org/DesignIssues/LinkedData.html
2. Bizer, C.: The emerging web of linked data. IEEE Intell. Syst. **24**(5), 87–92 (2009)
3. Cyganiak, R., Jentzsch, A.: The linking open data cloud diagram. http://lod-cloud.net/
4. The Best Open Data Releases of 2012. http://www.theatlanticcities.com/technology/2012/12/best-open-data-releases-2012/4200/
5. Graphity. http://graphity.org
6. Herrmannova, D., Knoth, P.: Visual search for supporting content exploration in large document collections. D-Lib Mag. **18**(7/8) (2012)
7. LodLive. http://en.lodlive.it/
8. ::oobian::. http://oobian.com/
9. VisualExplorer. http://academic.research.microsoft.com/VisualExplorer
10. VisualDataWeb tools. http://www.visualdataweb.org/tools.php
11. jsPlumb. http://jsplumbtoolkit.com/
12. jQuery. http://jquery.com/
13. De Vocht, L., Coppens, S., Verborgh, R., Vander Sande M., Mannens E., Van de Walle R.: Discovering meaningful connections between resources in the web of data. In: Proceedings of the 6th Workshop on Linked Data on the Web (2013)

Content Visualization of Scientific Corpora Using an Extensible Relational Database Implementation

Theodoros Giannakopoulos$^{(\boxtimes)}$, Eleftherios Stamatogiannakis,
Ioannis Foufoulas, Harry Dimitropoulos, Natalia Manola, and Yannis Ioannidis

Management of Data, Information, and Knowledge Group,
Department of Informatics and Telecommunications,
University of Athens, Athens, Greece
tyiannak@di.uoa.gr
http://www.madgik.di.uoa.gr/

Abstract. A method for supervised classification and visualization of collections of scientific publications is presented. By integrating a text classification module, which leads to class probability estimation, along with a dimensionality reduction technique, which represents each class in the 2-D space, any collection of unlabelled documents can be visualized. The classification and visualization modules have been trained on three different datasets and respective categorizations. We provide an example of our system's functionality by visualizing the content of collections of publications which share a common funding scheme. In order to implement this, we have developed a funding mining submodule which identifies documents of particular funding schemes. All the individual modules have been implemented using the madIS system, which provides data analysis functionalities via an extended relational database.

1 Introduction

Visualization of textual content is a rather important task in data mining, since it constitutes a way to represent what particular document corpora refer to. Among the wide range of textual information available in the web, scientific documents form a subject of major interest, making the text analytics task for such content more complex and interesting, mainly due to their content richness and diversity. In this work we present a method for supervised classification and visualization for collections of scientific publications. The classification and visualization modules have been trained using a series of taxonomies and respective datasets (e.g., the arXiv dataset [1]). In addition, special focus has been given on the integration of both the classification and visualization modalities: in particular this is achieved in the context of a data processing workflow. We demonstrate intermediate results of this procedure, applied on a particular use case, according to which we are interested in visualizing the content of collections of publications which *share a common funding scheme* (e.g. FP7-ICT). Towards this end,

L. Bolikowski et al. (Eds.): TPDL 2013, CCIS 416, pp. 101–112, 2014.
DOI: 10.1007/978-3-319-08425-1_10, © Springer International Publishing Switzerland 2014

we have also implemented a fast and accurate fund mining submodule which is responsible for detecting funding information in scientific publications.

The proposed system has been implemented under the `OpenAIREplus` EU project titled: "2nd-Generation Open Access Infrastructure for Research in Europe" (283595)[1]. This project aims to build an information infrastructure of scientific publication and data repositories. In addition, it implements EC's *open access* policies through services that effectively connect publications to scientific data and funding information. This is achieved through data mining techniques towards the automatic classification, indexing and clustering of scientific publications, funding information mining and content visualization. In the context of such an infrastructure, content classification and visualization can be a rather powerful tool for research administrators, if such techniques are connected to funding schemes. In other words, automatic content visualization can assist the research administrators in the process of strategy or policy making, since it will provide them with "an image" of the content distribution for particular funding schemes or any other categorization of interest (e.g., by country, institutes, etc.).

2 Methodology

2.1 Content-Based Classification

The purpose of this submodule is twofold: (a) To provide a simple way of text classification: towards this end a rather straightforward technique is adopted. (b) To represent the content of each document class. This representation will be also used in the visualization step.

Feature Extraction. The feature extraction is rather straightforward, since it only involves the extraction of term frequencies, which will be later used to estimate the respective probabilities used in the classifier. Towards this end, some typical text mining steps are adopted. In particular, the following steps are executed for each document d:

1. Tokenization: the initial stream text is broken into individual words. Also, a separate process for detecting frequent word 2-grams is used.
2. Stop word removal: towards this end, we have adopted the NLTK's stop words list [2]
3. Stemming: for this preprocessing step the Wordnet lemmatizer of NLTK has been adopted [2]
4. A list of unique terms is generated after the first preprocessing steps
5. For each unique term t its frequency $df_d(t)$ is extracted

As the above process continues for a corpus of documents, a global list of unique terms is updated, along with the respective term frequencies for each document. By "terms" we mean single words or 2-grams, as explained above.

---

[1] http://www.openaire.eu/en/component/content/article/
   326-openaireplus-press-release

Classification. Since we are interest in a supervised learning scheme we obviously make the assumption that each document is mapped to one or more classes. There are several of such available datasets (and respective taxonomies) which will be discussed later. In the context of a supervised task, we execute for each class c the process described in Sect. 2.1 in order to compute the list of terms and the corresponding frequencies for each document in the corpus (df_d). Then, based on these term frequencies, the following probabilities are estimated (a) $P(t)$: the a-priori probability that term t can appear in the whole corpus and (b) $P(t|c)$: the probability that term t appears in some document of a particular class c.

These probabilities are used to produce a set of dictionaries (D_c) and respective weight arrays (W_c) for each class c. In particular, for each class c and for each term t in the list of corpus terms, if $\frac{P(t|c)}{P(t)} > T$, where T is a user-defined threshold, then the term t is added to dictionary D_c. Also, the respective weight vector (W_c) is updated according to: $W_c(t) = \frac{P(t|c)}{P(t)}$. In this way, each class obtains a dictionary-based representation which is used both for classification and visualization. In the case of document classification, for the document d, with terms $t_1, \ldots, t_N$ the probability

$$P_d(c) = \sum_{i=1}^{N} log(W_c(j : D_c(j) = t_i))$$

is computed. This classification step is actually equivalent to the Naive Bayes classifier [3].

2.2 Content Visualization of Text Corpora

Class Numerical Representation and Dimensionality Reduction. As explained in the previous Section, each content class is represented through a pair of term dictionaries and respective weights. Our final purpose is to represent a corpus of scientific publications in a human perceptible dimensionality. In particular, the visualization module aims to map each of the content classes (through their dictionary representation) to a particular point in the 2D space, so that similar classes (in terms of textual content) are close to each other. This is actually a dimensionality reduction task.

Let us first create a numerical representation of the content classes. Towards this end, a similarity-between-classes matrix is extracted. This matrix is defined based on the extracted class dictionaries and respective weight arrays (Sect. 2.1). In particular, let c_1 and c_2 be a pair of content classes and D_{c_1}, D_{c_2}, W_{c_1} and W_{c_2} the related dictionaries and weights respectively. N_1 and N_2 are the number of dictionary terms for the two classes. The transition from the "dictionary space" to a purely numerical representation is achieved through the similarity measurement calculation:

$$S(c_1, c_2) = \frac{\sum_{i=1}^{N_1} W_{c_2}(k : D_{c_1}(i) = D_{c_2}(k))}{\sum_{i=1}^{N_2} W_{c_2}(i)} + \frac{\sum_{i=1}^{N_2} W_{c_1}(k : D_{c_2}(i) = D_{c_1}(k))}{\sum_{i=1}^{N_1} W_{c_1}(i)}$$

In other words, we directly use the extracted dictionaries to calculate the similarity between any pair of classes. An alternative of this similarity technique would be some type of sample-to-sample similarity measurement. However, the extraction of the adopted class-based similarity matrix is of low computational cost, which makes it attractive in the context of a system that processes very large corpora. In addition, this approach makes direct use of the information extracted in the training phase of the content classifier.

Using matrix S we have managed to numerically represent the class distributions in the $\mathbb{R}^M$ space, where M is the total number of classes, from a simple dictionary representation. Now, we need to find a combination of the dimensions of this space to a 2D space which will provide us with the visualization results. However, since M can be quite high for most of the taxonomies (e.g. the arXiv dataset has almost 150 classes) the dimensionality task cannot be achieved directly, due to numerical issues. So instead of proceeding with the final dimensionality reduction procedure, we firstly reduce the feature space via a clustering technique. In particular, we first apply a k-means clustering algorithm [4] on S. Towards this end, we assume rows are samples. k is selected to be equal to 20. Therefore, this clustering procedure leads to a set of k cluster centers, say $Cl_i, i = 1, \cdots, k$. This clustering is a grouping of similar content classes, based to the dictionary-based similarity criterion. As a next step, we compute the Euclidean distance between each row i of the S matrix and each cluster j: $d(i, j)$. d can be assumed as a set of M samples in the k feature space.

The clustering procedure described above leads to a new numerical (lower dimension) representation of each class based on its distances from the extracted content clusters. A self organizing map (SOM) is then used in order to extract a 2-D discretized representation of the classes [5], based on that lower dimensional space. Now each class, is represented by a pair of discretized coordinates in the 2-D feature space. The reason why we selected to express the original feature space as a linear combination of distances from cluster centers, before proceeding with the main SOM algorithm, is to avoid numerical and computational issues that stem from the high initial dimensionality and the large number of classes involved in the SOM training procedure. Reducing the class dimensionality to $k = 20$ makes the training of the SOM faster and more accurate.

Content Visualization of Unlabelled Corpora. The classification-visualization submodules described above classify an unknown document to a set of classes, providing soft outputs (probability estimations) and represent each of the classes in the 2-D space. If these two submodules are combined and applied for a corpus of unknown scientific documents, they can provide a visual interpretation of the corpus content. In more detail, the content classification module is firstly applied for every document $i, i = 1, \ldots, N_d$. N_d is the total number of documents in the collection. This leads to a set of output probabilities $P_i(c)$ for each class $c = 1, \ldots, M$. When the classification stage is completed for each document, the corpus content is represented using a 3-D vector for each class c: $[X_c, Y_c, \frac{\sum_{i=1}^{N_d} P_i(c)}{N_d}]$, where, X_c, and Y_c are the estimated 2-D class coordinates extracted from the training phase of the visualization module. According to that, each document corpus is represented for each class of the adopted taxonomy, using: (a) the 2-D estimated coordinates and (b) the accumulated (average) estimated content class probability. This can be illustrated in the 2D plane using a "balloon" representation for the visualization of this type of 3-D data, provided by Google.[2]

2.3 Fund Mining

The purpose of the fund mining submodule is to detect documents of particular funding schemes. The initial aim was to identify EU FP7-funded[3] documents, however, recently this was extended to also include Wellcome Trust[4] projects. We have now further enhanced the module so that it is able to handle an arbitrary number of funding bodies and institutions. As explained in the introduction, funding information is a rather important type of metadata that can be useful in article, authors, institutions and funding statistics and visual analytics. Consider for example the task of discovering and presenting trends in a temporal way, or tracking statistics for different funding bodies and calls. In the context of the present work, funding information is used to specify the types of documents being visualized.

The funding mining module can either be used on individual publications (e.g., at the time a publication is deposited to facilitate authors in adding metadata information), or in batch mode (e.g., in order to processes all documents found in a collection/repository). In both cases, the module does some preprocessing (such as stop word removal, tokenization, etc.) on the text of each publication. Then it scans the text to extract possible matches using patterns, and it finds matches against the current known lists of project grant agreement numbers and/or acronyms for various funding bodies. In addition, contextual information is used to provide a confidence value for each match and to filter out any false matches. Specifically, the context is considered as a bag of positioned weighted words/n-grams. Some terms have positive weights (ex. fp7, european research council) whereas some others have negative (ex. postal code, telephone number etc.). The absolute weights may also increase according to their distance from the matching grant id/acronym. For the selection of terms we use a naive bayesian method on the contexts of manually classified matches. Typical examples of false matches are: gene accession numbers, postcodes, report numbers, other identifiers, etc., which may appear identical to valid grant numbers. Matching by acronym only (in publications where a corresponding grant number is not given) is even more prone to false matches, since acronyms can frequently be identical to regular words. Also, publications may reference project grants in a literature survey section or the references section, without actually being funded by those particular projects; these situations must be identified as false matches.

---

[2] https://developers.google.com/chart/
[3] http://cordis.europa.eu/fp7/
[4] http://www.wellcome.ac.uk/

3   Implementation Issues

All the training submodules (classification and visualization) have been entirely implemented in Python using a wide series of external libraries (e.g. NumPy[5] and NLTK). However, a seperate release version is needed for the testing case so that:

– implementation is achieved in the context of a data processing workflow
– it can be easily transferred to a distributed environment

Since the adopted scheme only involves text segmentation, dictionary terms retrieval, a simple computation of frequency-related weights and a computation of average soft probabilities, the implementation of the testing phase of both the classification and the visualization modules can be achieved in the context of a data processing workflow. Towards this end, we have used the madIS [6] system which provides data analysis functionalities via an extended relational database. madIS is built on top of the SQLite database with several Python extensions and it feels like Hadoop SQL, without the overhead but also without the distributed processing capabilities.

In madIS, queries are expressed in madSQL: this is an SQL-based declarative language extended with UDFs (User Defined Functions). UDFs are also supported by database systems for a long time; however, their use is limited due to their complexity and limitations. One of the goals of madIS is to eliminate the effort of creating and using UDFs by making them a first class citizens in the query language itself. These features combined, make madIS an agile data analysis environment that encourages rapid experimentation. madIS supports the following three types of UDFs:

– *Row functions.* These take as input one or more columns from a row and produce one value (e.g. the UPPER() function). They are analogous to the Map operator of Map/Reduce systems.
– *Aggregate functions.* These can be used to capture arbitrary aggregation functionality beyond the one predefined in SQL (i.e., AVG(), etc.). They are analogous to the Reduce operator of Map/Reduce systems.
– *Virtual table functions.* These are adopted in order to create virtual tables that can be used in a similar way with tables.

Using this UDF functionality along with the traditional database functionalities, and since the UDFs are closely tied to the relational DB engine in madIS, the communication cost between the two execution layers (functional and relational) is eliminated. In this context, the classification module for example, can be implemented by using (a) a UDF to split document into words, (b) the relational facilities to calculate word frequencies and (c) aggregate UDFs to compute sum of logs. Note that the whole process can be achieved in one single madSQL query, completely within madIS. Finally, apart from the testing phases of the classification and visualization modules, the funding mining module has been entirely built on top of the madIS system.

---

[5] http://www.numpy.org/

4   Datasets and Taxonomies

Both the classification and visualization modules have been trained on three different datasets and respective taxonomies, namely:

- arXiv (https://www.arxiv.org). This is a large archive for electronic preprints of scientific publications, covering a wide range of fields. The arXiv categorization is rather simple: 2 levels of hierarchy with a total of almost 130 class labels in the second level. These 2nd level labels are organized in 7 general categories, for example "Computer Science - Data Structures and Algorithms". We have simply used the 2nd level labels, without taking into consideration the hierarchical structure of the taxonomy. In total, around 450 K abstracts have been used.
- BASE (www.base-search.net). This is an open access archive of scientific documents operated by Bielefeld University Library. The adopted categorization method is DDC (http://dewey.info), which is rather old but it covers a wide range of scientific material. We have adopted the first 2 DDC levels, i.e. 100 content classes were used in total. The BASE dataset contains manually annotated data in several languages, however since the current classifier version functions on English texts, we have used almost 35 K annotated documents in the English language.
- WoS (Web of Science, http://thomsonreuters.com/web-of-science). This is a large citation index categorized in approximately 180 class labels (non-hierarchical). We have used about 18 K labelled abstracts.

These datasets have been used to train the classification and visualization modules. Furthermore, arXiv was used by the funding module to detect the fundings of all related publications. *Only the abstracts* have been used for training and testing our methods.

5   Results

5.1   Content Classification Performance

In order to evaluate the classification submodule, we have used the arXiv dataset (the largest among all three datasets). It has to be noted the arXiv dataset is a multi-label one: this means that each document can belong to more than one class labels at the same time. However, it has been found that in 95 % of the cases the arXiv abstracts are annotated to a single label. Therefore, the classification task is quite hard for that case (only most dominant classes are counted as correct). However, we have computed the recall rate for a number of returned results by the classification module. Also, we have used several thresholds of the probabilistic ration described above. These results are presented in Fig. 1. Note that, since most of the arXiv abstracts are single-label, there is no meaning computing the precision rate for this dataset.

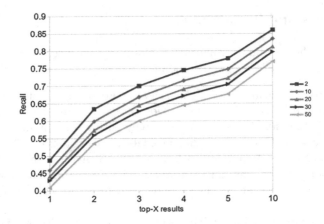

Fig. 1. Classification performance for different probability ratio thresholds. The arXiv dataset has been used.

A first obvious observation of the classification performance results is that if larger dictionaries are used (lower threshold in the dictionary compilation procedure) the performance is boosted. However, the more dictionary terms used, the more the computational time cost. To make this clearer, in Table 1, we present the average classification times per abstract (in milliseconds) for different dictionary sizes (i.e., different thresholds adopted in the dictionary training procedure). Two general conclusions can be drawn from the Table: first, the average execution time per abstract is not increased when the process is batch-executed for a very large number of abstracts (actually it decreases - 10 % to 40 % in some cases); second, there is a huge drop (50 %) in the average execution time per abstract for $T = 10$ (related to the $T = 2$ case).

Table 1. Average execution times (msecs) per abstract of the classification module. Higher dictionary thresholds (less dictionary terms) lead to faster classifications.

	Threshold				
#abstracts	2	10	20	30	50
10	63	27	21	20	17
15000	57	23	15	13	10

5.2 Funding Mining Performance

The funding mining submodule has been extensively evaluated against a large number of publication corpora from library resources, some of which are: ArXiv, PLoS, PUMA, OA set from Europe PubMed Central, etc. The resulting accuracy was over 99 %, with almost all mistakes or false alarms given with very low confidence values. Therefore, they can easily be identified and removed during a

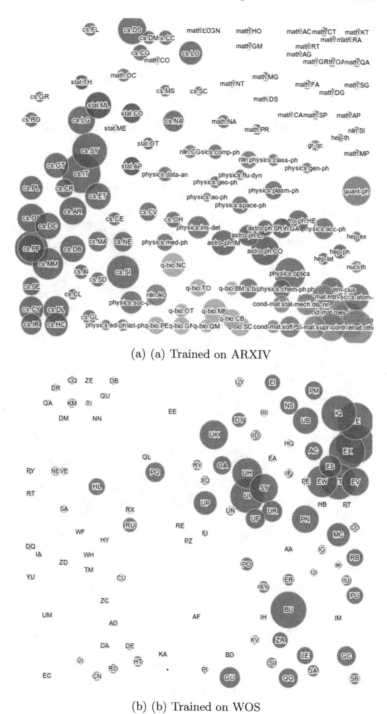

(a) (a) Trained on ARXIV

(b) (b) Trained on WOS

Fig. 2. Content distribution of the **ICT**-funded (FP7) publications from the arXiv dataset, using classification and visualization models that have been trained on two taxonomies: ARXIV and WOS

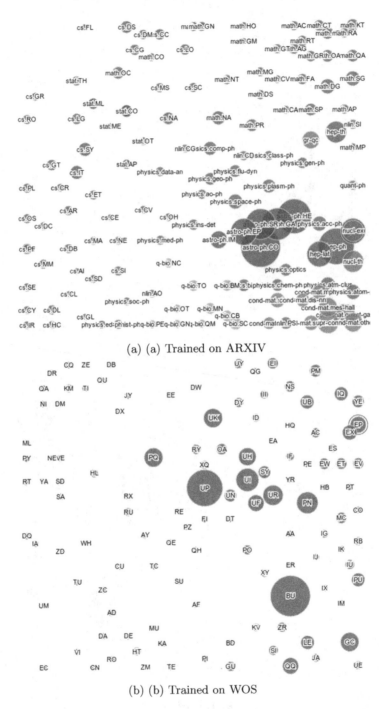

(a) (a) Trained on ARXIV

(b) (b) Trained on WOS

Fig. 3. Content distribution of the **PEOPLE**-funded (FP7) publications from the arXiv dataset, using classification and visualization models that have been trained on two taxonomies: ARXIV and WOS

curation phase. The estimation of this performance has been found by verifying each funding match/results given by the algorithm by manual curation. However, we cannot give precision and recall figures because the datasets are not labelled. We are only able to check the matches returned by the text mining. Furthermore, as we continue to process more and more publications, the module's filtering rules can be further fine-tuned, based on the feedback received after curation. As far as the time complexity is concerned, the module's processing times are very short: between 2180 and 5090 full text articles per minute depending on the dataset (about 3600 full text publications/min on average).

5.3 Content Visualization Examples

Figures 2 and 3 present the content visualizations for two different funding categories, namely the FP7-ICT and FP7-PEOPLE calls. Both corpora have been built using the funding mining submodule, applied on the whole set of the ARXIV dataset. The result was more than 4000 fund-related publications for both funding cases. These two corpora of publications have been automatically classified and visualized using the proposed method (for classification threshold

Table 2. Some of the category labels and names from the arXiv and WOS taxonomies

arXiv		WOS	
astro-ph.GA	Astroph. - Galaxy Astrophysics	BU	Astronomy - Astrophysics
astro-ph.SR	Astroph. - Solar and Stellar	GC	Geochemistry and Geophysics
cs.DB	CS - Databases		
cs.DL	CS - Digital Libraries	GU	Ecology
cs.IT	CS - Information Theory	IQ	Engineering, Electrical and Electronic
cs.LG	CS - Machine Learning		
cs.PF	CS - Performance	EX	Computer Science, Theory and Methods
cond-mat.other	Condensed Matter - Other	HL	Health Care Sciences
hep-lat	High Energy Physics - Lattice	LE	Geosciences, Multidisc.
hep-th	High Energy Physics - Theory	PU	Mechanics
physics.geo-ph	Physics - Geophysics	RU	Neurosciences
physics.optics	Physics - Optics	UB	Physics, Applied
physics.space-ph	Physics - Space Physics	UK	Physics, Condensed Matter
quant-ph	Quantum Physics	UI	Physics, Multidisc.
q-bio.CB	Quantitative Biology - Cell Behavior	UP	Physics, Particles and Fields
stat.ML	Statistics - Machine Learning	YE	Tellecom.

$T = 20$). In each case, two classification-visualization models have been adopted: one trained on the ARXIV dataset and another on the WOS dataset. Therefore, for each of the two funding categories we show two visualizations. Note that the meaning of the colors for the arXiv model are not important; they just indicate the first-level (general) classes of the arXiv taxonomy. In the case of the WOS visualization model a single color is presented, since that taxonomy is composed of a single level of classes. Finally, Table 2 presents a list of classes (for both taxonomies), in order to make the interpretation of the figures more clear. This is not the whole list of classes but the most representative in the visualization results[6].

6   Conclusions

We have presented a system towards visualization of corpora of scientific publications using supervised knowledge. Special focus has been given on implementing the whole system in the context of a data processing workflow, through the utilization of an extensible relational database. In order to achieve direct integration of both the classification and the visualization modules in the data processing workflow, we have selected to implement simple but effective approaches (e.g. the Naive Bayes classifier). Performance results have been given on the individual submodules, and a series of visualization results has been presented for specific funding schemata. Our future research efforts will focus to the following directions: (a) evaluation of the content visualization results (b) embedding more semantically important information in the results (e.g. text tags) (c) model temporal evolution of the extracted visualizations to discover trends.

Acknowledgments. The research leading to these results has received funding from the EU's FP7 under grant agreement no. RI-283595 (OpenAIREplus).

References

1. arXiv: (https://www.arxiv.org) Cornel University Library article archive
2. Bird, S.: NLTK: the natural language Toolkit. In: COLING/ACL on Interactive Presentation Sessions, pp. 69–72. Association for Computational Linguistics (2006)
3. Rish, I.: An empirical study of the Naive bayes classifier. In: IJCAI 2001 Workshop on Empirical Methods in Artificial Intelligence, vol. 3, pp. 41–46 (2001)
4. Theodoridis, S., Koutroumbas, K.: Pattern Recognition, 4th edn. Academic Press Inc., New York (2008)
5. Kohonen, T.: Self-Organizing Maps, 3rd edn. Springer-Verlag New York Inc., New York (2001)
6. Madis: https://code.google.com/p/madis/Complex data analysis/processing made easy

---

[6] More visualization examples are available in http://www.di.uoa.gr/~tyiannak/PubVisulatisations/contentAnalysis.html.

CERIF for Datasets (C4D)

Linking and Contextualising Publications and Datasets, and Much More...

Scott Brander[1], Anna Clements[1], Valerie McCutcheon[2],
Paul Cranner[3], Ryan Henderson[3], and Kevin Ginty[3(✉)]

[1] University of St Andrews, St Andrews, Fife, UK
{scott.brander,akc}@st-andrews.ac.uk
[2] University of Glasgow, Glasgow, UK
valerie.mccutcheon@glasgow.ac.uk
[3] University of Sunderland, Sunderland, UK
{paul.cranner,ryan.henderson,
kevin.ginty}@sunderland.ac.uk

Abstract. The overall aim of CERIF for Datasets (C4D) is to develop a framework for incorporating metadata into CERIF (the Common European Research Information Format) such that research organisations and researchers can better discover and make use of existing and future research datasets, wherever they may be held. CERIF provides a standardised way of managing and exchanging research information and has been widely used for recording and exchanging information about research projects and publications. C4D looks at the suitability of CERIF for recording datasets, suggests ways that the model could be improved and implements pilot functionality based on the findings of C4D at the three partner Universities in the UK.

Keywords: Datasets · CERIF · Research information systems · Current research information systems (CRIS) · Institutional repositories (IR) · CERIF for datasets (C4D)

1 Project Context

1.1 Background and Aims

The overall aim of CERIF for Datasets (C4D) is to develop a framework for incorporating metadata into CERIF (Common European Research Information Format) such that research organisations and researchers can better discover and make use of existing and future research datasets, wherever they may be held.

This project is funded by JISC, '... the UK's expert on digital technologies for education and research' [1] with partners: the Universities of Sunderland, Glasgow and St Andrews, Research Councils (NERC and EPSRC), and euroCRIS as expert advisors. Originally running for 18 months from October 2011, it has now been extended to September 2013.

CERIF provides a standardised way of managing and exchanging research information. The UK is leading the way in promoting and adopting CERIF as the

Ł. Bolikowski et al. (Eds.): TPDL 2013, CCIS 416, pp. 113–126, 2014.
DOI: 10.1007/978-3-319-08425-1_11, © Springer International Publishing Switzerland 2014

research information exchange format of choice. This underpins efforts to open up access to research publications and data, as signalled in the UK Government's 'Open Data White Paper [2] published in June 2012; and JISC have been providing significant funding and strategic support for projects to investigate and implement practical CERIF solutions since 2009 [3].

1.2   Reporting and Assessment Landscape

In March 2012, a report by UKOLN found that almost a third of UK Higher Education had implemented a CERIF-compliant CRIS since 2009 [4].

This rapid adoption has been driven by the desire to better support research management at the institutional level and in particular to streamline reporting to funders. The UK operates a dual funding strategy for research [5]; with approximately $1/3^{rd}$ of funding (quality-related research [QR] money) being distributed as a result of national quality assessment exercises taking place every 5 years or so (the next being REF2014) and a $1/3^{rd}$ distributed via the 7 discipline-based research councils through competitive application. The remaining $1/3^{rd}$ comes from charities, business and other sources.

The UK funders are increasingly interested in datasets as well as the more traditional outputs, such as journal articles. In 2011, the research councils, collectively known as RCUK [6], published a set of common principles on data policy[1] and in April 2013, their new policy on open access came into force. This policy requires articles to be made open access and also requires that each article provides a statement on how underlying research materials, such as data, samples or models, can be accessed.

All these developments are part of the national and – and indeed international - agenda to make research more open and accessible. The C4D project looks specifically at three different CERIF-compliant CRIS/IR infrastructures and how these can be extended to include linkages to datasets and so facilitate the existing open access and reporting requirements, anticipate new requirements from other funders, and provide rich contextual information for other researchers and research users looking for relevant research outcomes to explore, reuse and build upon.

1.3   Questions We Want to Answer

The main questions we wanted to answer in the project were:

1.   What metadata do we want to capture?
2.   What vocabularies do we need?
3.   Can CERIF provide what we need?

Given that our aim is to use the outcomes of the project in our existing research information infrastructure, we had the following principles guiding us in exploring these questions:

---

[1] RCUK: RCUK Common Principles on Data Policy.

- Use established standards where possible; i.e. do not reinvent the wheel
- Be realistic ... if we ask for too much we may get nothing and we need to implement **now**
- Design for change as this is a rapidly developing field

All three institutional partners have existing data sets from marine research funded by one of the funder partners, NERC (National Environment Research Council). NERC also runs 6 national data centres which are responsible for the long-term management of research data resulting from their funded research. The marine science data centre is the British Oceanographic Data Centre [7], which expects data deposited to conform to the MEDIN[2] format [8]. See Sect. 3 for more details on mapping MEDIN to CERIF.

Throughout the project we have engaged with others working in this area, including the Universities of Oxford and Bristol, and reviewed the emerging consensus in the minimum metadata required for identifying and discovering research data. The University of St Andrews also consulted with the other Pure Users and Atira, the makers of Pure, to agree a common set of metadata that was sufficient to provide the level of contextual reporting required by the funders but not so burdensome that researchers would be reluctant to or be unable to provide the information. Similarly, the University of Glasgow has consulted with other ePrints Users.

In term of vocabularies, we were particularly keen to find a common way of categorising research areas or themes. The related JISC-funded Engage project [9] looking at research clusters[3] at the University of Glasgow looked at this topic [10] and recommended the use of the recently harmonised RCUK Classification scheme.[4] In addition, there are further vocabularies required such as those for defining data types and access to research datasets.

The third question, i.e. whether CERIF can provide what we are looking for, is the main focus of the rest of this paper.

2   What is CERIF and What Is a CERIF-CRIS?

2.1   Description

CERIF is a conceptual model describing the research domain and is maintained formally as an entity relationship model (ERM). It is a standard, living model for the development, implementation and interoperability of current research information systems (CRIS). There have been several iterations of the CERIF model since 1991 [11], with the latest version (v1.5) released earlier in 2013.

The main entities of CERIF are represented in Fig. 1 below:

A Current Research Information System (CRIS) is a database or other information system storing data on current research by organisations and people.

---

[2] Marine Environmental Data and Information Network (MEDIN); http://www.oceannet.org/.

[3] http://researchclusters.wordpress.com/

[4] http://eprints.gla.ac.uk/69724

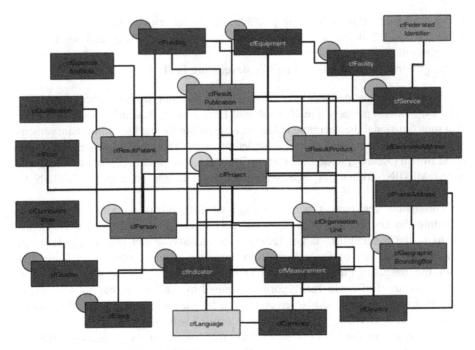

Fig. 1. CERIF research information entities

In order to gain a holistic view of research information, we have presented a view of the research information system as the centre of research-related activity within an institution (or region, or country...) which integrates and interoperates with other systems.

For example, at the University of St Andrews we have the model represented in Fig. 2. The dashed lines indicate the current work in C4D to integrate research datasets.

CERIF is maintained by euroCRIS, a not-for-profit community of users, experts and developers of research information systems and dedicated to supporting all members of the research community by advancing interoperability between CRIS and related systems using CERIF. At the end of 2012, euroCRIS had over 170 members (institutional and personal) in 43 countries, including in North America, Asia and Africa, as well as Europe [12].

2.2   CERIF Advantages

CERIF has many advantages as the canonical model (the research information entities, attributes, associations and semantics) for contextual metadata for datasets:

- Covers all aspects of research information: researchers, projects, organisations, funding, outputs (publications, patents, products including data sets), equipment, services, and so on;

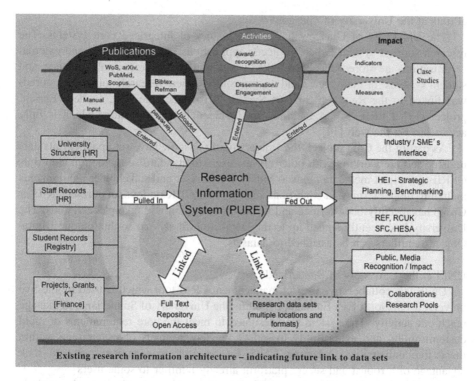

Fig. 2. CRIS model at University of St Andrews

- An optimal (relational) architecture allowing the expression of any kind of relation between entities/attributes with every relation "time-stamped" and semantically defined;
- Very fine-grained structure, allowing output of the metadata to virtually any format;
- A separated "semantic layer" allowing the use of multiple (any) controlled vocabularies (classifications, typologies) as well as their cross-linking and mapping;
- Ability to cope with multiple languages.

2.3   Current Use Cases

Pure at the University of St Andrews

The University of St Andrews purchased Pure in 2009 (the first to do so in the UK as part of a joint project with the University of Aberdeen) having identified the need for a fully functional and integrated research information system to replace their existing in-house research expertise database. Pure is a user-driven enterprise-class CRIS based on CERIF and currently covers projects, outputs, staff, students, organisations (internal and external), equipment, activities and awards and the relationships between them.

Datasets are not currently captured sufficiently in Pure, although there is a growing need by funders and institutions for them to be preserved, alongside sufficient metadata to enable the data to be understood and discovered.

ePrints at the University of Glasgow

The University of Glasgow has a long history of integrated core systems. The research support system (where projects, applications, awards, internal and external organisations are stored) has been linked to the human resources (staff), finance, and student systems for many years and the repository (where research outputs are stored) was linked to the Research Support System 2010 under the JISC funded 'Enrich' project [13]. CERIF export facilities are included in the repository which is fully accessible via the web [14].

As part of the C4D project, the University of Glasgow have set up an ePrints data registry and are working with other ePrints users to standardise the common ePrints CERIF-compliant metadata fields to satisfy ePrints user and stakeholder requirements including funder terms and conditions such as the RCUK policy. An ePrints UK User Group has recently been formed and further consultation will take place via this. The University has recently signed up to the DataCite [15] service so that unique Digital Object Identifiers can be assigned to datasets.

UNIS at the University of Sunderland

UNIS is a collaborative project management/CRM tool which is used by the five universities in North East England, including the University of Sunderland, to manage reach-out activity. The system was designed to meet the core requirements of rapid customisability and extensibility to satisfy the requirements of user groups within those five universities. Adapting UNIS for research management purposes took advantage of a robust and secure platform already familiar to some users.

Over a period of time the UNIS platform has been adapted and extended to include research information by supporting the import and export of Research Council data in CERIF format, and the linking of research grant information and publications together. In C4D, Sunderland extended the platform adding the capacity to store research data metadata in an environment which already holds data on research projects and research outputs. C4D also provides functionality to link the metadata to grant information and an interface to search the repository.

3 CERIF: Where Datasets Fit

3.1 CERIF – The Current Model

There are numerous ways of defining a dataset, but in its simplest form a dataset is a set of data that is collected for a specific purpose. The dataset can be collected in many ways, and may take the form of surveys, interviews, observations, census data, raw data from equipment, and so on. A dataset may also be a research input as well as an output.

For the purposes of C4D we concentrated on datasets resulting from funded research; with the emphasis on data underlying research publications - this being a pragmatic approach to allow us to fulfil existing funder policy requirements.

The key aspects of such datasets are that they should be discoverable and citable; therefore easily identifiable, stable, complete and be seen in context i.e. related to the project and funder, the researchers, the output(s) and publisher(s), even the equipment and other activities involved in the research which produced the research data.

The central CERIF entity behind the concept of a dataset is cfResultProduct and it maintains multiple relationships with other entities such as publications, persons, organisations, patents, projects, equipment and funding in line with CERIF's fully relational capability. Fig. 3 below is a subset of CERIF entity relationship model showing the ResultProduct entity and its relationships.

3.2   Mapping MEDIN to CERIF

A detailed mapping exercise was conducted from the C4D use case – marine metadata from the Marine Environmental Data and Information Network (MEDIN), a profile of the GEMINI2 metadata standard – and the elements were mapped largely to cfRe-sultProduct. The full mapping is available at the C4D project blog [16]. An abridged version can be viewed in Appendix A.

This exercise was largely successful with 24 of the 30 elements mapping across directly. The remaining 6 elements require extensions to CERIF and these have been recommended to euroCRIS and discussed in the CERIF Task Group which maintains the standard. Three of the extensions have already been approved and will appear in the next release of CERIF v1.6. The remaining items are still being discussed within the CERIF TG. Further detailed documentation on the C4D mappings and recommendations can be found at the project blog including an implementation example [17] (Fig. 4).

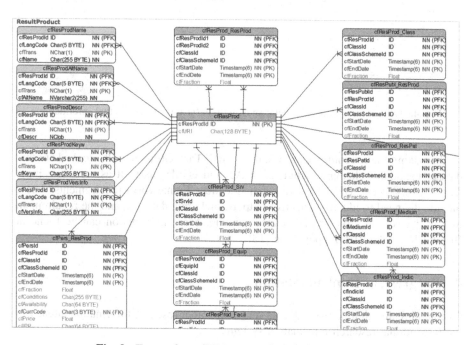

Fig. 3. Extract from CERIF 1.6 entity relationship model

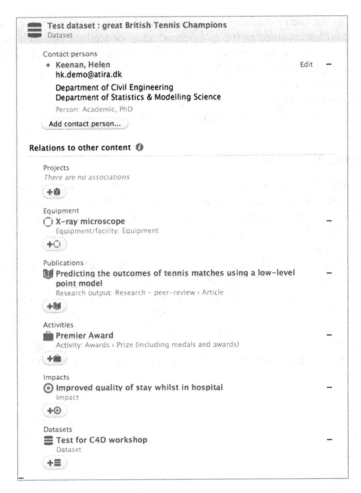

Fig. 4. Extract from Pure 4.17 beta: showing dataset links to contextual information

In making their recommendations, the CERIF Task Group has also looked at other dataset metadata schemas, including DCAT and eGMS, as well as receiving input from OpenAire and UK REF (Research Excellent Framework) requirements. These include the need to identify sensitive outputs, including datasets, and the requirement to link datasets to projects and related funding. More information can be found at Brigitte Jörg's CERIF Support blog [18].

4   Progress in Implementation

Overarching aim to link research data sets to the other research information already in the institutional research information systems.

4.1 University of St Andrews: Commercial CERIF-CRIS

The C4D application profile is being implemented in phases in the commercial Pure CRIS with first phase due for release in v4.17, Oct 2013.

4.2 University of Glasgow: Open Source IR Software

A sub-set of the key fields was implemented in January 2013. Discussions with other ePrints sites and feedback from users allow ePrints to modify the look and feel periodically [19].

4.3 University of Sunderland: In-House CERIF-CRIS

The UNIS/C4D system extended the research information infrastructure, going beyond what was available and resulting in an integrated metadata repository. The current Sunderland platform is available as a beta demonstrator system (Fig. 5).

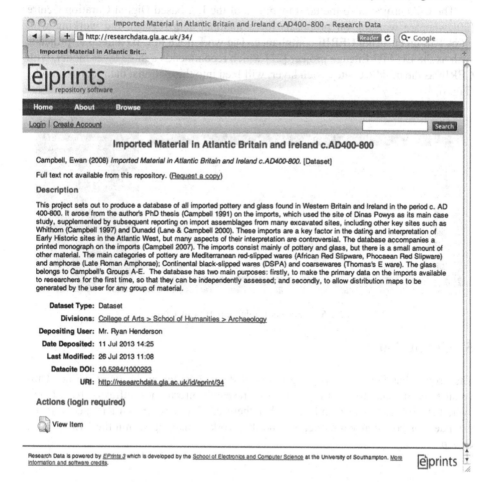

Fig. 5. Example from Glasgow research data repository

4.4   Next steps

The C4D project has demonstrated that CERIF can be used to record rich metadata about datasets and, crucially, relate these datasets to the many other pieces of the information jigsaw in the research landscape. All three partner institutions are implementing some or all parts of the C4D profile within their respective research information frameworks as described in Sect. 4.3.

The flexibility of CERIF does mean that there are some areas which still need more consultation with euroCRIS in order to agree the best approach. In some cases this is because it is not clear what type of information needs to be recorded e.g. element 21: "Conditions applying for access and use" - should this be picked from a pre-defined list (i.e. a classification) or a free-text field? In another example e.g. element 18: "Lineage", more comprehensive modelling work is required, although the building blocks, such as cfMeasurement and cfGeoBBox, exist to capture this information; but not all the necessary linkages. It is also questionable as to how generic such a metadata element is.

The C4D project also includes members of the UK-based Digital Curation Centre [20] who are working on proposals for a national data register and working with euroCRIS on ensuring CERIF-compliance. The work done in C4D and other projects, such as the EU FP7 Engage project [21] which recommends a three layer model, with CERIF as the middle context-rich layer, will feed into this national data register model (Fig. 6).

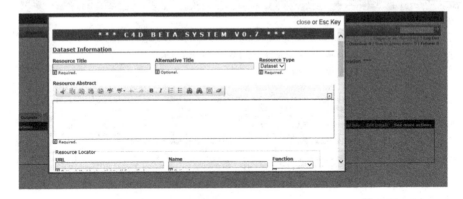

Fig. 6. Datasets implementation in UNIS

5   Conclusion

The project has delivered working pilots of data registries at the three partner Universities, with links to existing contextual research information infrastructure. However, the project has also indicated that there are areas where CERIF needs to be extended, or potentially remodelled, and this work is ongoing within the CERIF Task Group.

5.1 The Future of Datasets in CERIF

C4D has looked at datasets as a research output and this is how it is currently modelled in CERIF i.e. as cfResultProduct. However datasets can also be inputs to research. Should a new entity, cfDataSet, for example be introduced? C4D has also demonstrated that the current dataset model requires additional linkages to areas of CERIF that cfResultProduct does not currently provide - again, an argument that a new 'cfDataset' entity may be required.

As with other entities in CERIF, there is a need for agreed definitions and vocabularies (CERIF classification schemes [cfClassScheme]) in order to allow true interoperability between systems. euroCRIS works closely with CASRAI [22], the standards organisation which develops and maintains a common data dictionary for full lifecycle of research activity. One of the profiles currently being looked at within the CASRAI UK chapter is on data management.

Funding Acknowledgement. This work was supported by JISC [grant number DIINNAA].

Appendix A: Table Mapping MEDIN (GEMINI) Metadata to CERIF v1.5

See Table 1.

Table 1. Mapping of MEDIN elements to CERIF and DataCite

	MEDIN	DataCite v3.0 Mandatory Recommended Optional	CERIF v1.5	Notes
0	Identifier	M	cfResProdId	
1	Resource title	M	cfResProd, cfResProdName.cfName	
2	Alternative resource title		Not supported – proposed to CERIF Task Group	Approved and due v1.6, summer 2013
3	Resource abstract	R (Description)	cfResProd.cfResProdDescr.cfDescr	
4	Resource type	R	cfResProd.cfResProd_Class	
5	Resource locator		cfResProd_Srv.Srvid	
6	Unique resource identifier		cfResProd.URI	
7	Coupled resource		cfResProd_ResProd.classId	
8	Resource language	O	cfResProd_Class.cfLang with appropriate cfLangCodes	
9	Topic category	R (Subject)	cfResProd_Class.cfClassId with appropriate classification scheme	
10	Spatial data service type		cfResPubl_Srv.cfClassId linked to cfResProd	
11	Keywords		cfResProd.ResProdKeyw.Keyw and cfResProd.cfResProd_Class.cfClassId	
12	Geographic bounding box	R (GeoLocation)	cfResProd_GeoBBox.GeoBoxId	
13	Extent		cfResProd_Class.cfClassId	
14	Vertical extent information		Not supported in CERIF. CERIF has a GeoBBox element which can be used to record these attribute, but there is currently no cfResProd_GeoBBox linking element.	Approved and due in v1.6, summer 2013
15	Spatial reference		cfResProd_Class.cfClassSchemeId with spatial reference system classification scheme	
16	Temporal reference	M (Publication Year) R (other dates e.g. period of collection)	cfResProd_Class.cfClassSchemeId with temporal reference classification scheme	
17	Lineage		Not currently supported – proposed	CERIF TG still discussing
18	Spatial resolution		Not currently supported – proposed	Recommendation is cfResProd_GeoBBox

(continued)

Table 1. (*Continued*)

	MEDIN	DataCite v3.0 Mandatory Recommended Optional	CERIF v1.5	Notes
19	Additional information		cfResProd_cfResPubl.ResPublId with classification scheme	
20	Limitations on public access	O (Rights)	cfResProd_Class with appropriate classification scheme	
21	Conditions applying for access and use	O (Rights)	Not currently supported – proposed free text	CERIF TG still discussing
22	Responsible party	M (Creator, Publisher) O (Contributor)	cfOrgUnit_ResProd.OrgUnitId cfPers_ResProd.PersId	
23	Data format	O	cfResProd.cfResProd_Class with Data Format classification scheme	
24	Frequency of update		cfResProd_Class.ClassId with Frequency of Update classification scheme	
25	Conformity		cfResProd_Measurement.MeasId	
26	Metadata date		This is managed by the application	
27	Metadata standard name		No recommendation by CERIF Task Group, so was mapped to cfOrgUnit_cfresProd with linking roles	
28	Metadata standard version		As per 27	
29	Metadata language		Is cfLang entity but no link to cfResProd currently	CERIF TG still discussing
30	Parent ID	R (Related Identifier)	cfResProd_ResProd with appropriate classification scheme	

References

1. JISC. http://www.jisc.ac.uk
2. HM Government, Open Data White Paper: Unleashing the Potential. https://www.gov.uk/government/uploads/system/uploads/attachment_data/file/78946/CM8353_acc.pdf
3. JISC, Reseach Information Management: Towards a common standard for exchanging research information. http://www.jisc.ac.uk/publications/briefingpapers/2010/bpexriv1.aspx
4. UK UKOLN. http://www.ukoln.ac.uk/isc/reports/cerif-landscape-study-2012/CERIF-UK-landscape-report-v1.1.pdf
5. UK Innovation Research Centre. https://www.gov.uk/government/uploads/system/uploads/attachment_data/file/181652/bis-13-545-dual-funding-structure-for-research-in-theuk-research-council-and-funding-council-allocation-methods-andthe_pathways-to-impact-of-uk-academics.pdf
6. Research Councils UK (RCUK). http://www.rcuk.ac.uk/research/Pages/DataPolicy.aspx
7. NERC, British Oceanographic Data Centre. http://www.bodc.ac.uk
8. Marine Environmental Data and Information Network, MEDIN. http://www.oceannet.org
9. JISC Engage Project. http://researchclusters.wordpress.com/
10. Research Councils UK, RCUK. http://www.rcuk.ac.uk/research/Efficiency/Pages/harmonisation.aspx
11. CERIF Support Blog, Brigitte Joerg, CERIF in Brief. http://www.cerifsupport.org/cerif-in-brief/
12. euroCRIS Annual Report 2012. http://www.eurocris.org/Uploads/Web%20pages/annual_report/ANNUAL_REPORT_2012.pdf
13. JISC Enrich Project. http://www.gla.ac.uk/enrich/
14. Glasgow University ePrints repository. http://eprints.gla.ac.uk/
15. Datacite. http://www.datacite.org/whatisdatacite
16. Cerif for Datasets C4D project blog. http://cerif4datasets.files.wordpress.com/2012/09/c4d-cerif-mapping-v0-1.xlsx
17. Cerif for Datasets C4D implementation example. http://cerif4datasets.files.wordpress.com/2013/03/c4d-cerif-metadata-implementation.pdf
18. CERIF Support Blog, Brigitte Joerg, Datasets in CERIF. http://www.cerifsupport.org/2013/04/02/data-in-cerif
19. Glasgow University research data repository. http://researchdata.gla.ac.uk/
20. Digital Curation Centre DCC. http://www.dcc.ac.uk
21. Houssos, N., Jörg, B., Matthews, B. A multi-level metadata approach for a Public Sector Information data infrastructure. In: Jeffery, K.G., Dvořák, J. (eds.) Proceedings of the 11th International Conference on Current Research Information Systems. Prague, Czech Republic. pp. 19–31 (2012) http://www.eurocris.org/Uploads/Web%20pages/CRIS%202012%20-%20Prague/CRIS2012_2_full_paper.pdf
22. CASRAI. http://casrai.org

Investigations as Research Objects
Within Facilities Science

Brian Matthews$^{(\boxtimes)}$, Vasily Bunakov, Catherine Jones,
and Shirley Crompton

Scientific Computing Department, Science and Technology Facilities Council,
Harwell OX11 0QX, UK
{Brian.Matthews,Vasily.Bunakov,Catherine.Jones,
Shirley.Crompton}@stfc.ac.uk

Abstract. We consider the notion of data publication in the context of large-scale scientific facilities. Dataset publication allows access to and citation of data, but do not provide sufficient context. We propose instead to publish an investigation, a more complete record of the experiment, including details of the context and parameters of the experiment. We relate this investigation to the emerging concept of a research object, and consider how investigation research objects can be constructed to support the more complete publication of facilities science.

Keywords: Research data · Research lifecycle · Data publication · Digital preservation · Linked data · Research object

1   Introduction

Data publication is becoming an increasingly accepted part of the future data eco-system to support research. This involves enabling public access to data by other researchers, with appropriate guarantees of integrity in the management and persistence of the data, and encouraging researchers to cite the use of the data within publications. The intentions behind data publication include: assigning credit and recognition to the collectors of data; encouraging the inspection of data by peers to assess the quality of the data, and to validate the assertions of scientific insights claimed in published articles arising from the analysis of the data; enabling the reuse of the data by other researchers to re-analyse to discover new insights and reportable results, thus furthering the value of the research which arises from the data collection. As a consequence, a number of different approaches and infrastructures have been advocated for data publication (for example [1, 2]).

This is also becoming recognised in the field of "facilities science". We define facilities science as that science which is undertaken at large-scale scientific facilities, in particular in our case neutron and synchrotron x-ray sources, although similar characteristics can also apply for example to large telescopes, particle physics experiments, environmental monitoring centres and satellite observation platforms.

Ł. Bolikowski et al. (Eds.): TPDL 2013, CCIS 416, pp. 127–140, 2014.
DOI: 10.1007/978-3-319-08425-1_12, © Springer International Publishing Switzerland 2014

In this type of science, a centrally managed set of specialised and high value scientific instruments is made accessible to a community of users to run experiments which require the particular characteristics of those instruments. The facilities have their own dedicated staff and funding to supply a scientific service.

In this paper, we concentrate on neutron and x-ray sources, central facilities which supply beams of particles of a particularly intense (such as synchrotron x-ray radiation) or rare (such as beams of neutrons) nature which are otherwise unobtainable for individual research teams. These are then used to analyse the structure of matter at a micro- or nano-scale. These types of facilities differ from other "big iron" [2] science projects in that whilst the facility itself has the characteristics of "big science", including large long term investments, specialised support teams, large quantities of data, high-performance computing analysis requirements, the science itself is more characteristic of "small science" (or bench science), with many small experiments undertaken by small research teams taking readings of many samples, with diverse funding sources and intellectual objectives. This mixture of characteristics has influenced how facilities are approaching data publication.

In particular, the institutional nature of the facilities, with the provision of support infrastructure and staff, has allowed the facilities to support their user communities by systematically providing data acquisition, management, cataloguing and access, thus providing some of the advantages of "big science" to a small science community. This has been successful to date; however, as the expectation of facilities users and funders develop, this approach has its limitations in the support of validation and reuse, and thus we propose to evolve the focus of the support provided. We propose that instead of focussing on traditional artefacts such as data or publications as the unit of dissemination, we elevate the notion of "investigation" as an aggregation of the artefacts and supporting metadata surrounding a particular experiment on a facility to a first class object of discourse, which can be managed, published and cited in its own right. By providing this aggregate "research object", we can provide information at the right level to support validation and reuse.

In this paper, we discuss the facilities approach to managing and publishing data, concentrating on our approach which we have been developing at the STFC's facilities, in particular the ISIS Neutron Spallation Source[1]. We then discuss the limitations of this approach, and introduce the concept of an Investigation as a research object, as the unit of publication and access for facilities data. We discuss how this may be represented as Linked Data, comparing it with other similar approaches to research object in the literature. We then further consider how this Investigation may be used, and the tools support which would be required to collate, maintain and preserve such a research artefact.

---

[1] http://www.isis.stfc.ac.uk

2 Supporting Data Management and Publication

The neutron and synchrotron radiation facilities support a wide range of different experimental techniques (e.g. crystallography, tomography, spectroscopy, small-angle scattering), and experiments are undertaken within a wide range of different disciplines, including chemistry, bio-chemistry, materials science, earth science, biology, metallurgy, engineering and archaeology. However, from a data management perspective, they are all follow similar processes. User scientists apply for an allocation of time on an instrument supported by a science case, which, if accepted, is followed by one or more visits to the facility's site where a number of samples, prepared by the user in advance, are placed in the target area, and then exposed to the beam of particles for a desired period of time. During the exposure the beam particles are then blocked or deflected by the sample and then detected by banks of sensors arranged around the target area. These sensors then generate data on such parameters as particle counts, angle of deflection, time-of-flight of the particle, energy, or frequency. This raw data is then streamed off via data acquisition and data management systems which collect, aggregate and move the data to short or long term storage to await further analysis.

Traditionally, this process has been carried out with standard file systems; however, it has been recognised for some time that with the ever increasing data rates and volumes, and increase throughput of experiments, this approach was becoming increasingly hard to manage by hand with the accompanying risk of data loss or corruption. Consequently, we have systematised the process of data management by developing a data catalogue system, ICAT [3]. This cataloguing component, based on an information model capturing a view of a facilities experiment or "investigation" (the Core Scientific MetaData (CSMD) model [4]), within a relational database, provides a common point of gathering information about the experiment. This captures information on the experimental team and intent from the proposal system, and when the experimental visit takes place, will register the data sets, their locations in storage, and experimental parameters. This information is then exposed via an API, either for users to use for browsing and data download on or off site via a web interface (the "TopCat" tool), or else integrating with analysis tools and frameworks so that they can search for and access the data directly. This approach has been successful, and ICAT is being both augmented with additional components and also promoted as an open source tool for use in other similar facilities across Europe and beyond, and has been adopted as the reference data catalogue for the Pan-Data consortium of 13 European facilities[2].

Changes to data policy within ISIS have recognised the value of releasing data publicly; data is released for general use after an embargo period of exclusive use to the user. This can be done via the TopCat interface. However, to encourage citation of data and thus attribution and credit for data collection, ISIS issues Digital Object Identifiers (DOIs) for data issued via the DataCite consortium[3]. Thus for each

---

[2] http://www.pan-data.eu

[3] http://www.datacite.org

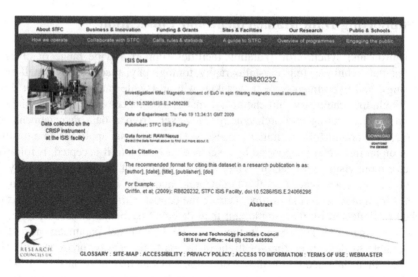

Fig. 1. DOI landing page for ISIS

investigation within ISIS, a DOI is issued, a minimal amount of metadata deposited with the DataCite search engine, and a suitable landing page produced as the "front page" of the data, as for example in Fig. 1. From this landing page, given suitable permissions for embargoed data, the data can be accessed. ICAT can provide a stable and quality source of metadata, and a route to archival storage. Thus this provides a suitable data publication channel for ISIS data.

2.1 The Changing Landscape of Facilities Science

This established process has been successful for data management and the data publication method via DOIs and landing page, whilst still evolving, should provide a mechanism to support basic data discovery, and support citation of data via DOI and a suitable recommended citation format, thus allowing credit to be attributed to experimenters in traditional publications, and following this, allow the facility to via citation tracking to monitor the value of the use of data generated. However, the landscape of facilities science is changing. We summarise some factors [5].

– Instrumentation and data analysis have become more user friendly than in early days of facilities science. This has led to a lesser significance of the instrumentation "gurus" with a current trend of not including them as the authors of papers; the estimate for biology papers is that about half of them do not now include any facility staff members as co-authors [6] so that new methods and forms may be required for the fair and inclusive attribution of research output.

– The advances of instrumentation and Internet have also led to services allows users to send their samples for remote investigation according to one of the service plans. The sample exposure on a large facility may be just one of the experimental techniques included in the service plan. The service provider then collects the experimental data and supplies them to the user in pre-agreed formats. This implies considering service providers the legitimate agents of facilities science with their inclusion in data management policy.

– Facilities use more than one service to collect data. The user monitoring exercise performed by PaNdata initiative showed that about 7000 (22 % of the total) of visitor researchers across Europe have used more than one neutron or synchrotron radiation facility for their investigations[4]. This makes actual the development of common user authentication and user authorization services, as well as experimenting with "virtual laboratories" for the collaborative data analysis.

– New experimental techniques like neutron tomography, or using robots for manipulating multiple samples, or studies of dynamics of materials. The new techniques produce larger volumes of data; they also raise potential opportunities for researchers to perform comparative and multi-aspect studies for the same samples using different experimental techniques, or using the same experimental technique for much wider variety of different samples. This scales up all three V's of Big Data: Volume, Velocity, and Variety, and makes their analysis more demanding from modelling and from computational points of view.

– Publishers and scholarly institutions such as the International Union of Crystallography are increasingly requiring traceability of published results through final result dataset to the raw data collected at the facility instrument, so that peers can test the validity of the claimed result.

Thus there is an increasing need to reuse and combine results from different sources; to provide sufficient detail to reviewers so that they can reconstruct the experiment to validate results; and to provide mechanisms to allow credit for various participants in the experimental process, suitable for their role, as in for example [7]. Much of this needs to be mediated via automated tools, so the record of the experiment needs to be available in a machine readable format. The current data publication mechanism based on DOIs and landing pages does not support this well as the context of the data collection, the relationships between various research artefacts, and the different roles of individuals in the process is not captured adequately, so we need to rethink what data publication means in this context.

3   Investigations as Research Objects

Our starting point is to consider the research lifecycle in facilities science, given in schematic form in Fig. 2 and given in more detail in [8]. From the point of view of the *Facility* (the user scientist may have a different view of their scientific process)

---

[4] http://wiki.pan-data.eu/CountingUsers

Fig. 2. Generic research lifecycle in facilities science

investigations tend to go through the same stages of proposals, preparation, experimental visit, data management, data analysis and visualisation, and publication.

The different stages of research lifecycle produce data artefacts (research proposals, user records, datasets, publications etc.) that are similar across research facilities. Different actors are also involved at the various stages. We also need to record the details of the experiment; which sample was analysed under which experimental conditions, to collect data representing which parameters. Thus by following through the lifecycle of a successful beam time application, we can collect all the artefacts and objects related to it, with their appropriate relationships. As this is strongly related to allocation of the resources of the facility, this is a highly appropriate unit of discourse for the facility; the facility want to record and evaluate the scientific results arising from the allocation is its scarce resources. Thus we propose that the appropriate unit of publication for facilities science is the Investigation.

At one level this is what we already do when we present a landing page for an investigation. Much of the information which is required can be recorded within the ICAT system. It can support describing which sample was used on which instrument to generate which data set under which experimental conditions to measure which parameters. However, the DataCite metadata does not include these, and while some of this information can be found on the landing page (e.g. instrument) and much more can be found by exploring the detailed metadata in TopCat itself, this is human accessible only, not straightforward to find or navigate, and is not distributed in a machine readable form. Further, related artefacts (derived data, publications, provenance information) is not systematically collected or presented, although now ICAT has the capability to collect this information [9, 10]. What we propose to do is publish the investigation as a single aggregated unit which can be identified and delivered to the user in a machine readable format and contain sufficient contextual information to support discovery of all the components of the investigation and their relationships, so they are available for validation and reuse; that is publish the investigation as a research object.

The notion of Research Objects has been explored in a number of projects in recent years (e.g. [11–13]), and Research Objects have been defined as:

> ... semantically rich aggregations of resources that bring together data, methods and people in scientific investigations. Their goal is to create a class of artefacts that can encapsulate our digital knowledge and provide a mechanism for sharing and discovering assets of reusable research and scientific knowledge[5].

---

[5] http://www.researchobject.org

Research Objects (ROs) as implemented can be seen to have the following characteristics.

- Information about research artefacts and their attributes and relationships are represented as Linked Data; thus RDF is used as the underlying model and representation, with URI used to uniquely identify artefacts. As ROs are linked data objects, they can link into to the existing Linked Data cloud to provide additional context information and be managed by the standard tools of Linked Data and the Semantic Web.
- Standard vocabularies are used to represent relationships describing the research process, such as workflow (workflow4ever[6]), provenance (e.g. Prov-O[7]), and citation (e.g. cito [14]). Use of standard vocabularies encourages shared understanding, enables reuse and allows the use of tools which are tailored for their specialised semantics.
- A bound is provided on the object as an aggregation, so we can determine membership of the research object; typically, OAI-ORE[8] is used for this purpose.
- The whole research object can be identified via a URI, so its own history and attributes can be related as a first class research artefact in its own right.

The notion of the boundary of a RO is particularly important. A research artefact can be linked to a number of research artefacts. An investigator or instrument can participate in a number of investigations; a publication may use the output of several investigations to support its results. If this is represented as a simple web of linked data, then it would be difficult to distinguish which artefacts and relationships are members of which research object. We need a notion of defining a boundary to determine membership of the RO; OAI-ORE, with its notions of Aggregation and Resource Map provides such a boundary. Research Objects are thus highly suitable as a mechanism to represent and publish Investigations.

4 Building an Investigation Research Object

We outline the major steps of building a research object to represent facility's investigations.

4.1 Representing CSMD in RDF

We can represent the CSMD as an OWL ontology. This will allow us to represent metadata as RDF triples within triple stores (or provide a triple based front end onto

---

[6] http://www.wf4ever-project.org/

[7] http://www.w3.org/TR/prov-o/

[8] http://www.openarchives.org/ore/

```
<owl:Class rdf:about="csmd:Investigation">
    <rdfs:label>Investigation</rdfs:label>
    <rdfs:comment>An investigation or experi-
ment</rdfs:comment>
    </owl:Class>

<owl:Class rdf:about="csmd:Facility">
    <rdfs:label>Facility</rdfs:label>
    <rdfs:comment>An experimental
facilty</rdfs:comment>
    </owl:Class>

<owl:Class rdf:about="csmd:Dataset">
    <rdfs:label>Dataset</rdfs:label>
    <rdfs:comment>A collection of data files and part
of an investigation</rdfs:comment>
    </owl:Class>

<owl:Class rdf:about="csmd:Datafile">
    <rdfs:label>Datafile</rdfs:label>
    <rdfs:comment>A data file</rdfs:comment>
    </owl:Class>
```

Fig. 3. A fragment of the CSMD ontology

metadata databases such as ICAT via for example a SPARQL endpoint) and allows us to publish data about investigations into Linked Open Data. Figure 3 gives a sample of the OWL representation; the full model can be found on the ICAT Google Code site[9]. The OWL representation has a base URI: http://www.purl.org/net/CSMD/ 4.0#

4.2   Constructing an Investigation Research Object

As the facilities lifecycle is enacted within an experiment, we can then construct the research object. Thus, immediately after an investigation has been approved, we can initialise the research object, assigning a DOI at this early stage, and providing some basic information from the proposal, such as instrument used and investigator, as in Fig. 4, which also includes a prototypical fragment in RDF-Turtle of the investigation object at this stage.

---

[9] https://code.google.com/p/icatproject/

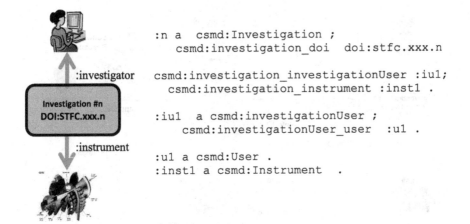

```
:n a  csmd:Investigation ;
    csmd:investigation_doi  doi:stfc.xxx.n

csmd:investigation_investigationUser :iu1;
    csmd:investigation_instrument :inst1 .

:iu1  a csmd:investigationUser ;
    csmd:investigationUser_user  :u1 .

:u1 a csmd:User .
:inst1 a csmd:Instrument  .
```

Fig. 4. Initialising the investigation object

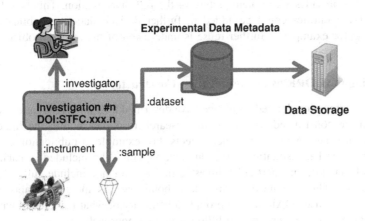

Fig. 5. Investigation object after the experiment

As the experiment in undertaken, we can add further information to the investigation object, to build a more complete picture of the collection of raw data on a sample, again as in a simplified view in Fig. 5. This step captures the information presented on the current DOI landing page.

As the experimental lifecycle goes on, as for example analysis of the data through software packages, and publications and other auxiliary content is added to the investigation, together with the parameters and configurations used, and provenance information collected, we can continue to add to the Investigation object, building an eventual object which may contain references to objects in different repositories, ownerships and locations, brought together in a single linked structure as in Fig. 6.

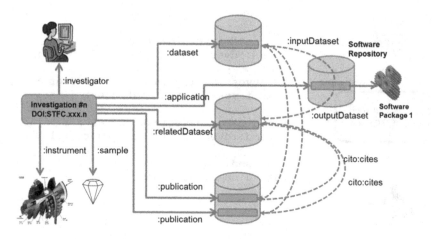

Fig. 6. Investigation Object after a complete lifecycle

Thus this provides a complete picture of the full investigation. This is a dynamic object; further entities could be added it, further derived datasets, publications, or annotations for example as further reuse is undertaken of the research object.

4.3   Using OAI-ORE as an Aggregation Constructor

Using the aggregation defined above we have described how an investigation research object can be constructed. However, the research resources within the linked data graph can also be connected to other objects. For example, a publication could use data from several investigations. The publication should be included in each investigation object, but any particular investigation should not include fully the other investigations. Thus we need to provide a boundary. As mentioned above, other approaches have used OAI-ORE to provide a boundary of what is included within the research object, and we propose to follow a similar approach.

OAI-ORE provides some core constructs for capturing aggregations. The class `ore:Aggregation` provides an abstract concept for aggregating resources (`ore:AggregatedResources` in OAI-ORE), with an object property `ore:aggregates` as the combining mechanism. `ore:ResourceMap` describes the aggregation, the resources and the relationships between them. Thus to represent an Investigation Research Object, which is an aggregation, we declare that the Investigation class is a subclass of `ore:Aggregation`:

   `csmd:Investigation rdfs:subClassOf ore:Aggregation.`

This follows the approach of the Core Research Object Model[10], and thus we can also declare:

   `csmd:Investigation rdfs:subClassOf ro:ResearchObject.`

---

[10] http://www.researchobject.org/ontologies/

Further, we can declare the core relationships between Investigations and other resources in the CSMD using sub-properties:

`csmd:investigation_dataset rdfs:subPropertyOfore:aggregates.`

We can thus use OAI-ORE to construct the investigation research object with minimal changes to our information model.

5 Using Investigation Research Objects

5.1 Supporting Multiple Viewpoints

Regardless of discipline there is an acknowledged "life cycle" of research, which is realised in many ways depending on the audience and purposes; a researcher, a funder, a research organisation, a publisher or a preservation institution will focus on different aspects of this life cycle and bring additional contextual links relating to their business process and requirements. For these different stakeholders the central object to which context is added will be different as their world viewpoint is different, for example a publisher will want to establish links from the publication; a funder may wish to do the same for grants. We have described building the links to the investigation from our viewpoint as a facility which is responsible for the creation, discovery and curation of the investigation undertaken at the facility.

The use of research objects supports well this notion of different points of view. Publishing data within a linked open data context in particular makes notions of what constitutes a coherent viewpoint of relevant resources and relationships hard to capture. By providing boundaries and criteria for membership, research objects can support multiple points of view within one data infrastructure. Thus different stakeholders can construct, use and reuse the context relevant to them, and also be credited to the portion of the object which is appropriate to their contribution.

5.2 Data Publication

We would propose to use investigation research objects as the unit of publication for our facilities data. Thus we would identify investigation and their related resource maps by persistent identifiers, and use them to generate a landing page. This would be extensible to provide access to the research object in its entirety and include related entities to provide more information in context which could be accessed by other automated agents. Metadata associated with the DOI would need to be changed. Currently, the Datacite metadata field ResourceType supports Dataset and Collection (amongst others), neither of which is correct[11] in this context. We would propose that the list of allowed values for this field is extended to include the notion of experiment, study or investigation.

---

[11] http://schema.datacite.org/meta/kernel-2.2/doc/DataCite-MetadataKernel_v2.2.pdf

Using the notion of research object as a more open ended bounded object raises the notion of what exactly is being published persistently in this case. If we add additional information are we maintaining stability? Research Objects are well suited to notions of versioning, where we can relate objects together as they change, thus keeping the old boundary stable. Further, we would propose to have different levels of assurance in our case. The core information on the experiment (sample, instrument, parameters, raw dataset) would remain constant, with other information being secondary and subject to possible extension; this would made clear in the presentation.

5.3   Data Preservation

Shifting the focus from the data to the investigation makes the data preservation activity a more complex one, as it moves from activities relating to the preservation of a well-defined digital object to include not only the digital object but also activities to ensure that the complex linked data, OAI-ORE resource map maintains it integrity and meaning, and links still point to resolvable objects. For preservation purposes it is important that these links are permanent to ensure the integrity of the object.

6   Discussion

The work presented in this paper represents a work in progress. Further discussions are required to agree the correct representation of Investigations as research objects, and design and implementation work to provide tools support so that investigation research objects can be constructed, maintained and published as linked data. However, we see that this could form the basis of a data publication route for facilities data via enhanced landing pages.

Despite the potential for Investigations to become daily "commodities" of the research discourse in facilities science, there are challenges for them, too:

– Universal IDs for Investigations are still a novelty: there is not many of them.
– Lack of IDs for other components like instruments, or experimental techniques.
– Proto-objects most circulate within a "native" facility (although projects of PANDATA collaboration raise hopes).
– Many researchers, data practitioners, publishers and policy makers are unaware of the potential of Research Objects as intellectual entities.

There is also a specific psychological challenge related to the Linked Data representation for Investigations that we mentioned as the most appropriate modelling technique. The flexibility of Linked Data allows re-use and re-combination of its granular parts in other information context so the boundaries of Linked Data information entities tend to be socially defined, and depend upon the role and the interests of the data modeller. Sharing Investigations as Linked Data implies the data publisher agreement for the modifications and derived objects to circulate along with what publisher thought was the best model for Investigation description.

Also the socially defined boundaries of Linked Data objects raise the importance of best practices that should accompany data modelling and system implementation effort. The best practices should be included in structured data curation framework for facilities science that will help the information departments of large facilities to perform a role of a conscious data curator helping to increase data value across the entire research data lifecycle for the variety of stakeholders [15]. Information technologies and services will be then an important means to underpin the data curation role but not the end in themselves.

Acknowledgements. This paper is related to the projects of PaNdata (www.pan-data.eu) collaboration, and SCAPE project supported by the EU 7th Framework Programme for Research and Technological Development. The authors would like to thank their colleagues for their input for this paper although the views expressed are the views of the authors and not necessarily of the collaboration.

References

1. Lawrence, B., Jones, C., Matthews, B., Pepler, S., Callaghan, S.: Citation and peer review of data: moving towards formal data publication. Int. J. Digit. Curation **6**(2) (2011). doi:10.2218/ijdc.v6i2.205
2. Parsons, M.A., Fox, P.A.: Is data publication the right metaphor? Data Sci. J. **12** (2013). doi:10.2481/dsj.WDS-042
3. Flannery, D., et al.: ICAT: integrating data infrastructure for facilities based science. In: e-Science: 5th IEEE International Conference on e-Science (2009)
4. Matthews, B., et al.: Using a core scientific metadata model in large-scale facilities. In: 5th International Digital Curation Conference, London, UK (2009)
5. Bunakov, V., Matthews, B.: Data curation framework for facilities science. In: Proceedings of DATA 2013: the 2nd International Conference on Data Management Technologies and Applications, Reykjavík, Iceland, pp. 211–216, 29–31 July 2013
6. Mesot, J.: A need to rethink the business model of user labs? Neutron News, **23**(4) (2012)
7. Marcos, E., et al.: Author order: what science can learn from the arts. Commun. ACM **55**(9), 39–41 (2012)
8. Matthews, B., et al.: Model of the data continuum in photon and neutron facilities. PaNdata ODI, Deliverable D6.1. (2012). http://pan-data.eu/sites/pan-data.eu/files/PaNdataODI-D6.1.pdf
9. Yang, E., Matthews, B., Wilson, M.: Enhancing the core scientific metadata model to incorporate derived data. Future Gener. Comput. Syst. **29**(2), 612–623 (2013)
10. Fisher, S.M., Phipps, K., Rolfe, D.: ICAT job portal: a generic job submission system built on a scientific data catalogue. In: 5th International Workshop on Science Gateways (2013)
11. Bechhofer, S., et al.: Why linked data is not enough for scientists. Future Gener. Comput. Syst. **29**(2), 599–611 (2013)
12. Shaon, A., Callaghan, S., Lawrence, B., Matthews, B., Osborn, T., Harpham, C.: Opening up climate research : a linked data approach to publishing data provenance. In: 7th International Digital Curation Conference (DCC11), Bristol, England (2011)
13. Belhajjame, K., et al.: Workflow-centric research objects: a first class citizen in the scholarly discourse. In: Proceedings of the ESWC2012 Workshop on the Future of Scholarly Communication in the Semantic Web (SePublica2012), Heraklion, Greece (2012)

Second International Workshop on Supporting Users Exploration of Digital Libraries

Supporting Information Access and Sensemaking in Digital Cultural Heritage Environments

Paula Goodale[1]([⊠]), Paul Clough[1], Mark Hall[1], Mark Stevenson[2],
Kate Fernie[3], and Jillian Griffiths[3]

[1] Information School, University of Sheffield, Sheffield, UK
{p.goodale,p.d.clough,m.mhall}@sheffield.ac.uk
[2] Department of Computer Science, University of Sheffield, Sheffield, UK
r.m.stevenson@sheffield.ac.uk
[3] MDR Partners, London, UK
{kate.fernie,jillian.griffiths}@mdrpartners.com

Abstract. User-centered design and evaluation of a system to improve information access and assist the wider information activities of users in cultural heritage digital collections is described. Extending beyond simple, standalone information seeking and retrieval tasks, the system aims to enhance content 'findability' and to support users' cognitive processes of sensemaking, learning and creativity, by embedding tools for information use at the point of access. A generalized user interaction model derived from requirements analysis is shown to be compatible with models of exploratory interaction and information seeking support, illustrating potential for a single system that can adapt to diverse use case scenarios. Controlled laboratory evaluations, whilst demonstrating support for a variety of information tasks, also reveal variance in information seeking behavior by task type and user profile, indicating a need for a system that lets users select their preferred interaction mode in context. Interactions with the path creation functionality highlight potential for sensemaking and creativity support tools to be embedded within digital library collections.

Keywords: Exploratory search · Information foraging · Sense-making · Interactive IR · User-centred design · Evaluation

1 Introduction

Information access can be divided into two main activities: (1) information seeking and retrieval, and (2) information use, including analysis and synthesis of results. Sensemaking pervades this wider process and is exhibited by expert and novice users in various domains as they validate and interpret information found. Current search systems do not support analytical and sense-making processes well [1], particularly when there is a risk of overload when attempting to select from vast collections of information [13]. There is therefore considerable scope to improve information access and cognition through the integration of sensemaking tools within search systems,

Ł. Bolikowski et al. (Eds.): TPDL 2013, CCIS 416, pp. 143–154, 2014.
DOI: 10.1007/978-3-319-08425-1_13, © Springer International Publishing Switzerland 2014

including, e.g. provision of collection overviews, and tools for arranging, grouping and annotating information objects [8].

In cultural heritage, interpretation, meaning-making and constructivist approaches to learning are implicit in the provision of access to cultural heritage (CH) collections. In digital environments these processes are increasingly participatory and collaborative, with opportunities for novice users to actively engage in knowledge creation [16]. Indeed, at a high level, expert and novice users have somewhat similar requirements in this domain, engaging in a range of fact-finding, more exploratory, and complex information tasks [2, 18]. It is therefore important that digital CH collections support both a variety of users and tasks.

This paper describes the design and evaluation of a novel system developed to enhance information access and use in digital CH environments. Support is given for a broad range of information needs, from focused fact-finding to exploratory browsing, with a particular focus on enabling more open-ended modes of interaction such as berry-picking [3] and information foraging [14]. Additional tools support users' more advanced cognitive processes of sensemaking and creativity that are integral to information and work tasks in areas such as curation, research, and inquiry-based learning, in both formal and informal contexts. A pathway metaphor is utilised to facilitate both information access and sense-making, and is particularly suited to the CH domain with its common use of guided tours and trails for interaction with exhibits in physical locations.

2 Related Work

2.1 Exploratory Search and Sensemaking

Exploratory search extends the idea of basic fact-finding or 'lookup' information tasks into the areas of 'learning' and 'investigation', which in turn incorporate extended information processing, evaluation and annotation activities [12]. Overlapping with this conceptualization of exploratory search are modes of information behaviour, such as information foraging [14], where the user uses a 'scent' to exploit an information source and find related items, and berry-picking [3], which is an extended, iterative and adaptive search process that also incorporates the idea of collecting information objects as the search progresses over time. Exploratory behavior is also presented in the context of the wider information seeking process, where it signals feelings of confusion and uncertainty, and constitutes investigatory behavior, as a precursor to formulating a more specific information need, and more directed collection of information [11]. This mode of exploratory searching as a means of overcoming uncertainty, developing mental models and exploring concepts about information needs has significant implications for system design [20].

Exploratory search is an integral part of the broader activity of sensemaking [12]. The four main elements of the sensemaking process in the context of analyst problem-solving [15] are: information gathering; re-representation of information into a schema; development of insight from analysis of the representation; and, creation of knowledge product or action based on insight. It is an iterative process incorporating a number of learning loops, including information foraging at the earlier stages of gathering, filtering and extracting information into an initial model, which might require exploration, browsing, collecting and filtering support within an information seeking system.

More general models, suited to both expert and novice information users are the 'information journey', which looks at information seeking within the context of interpretation and information use [1, 4], and the 'genex framework', focused more on gathering information for repurposing and reuse in the creation and sharing of new resources [17].

Designs of information seeking support systems (ISSS) to meet these more complex user needs are yet to be fully exploited, but could include tools for the provision of collection overviews, and tools for arranging, grouping and annotating information objects [8]. Key challenges in designing effective ISSS include developing tools for: finding information; filtering results via facets; visualization and exploration; learning about the subject area; collaboration; tagging and data sharing; revisiting search history; note-taking and collection building; providing novelty and comparison of information found; integrating with desktop software; and encouraging deeper user engagement and satisfaction [21]. Similarly, for creativity support, tools which enable eight core information tasks are required: searching; visualization; relating (communication); thinking; exploring; composition; reviewing; and, disseminating [17]. More specifically, visualization and representation tools could include spatial, argumentational (narrative), faceted, hierarchical, sequential and network forms [6]. Sensemaking and exploration are at the heart of all of these requirements for ISSS and creativity support systems.

2.2 User Requirements and Behaviour in Cultural Heritage

Research on user requirements and information behaviour in CH digital collections is relatively scarce, especially when considering the needs on novice users, i.e. those without detailed subject and domain knowledge. User requirements vary widely for users with different levels of expertise, knowledge and task [19]. In terms of information seeking, expert users regularly engage in both simple fact-finding and more complex information gathering tasks, amongst others, with the latter having multiple variations and components such as topic searches, exploration, collecting/combining [2], all of which are relevant to our current study. Similarly, novice users [18] also engage in known-item searching and exploration. Visual representations of artefacts are highly important in this context, and the process of meaning-making through contextual information and the derivation of personal inferences and connections is also strongly evidenced [15].

For known-item or fact-finding searches, some knowledge of the metadata and collection structure is imperative, but such knowledge is much less likely to be used effectively, if at all by novice users than expert users [10], although this may be overcome to some degree by technical or information seeking skills [9]. In addition, information retrieval tools in CH collections, and the web more generally, are much less likely to effectively support the needs of users more in more open-ended exploratory tasks [8].

There is considerable scope then for systems to support more exploratory forms of information seeking within digital libraries generally, and within CH digital collections. In addition, there is scope to consider additional tools to support the wider information seeking and sensemaking processes, to aid information use in various contexts.

3 System Design

A user-centered design process has been employed, comprising two iterations of a cycle of user requirements, design, implementation and evaluation. Here we focus on the first prototype, and will report on the second prototype in due course, once evaluations are completed. User requirements were gathered from novice (lower domain and subject knowledge) and expert users (higher domain and subject knowledge) across cultural heritage, education and commercial domains. An online survey of 79 expert and novice users, and qualitative interviews with 22 expert users, identified typical information behaviours and preferences relating to exploration, sensemaking and use of CH collections in different contexts [7]. These findings detail a number of interpretations of the path construct by CH professionals, and inform a high-level interaction model and functional specification for the first prototype. The interaction model incorporates five core activities carried out by users and can be used to illustrate a range of exploratory and sense-making information interactions specific to various different work and leisure tasks [reference removed]. An important feature of the model and interaction design is that they support diverse navigational paths, according to the users' varying tasks, needs and preferences (Fig. 1).

The PATHS UI model is compared with established models of user behavior in complex information work (Table 1), and can be seen to address all aspects of information seeking, exploration, sensemaking, creativity and information use, to some degree. It is however, a relatively high level generalized model, designed specifically for users in the CH environment. It would therefore benefit from a more detailed representation of the 5 core activities, based upon observations and feedback

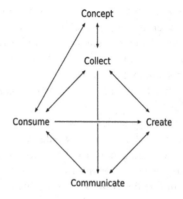

Fig. 1. PATHS generalized user interaction model.

Table 1. Comparison of the PATHS user interaction model with the exploratory search [12], information journey [4], and genex framework [17] models (primary, secondary elements)

PATHS UI model	PATHS design features	Exploratory search	Information journey	Genex framework
Concept	-Follow path -Explore modes -External links -Search	Investigate Learn	Recognise need Find info Use	Relate
Collect	-Search -Explore modes -Add to workspace -Facets -Similar items -Follow keywords -External links	Learn Lookup	Find info Validate/interpret	Collect
Create	-Create path -Re-order -Add text node	Learn Investigate	Validate/ interpret Use	Create Relate
Consume	-Follow path -Similar items -External links	Learn Investigate	Use Recognise need Find info	N/A Collect Relate
Communicate	-Publish path -Share content/path -Annotate path -Add comments	Learn	Use Validate/ interpret	Donate Relate

from user evaluations of a more sophisticated prototype in due course, as well as modification for other information domains.

Functional specification and interface design for the first prototype focused on three core interactions underlying this model; search, explore and create (Fig. 2). Search and Explore provide much of the functionality for the Concept and Collect elements of the model, whilst Create (interface) incorporates elements of Create, Consume paths, and Communicate (interaction model). Search is enabled via a simple search box (one for primary content and another for paths created by users), with faceted search results for additional filtering. The primary explore function at this stage is a tag cloud, but we also provide links to topics, similar items, and related external content at the item record level. Create is a more complex function that is supported by numerous tools, including a collect (add to workspace) feature, annotations, and a path creation workspace (Fig. 3) with add/edit/delete/reorder and annotation facilities.

As is usual in any complex information environment, we expect that the more advanced tools will be used initially by more expert users, with paths created by, for example, curators, teachers and amateur enthusiasts. These path-based information objects will provide exploration, learning and way-finding support for novice users. In time, it is hoped that novice users will be encouraged to try creating their own paths.

In terms of content, the first prototype incorporated data from the English and Spanish collections held in the Europeana digital library. This paper focuses on the

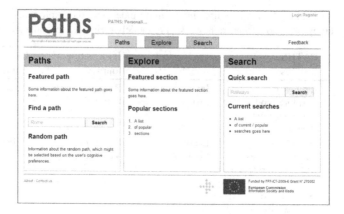

Fig. 2. Interface for first PATHS prototype: home page

Fig. 3. Interface for first PATHS prototype: path creation workspace

English collections, comprising some 800,000 objects from a wide variety of smaller- and medium-sized UK-based CH institutions.

4 Evaluation

The first PATHS prototype, described above, was evaluated under controlled laboratory conditions using a protocol informed by the Interactive IR Evaluation framework [5]. A total of 31 expert and novice users were recruited according to their use and knowledge of CH information for work, study or leisure purposes. The sample was evenly split the two groups. Almost 60 % of users self-identified as advanced internet users, which may help overcome a lack of domain subject knowledge to some degree [9]. Evaluation sessions were conducted on a one-to-one basis, lasting 2 h, comprising data collection as follows:

- User profile: questionnaire and cognitive style analysis
- 4x short simulated work tasks (simple fact-find; extended fact-find; browsing a topic; free exploration)
- 1x long complex simulated work task (path creation)
- Post-task questionnaire: feedback on all 5 tasks
- Post-session questionnaire: feedback on the system
- Think-after interview: reflection on the path task

Simulated work tasks allow for evaluation of somewhat realistic user behaviour in a controlled environment, and activity was captured via screen-recording software and log file data. All tasks were undertaken by all users, with the short tasks rotated in a latin square, and the longer path creation task at the end. An example of the path task for general museum visitors (novice users) follows:

> "Imagine you are a history or art enthusiast who wants to share their knowledge and interests with friends and other web users. You are to create a path which you will share via a blog and/ or social media, on a topic such as a famous person or event from history, an artist or art topic, or a historical guide to a place, activity or object."

Our goals in evaluating the system in this way were three-fold: (1) to assess interaction design and overall usability of the system in support of different information tasks; (2) to gain a more in-depth understanding of information seeking behavior in the CH context, including any differences in behaviour between different types of users; and, (3) to ascertain the typical attributes and potential uses of paths as information objects in cultural heritage collections.

5 Results

In this section we present and discuss the key findings of the laboratory evaluations in relation to the three research goals relating to usability, information behavior, and paths as information objects.

5.1 Usability and Support for Tasks

A series of sixteen different 7-point semantic differential scales (+3 to 0 to −3) were used to gauge elements of usability and user satisfaction, from a variety of opposing word pairs. Median values across all 16 scales were broadly positive, or neutral, with a −1 score only for efficiency (novice users) and familiarity (expert users). Overall, expert users rated their experience more positive than novices, with a median of +2 for exciting, interesting, enjoyable, creative, inventive and useful. This discrepancy between expert and novice users is perhaps to be expected at this stage, when the system is unknown, due to greater domain knowledge, and the appeal of the more advanced functionality which is likely to be adopted first by those with experience.

Table 2. Time taken for completion of simulated work tasks

	Mean	Maximum	Minimum
Simple fact-find	4.53	5.00	2.83
Extended fact-find	4.07	5.00	1.83
Open-ended browsing	4.78	5.00	2.28
Exploration	4.36	5.00	2.34
All tasks A-D	4.44	5.00	1.83
Path creation	25.33	33.6	11.73

As a gauge of effort to complete the simulated work tasks, time taken and number of mouse clicks were measured. Time taken for the shorter tasks varied between users and between tasks. The mean average for all short task types was over 4 min. The maximum time taken for all four of these tasks was 5 min (the maximum time allowed) and this time was recorded for 60 % of all tasks undertaken. However, there was a proportion of users who used much less than the 5 min allocated, with a minimum time of 1.83 min for the extended fact-find task, to 2.83 min for the simple fact-find task (Table 2).

It is possible that a longer time taken on a task indicates one of two things; either the task was difficult to complete, or the user was engaged in the task and enjoying the experience. Ratings of task experience on 7-point semantic differential scales, show that the two fact-finding tasks were marginally easier to complete that the browsing and explorations tasks, but that the browsing tasks was somewhat less enjoyable than the other three tasks. On further examination, it is found that there is a statistically significant positive correlation (Spearman's Rank) of 0.417 at the 0.01 level between ease of task completion and enjoyability.

Ratings of how well PATHS supports different information tasks were encouraging. Positive responses were given by more than 50 % or more of users for serendipity and discovery, finding items related to a topic, creating resources, using content created by others, sharing content, and exploration. Exploration also received one of the highest negative responses (34 %), along with fact-finding (40 %). More detailed feedback on ease of use, and inventiveness of individual elements of PATHS functionality, also showed exploration lagging behind some other areas, although it was rated highly for usefulness, and when selecting the three tasks for which they would be most likely to use PATHS, all users selected exploration as one of their three choices, followed by finding items relating to a topic, and creating resources (Fig. 4).

5.2   User Behaviour

Observations of user behavior in completing the evaluation tasks show that browsing strategies are used considerably more widely for open-ended browsing and exploration tasks than for fact-finding tasks, and that more item records are viewed for the latter, suggesting a need to verify information, rather than simply selecting based upon the thumbnail image. The action of browsing multiple pages of search results was highest for exploration tasks, and browsing behavior was more evident overall for

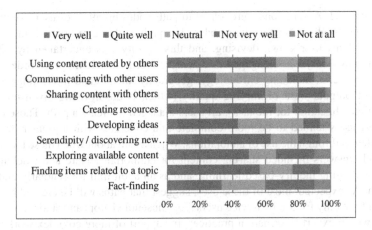

Fig. 4. How well does PATHS support different information tasks

those with a wholist (divergent thinking) cognitive style, along with associated higher use of the tag cloud for additional exploration. These findings are unusual in the context of general web searching behavior, but compatible with the profile of CH users preferring visual content [18], especially in the context of looking for interesting or unusual examples.

Looking more closely at strategies for finding materials for a path, there is evidence that 33 % of users employed serial browsing techniques (viewing multiple pages of search results), 39 % used serial searching techniques (regular query reformulation, few pages of search results), only 6 % opted for exploring via the tag cloud, and 22 % used a combination of these strategies. It was also found that although wholist types browsed much more widely through the collection (up to page 40 in one instance) than their opposite analyst (narrow convergent thinking) cognitive style types, they added much fewer items to their workspace. This suggests that analyst types desire to find everything available before they decide what to include, whilst wholists are happy with fewer, more interesting items. These findings also may present interesting opportunities for system design and adaptivity, as at one extreme, analytic users are presenting a preference for high recall, whereas users with a wholist cognitive style are interested in neither precision, nor recall, but instead appear to seek for novelty.

5.3 Path Creation and Use

Lastly, we consider sensemaking and information use activities in relation to the path creation task. Tools were available for collecting, organizing and connecting, and, annotating the path and it's individual nodes. All elements of the path creation activity were optional and unprompted, yet it was found that the majority of users engaged with many of the sensemaking aspects to some degree.

The simple activity of adding a path summary was completed by 91 %, metadata (tags) was added by 82 %, and 33 % attempted to add more items after their path was initially created. Annotations were added to path nodes by 59 % of users, with 36 % adding notes to all or most of their nodes. The path could be re-ordered into a linear sequence of the user's own devising, and this activity was undertaken by 72 % of users, although only 17 % engaged in extensive reordering. Items were ordered by a variety of criteria, including chronology, geography, theme, and interestingness.

Whilst outputs were of varying quality (which is unsurprising given only a 30 minute time allocation for the task), all users managed to create a path. Those created by expert users tended to be more complete and coherent, with a greater degree of interpretation through the use of annotations. When asked about when these tools might be useful, answers included sharing content for curatorial, leisure and teaching purposes, facilitating inquiry-based learning, and as an audit trail for scholarly and other research. As expected, most of these uses, suggest that paths will be created by expert users, but not only for use by novice users (e.g. museum visitors and students), but also for use within expert information practices, in support of more complex work tasks.

6   Conclusions

A prototype information seeking support system has been created for digital CH environments, emphasizing exploration, sensemaking and creativity. Evaluation of the system suggests that these activities are initially well-supported, but there is room for improvement, particularly in exploration, Users have also expressed a desire for greater integration between the search and explore functions to allow for seamless movement between the two activities, and have requested more advanced and flexible path creation tools. These requirements have been addressed within the second PATHS prototype, including new thesaurus and map based exploration tools, and an enhanced visual path creation tool, with options for hierarchical structures. The thesaurus and map aim to provide clearer overviews of the content within large scale CH collections and the enhanced path creation tools will enable more diverse path forms and support more complex sensemaking activities (Figs. 5 and 6).

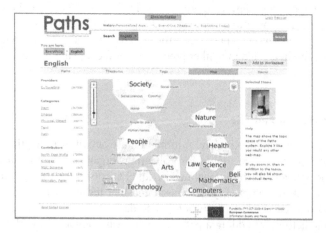

Fig. 5. Interface for second PATHS prototype: map exploration

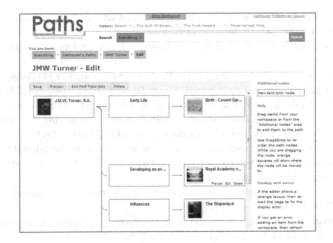

Fig. 6. Interface for second PATHS prototype: path creation

Acknowledgments. The research leading to these results has received funding from the European Community's Seventh Framework Programme (FP7/2007–2013) under grant agreement n° 270082 relating to the PATHS project.

References

1. Adams, A., Blandford, A.: Digital libraries' support for the user's 'information journey'. In: Proceedings of 5th ACM/IEEE-CS Joint Conference on Digital Libraries, Denver, Colorado, 7–11, June 2005, pp. 160–169. ACM, New York (2005). doi:http://dx.doi.org/10.1145/1065385.1065424
2. Amin, A., van Ossenbruggen, J., Hardman, L., van Nispen, A.: Understanding cultural heritage experts' information seeking needs. In: Proceedings of 8th ACM/IEEE-CS Joint Conference on Digital Libraries, Pittsburgh, PA, 16–20, June 2008, JCDL'08. ACM, New York (2008). doi:http://dx.doi.org/10.1145/1378889.1378897
3. Bates, M.J.: The design of browsing and berrypicking techniques for the online search interface. Online Inf. Rev. **13**(5), 407–424 (1989)
4. Blandford, A., Attfield, S.: Interacting with information. Synthesis Lectures on Human-Centered Informatics. **3**(1), pp. 1–99. Morgan Claypool Publishing, San Rafael (2010)
5. Borlund, P.: The IIR evaluation model: a framework for evaluation of interactive information retrieval systems. Inf. Res. **8**(3), 8–3 (2003)
6. Faisal, S., Attfield, S., Blandford, A.: A classification of sensemaking representations. In: Proceedings of CHI '09 Workshop on Sensemaking (2009)
7. Goodale, P., Hall, M., Fernie, K., Archer, P.: Paths Project D1.1 User Requirements Analysis. PATHS Project (2011). http://www.paths-project.eu/eng/Resources
8. Hearst, M.A.: Search User Interfaces. Cambridge University Press, Cambridge (2009)
9. Hölscher, C., Strube, G.: Web search behavior of internet experts and newbies. Comput. Netw. **33**(1), 337–346 (2000)
10. Koolen, M., Kamps, J., de Keijzer, V.: Information retrieval in cultural heritage. Interdisc. Sci. Rev. **34**(2–3), 268–284 (2009)

11. Kuhlthau, C.C.: Inside the search process: information seeking from the user's perspective. J. Am. Soc. Inf. Sci. **42**(5), 361–371 (1991)
12. Marchionini, G.: Exploratory search: from finding to understanding. Commun. ACM **49**(4), 41–46 (2006)
13. Patterson, E.S., Roth, E.M., Woods, D.D.: Predicting vulnerabilities in computer-supported inferential analysis under data overload. Cogn. Technol. Work **3**(4), 224–237 (2001)
14. Pirolli, P., Card, S.: Information foraging in information access environments. In: Proceedings of SIGCHI Conference on Human Factors in Computing Systems, pp. 51–58 (1995). ACM, New York. doi:http://dx.doi.org/10.1145/223904.223911
15. Pirolli, P., Card, S.: The sensemaking process and leverage points for analyst technology as identified through cognitive task analysis. In: Proceedings of the International Conference on Intelligence Analysis (2005)
16. Proctor, N.: Digital museum as platform, curator as champion, in the age of social media. Curator Mus. J. **53**(1), 35–43 (2010)
17. Shneiderman, B.: Creating creativity: user interfaces for supporting innovation. ACM Trans. Comput. Hum. Interact. **7**(1), 114–138 (2000)
18. Skov, M., Ingwersen, P.: Exploring information seeking behaviour in a digital museum context. In: Proceedings of 2nd International Symposium on Information Interaction in Context, London, 14–17, October 2008, IIiX '08. ACM, New York (2008). doi:http://dx.doi.org/10.1145/1414694.1414719
19. Sweetnam, M.S., Agosti, M., Orio, N., Ponchia, C., Steiner, C.M., Hillemann, E.-C., Ó Siochrú, M., Lawless, S.: User needs for enhanced engagement with cultural heritage collections. In: Zaphiris, P., Buchanan, G., Rasmussen, E., Loizides, F. (eds.) TPDL 2012. LNCS, vol. 7489, pp. 64–75. Springer, Heidelberg (2012)
20. Vakkari, P.: Exploratory searching as conceptual exploration. In: Proceedings of 4th Workshop on Human-Computer Interaction and Information Retrieval (HCIR 2010), Rutgers University, New Brunswick, NY (August 22, 2010), pp. 24–27 (2010)
21. White, R.: Designing information seeking support systems. In: NSF Workshop on Information Seeking Support Systems, Chapel, Hill, NC, pp. 55–58. National Science Foundation (2009). doi:http://ils.unc.edu/ISSS/ISSS_final_report.pdf

The CULTURA Portal
Exploring Cultural Treasures

Gary Munnelly[✉], Cormac Hampson, Seamus Lawless,
and Owen Conlan

Knowledge and Data Engineering Group, SCSS, Trinity College,
Dublin 2, Ireland
{munnelg, Cormac.Hampson, Seamus.Lawless,
Owen.Conlan}@scss.tcd.ie

Abstract. This paper introduces the CULTURA system which is pioneering the next generation of online tools for interacting with the cultural treasures of Europe. An overview of the architecture is presented which highlights some of the key features of the CULTURA environment. This is accompanied by a brief description of the intended workflow of both the user and the services. A live version of the portal can be found at http://cultura-project.eu.

Keywords: CULTURA · Personalization · Digital heritage · User modelling

1 Introduction

The information age has provided humanity with a level of access to knowledge that is incomparable with any other period in recorded history. Documents about almost any subject, from detailed information about the life of Henry VIII to instructions regarding how to eat an orange can be located and consumed within moments by those who are interested in such things.

This information explosion has resulted in an empowered community of users who are confident that when they wish to learn about a subject, relevant data is little more than a Google search away. However, some resources that have remained inaccessible to the average individual include many of the original, primary sources of cultural heritage. While efforts have been made to digitize these documents, either by scanning the originals or transcribing the text, the content itself can present a barrier to the would-be scholar.

Depending on the specific era, such documents may be challenging due to the density of their information, their inconsistent use of language, archaic spelling or terminology, the assumption of a certain amount of prior knowledge on the part of the reader and more [1]. This is an unfortunate circumstance as users who wish to study these texts can locate them by traditional means of searching, but often lack the tools to consume them in a more forensic manner. This paper describes CULTURA (http://cultura-project.eu) [2], a dynamic, customizable web portal which provides a suite of tools designed with the goal of empowering and assisting the user in their exploration of these cultural treasures.

Ł. Bolikowski et al. (Eds.): TPDL 2013, CCIS 416, pp. 155–158, 2014.
DOI: 10.1007/978-3-319-08425-1_14, © Springer International Publishing Switzerland 2014

2 An Overview of CULTURA

CULTURA is a three year, FP7 funded project, whose main objective is to pioneer the development of personalized information retrieval and presentation, contextual adaptivity and social analysis, all in a digital humanities context. To that end, it employs a wide array of tools and services which are designed to aid and inform the user in their exploration of digital collections. At present, CULTURA is being trialled using two digital cultural collections – the 1641 Depositions from Ireland and the Imaginum Patavinae Scientiae Archivum (IPSA) from Italy. These collections present very different challenges for CULTURA, due to the depositions being textual in nature and IPSA being largely pictorial. Transcription of the depositions was performed manually by a team of expert historians.

The architecture of CULTURA is service oriented, allowing the portal to be tailored to suit a particular collection. For example, if inconsistent language is not a problem in a corpus of documents, then normalization may not be a required component and can be decoupled from the rest of the site as required.

2.1 Pipeline and Data Layer

Before the data is exposed to the user, it undergoes some preprocessing to extract meaningful information which can be used by both the system and the researcher.

The raw data, (which is comprised of historical documents, text etc.) is passed in both its original and normalized form to the entity extraction service. The process of normalization is intended to introduce consistency into the document language by resolving some of the variant spelling into a more modern form. This is particularly important for textual corpora in which the language is so archaic that standards are absent even within the work of an individual scribe. However, as a result of this process, some information can be lost from the artefacts, (e.g. Smythe being normalized to Smith, despite being a distinct and different name), hence the parallel analysis of the text in its original form.

Entity extraction is employed to identify the named entities within the texts including people, places, dates, etc. These entities provide an important insight into the nature of the text and can be used to guide a user towards resources which are relevant to their research as well as link documents which cover similar or related subjects. Social network analysis (SNA) is also applied to the output of this process in order to help amalgamate multiple individual entities into a single overall reference. For example, it may be possible to discern that the Phelim O'Neil whose activities in Louth are extensively documented in 1641, is the same man whose execution in 1653 is recorded elsewhere. The PreMapper tool developed in CULTURA provides a means by which the data curator can manually establish links which were not automatically detected by CULTURA.

As can be seen in Fig. 1, the data layer is largely a repository for the information extracted by the pre-processing layer. Data such as the normalized version of the corpus, entities identified and how these entities relate to one another (SNA) are stored along with the original copies of the source material. This data is drawn upon by the remaining layers of the architecture for their respective purposes.

The importance of the underlying user model should also be noted. This important feature of CULTURA is a major driving force behind many of the components in the control layer. Information about a user's browsing history within the site, inferred research interests and exhibited level of expertise is persistently stored in the data layer, thus allowing a user's personalized experience to span several sessions.

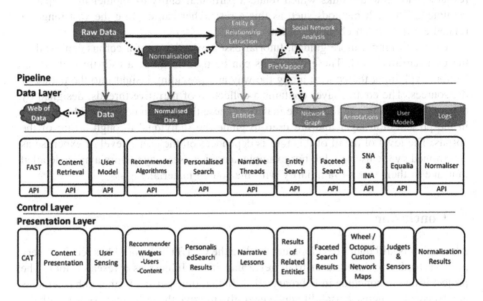

Fig. 1. Overview of the CULTURA architecture

2.2 Control Layer and Presentation Layer

The control layer services run as components of the live site and are interfaced with via a series of API calls from the client's computer. They can be invoked by the user to produce an effect within the CULTURA portal, e.g. annotation, normalization, etc. or they may be availed of by CULTURA itself as it attempts to personalize the user's experience, e.g. content retrieval, content recommendation, user model modification etc.

The user model is CULTURA's representation of the user. It is constructed based on a user's behaviour within the site in an attempt to discern how familiar they are with the source material, what entities and documents within a collection interest them etc. Based on this representation, CULTURA can tailor the experience of the individual to suit, not only their research interests, but also their level of expertise. For example, for a user who is exhibiting a particular interest in County Louth, both by bookmarking documents which relate to it and annotating bodies of text which contain references to it, CULTURA will attempt to establish what aspects of Louth are of interest to them by correlating the user model with the entities extracted by the pipeline. The relationships determined by entity extraction can then be used to produce lists of alternative sources which may interest the user. These are presented to the user in a recommender block and also influence the results of personalized searches.

The presentation layer is the user facing façade of the portal though which they are given transparent access to the various services that CULTURA provides. Simple user interface controls allow users to interact directly with documents and the environment in general through annotating, sharing, bookmarking and searching. SNA widgets such as the Wheel and the Octopus can be used to visualize the entities within a resource and view the links which relate a particular entity to another in a separate document. Through methods such as this a researcher can explore the vast range of related entities which chain documents together.

User's seeking a more guided, tutorial based experience of a corpus can avail of the user narratives [3]. These narratives can be used to guide a user through a collection, explaining the content along the way and providing insight into the nature of the sources. The control layer contains a collection of narrative threads, designed by experts in the domain of the source material. These threads can be selected by the user in the presentation layer and are used to guide the individual through a tour of the corpus. The level of detail of this tour is dependent on the user's level of expertise as determined by the user model. For example, a novice user may require a more detailed tour due to their lack of familiarity with the source material.

3 Conclusion

Although it is still under development, to date the CULTURA portal has received very positive feedback during user trials regarding its usefulness as a research tool. The project is due to conclude in February 2014. In that time period, further enhancements are expected to increase usability and generally improve the user's experience with the portal. In addition, work is underway to deploy a new collection, the 1916 Enniscorthy depositions, using the portal. This corpus, like the 1641 depositions, is textual in nature but contains a different quality of language. It is expected to demonstrate the transferability of the CULTURA platform for other domains.

A current version of the site can be found at http://cultura-project.eu.

References

1. Gotscharek, A., Neumann, A., Reffle, U., Ringlstetter, C., Schulz, K.U.: Enabling information retrieval on historical document collections: the role of matching procedures and special lexica. In: 2009 Proceedings of The 3rd Workshop on Analytics for Noisy Unstructured Text Data (2009)
2. Hampson, C., Agosti, M., Orio, N., Bailey, E., Lawless, S., Conlan, O., Wade, V., Ding, W., Marchionini, G.: The CULTURA project: supporting next generation interaction with digital cultural heritage collections. A Study on Video Browsing Strategies. Technical Report. University of Maryland at College Park (1997)
3. Conlan, O., Staikopoulos, A., Hampson, C., Lawless, S., O'Keeffe, I.: The Narrative Approach to Personalisation, New Review of Hypermedia and Multimedia [In Press]

The Tony Hillerman Portal: Providing Content Enrichment and Digital Access to Archival Manuscripts

Kevin J. Comerford[✉]

Center for Southwest Research, University of New Mexico, Albuquerque, USA
kevco@unm.edu

Abstract. Tony Hillerman (1925–2008) was a noted author from the American Southwest. In 2005, he formally donated his entire collection papers to the Center for Southwest Research, the special collections division of the University of New Mexico Libraries, with the understanding that they be used for educational purposes. This donation led to the creation of the Tony Hillerman Portal (http://ehillerman.unm.edu), a website that features digital facsimiles of Hillerman's manuscripts and provides a realistic document examination and content manipulation experience for students and researchers. The portal is built on the Drupal 7.22 Content Management System, and utilizes a variety of supporting technologies, including a streaming media server and eBook display application. Future enhancements to the site will include text and content analysis tools that will be of interest to Digital Humanities researchers, and additional photographs, videos and oral histories that help document Tony Hillerman's life and work.

Keywords: Archives · Content analysis · Content enrichment · Content management systems · Digital access · Digital humanities · Digitization · Drupal · eBooks · Manuscripts · Text analysis · Tony Hillerman

Tony Hillerman (1925–2008) was a noted author from the American Southwest. He wrote both fiction and non-fiction works, but he is best known for his series of criminal detective and mystery novels that take place on the Navajo Nation, in Arizona and New Mexico. A unique feature of Hillerman's work is how he imbibes his stories with Navajo and other Native American cultural and religious beliefs and practices. Readers of Hillerman's work have frequently remarked that they take an interest in Hillerman's work because they love a good detective story, but they become fans of his work because of what they learn about Navajo life and culture.

In addition to being an award-winning author, Hillerman was also a college professor who taught writing and was chair of the Department of Journalism at the University of New Mexico in Albuquerque for many years. In 2005, he formally donated his entire collection of manuscripts and personal papers to the Center for Southwest Re-search, the special collections division of the University of New Mexico Libraries, with the understanding that they be used for educational purposes, to help students learn about the creative and editorial processes of writing monograph-length works. Hillerman's papers include four to six completed manuscript drafts for

Ł. Bolikowski et al. (Eds.): TPDL 2013, CCIS 416, pp. 159–162, 2014.
DOI: 10.1007/978-3-319-08425-1_15, © Springer International Publishing Switzerland 2014

each of his twenty-two novels and eighteen non-fiction works, as well as screenplays, idea note-books and personal correspondence with his publishers and fans.

With a view toward honoring Hillerman's wishes, after several years of planning and seeking external funding for the project the Center for Southwest Research began a digital library initiative called the Tony Hillerman Portal (http://ehillerman.unm. edu), a web-based online resource providing digital access to all of Hillerman's manuscripts and papers, as well as centralizing access to online text and audiovisual resources about Tony Hillerman's life and work. The overarching goal of the project was to create the most comprehensive information resource about Tony Hillerman that had ever been published, in print or online, accessible through a single website. This goal presented a number of challenges to the project team; not only would the website be a discovery system that provided access to digitized copies of Hillerman's manuscripts and papers, it would also have to support and integrate a variety of content types and delivery formats, which could be hosted locally or linked to across the Internet. This approach also necessarily implied that a great deal of third-party content would have to be licensed for use on the site (Fig. 1).

Fig. 1. Front page of the Tony Hillerman Portal

However, while the website would collocate a variety of media, biographical, historical and literary resources, it was determined that from an information architecture standpoint, the focus of the website – in terms of content presentation, visual theme and end-user navigation - should primarily center on Hillerman's published works and in particular the manuscript drafts, as these resources would be the substantial digital artifacts for both students and researchers of Hillerman's work. After discussing what types of tools and features would be required to make optimal use of the online versions of the manuscripts with an advisory group of humanities researchers, it was determined that the manuscripts should be digitized at moderately high resolution (600 dpi), and that each page should be made full-text searchable through Optical Character Recognition (OCR), which would also be performed during the initial digitization process. Once technical specifications for the manuscripts were determined, the full scale digitization of the entire manuscript collection was started in September, 2012 (Fig. 2).

Students and faculty members who utilize archival materials in their research typically enjoy making close examination of artifacts so they can identify features such as author's marks and editor's notes – for most archival research, scholars are frequently required to travel long distances to perform detailed examination of archival collections. One of the opportunities identified for the Hillerman portal was to be able to provide a realistic content exploration and document examination experience for end users – providing the comparable level of content manipulation and visual resolution that one would experience if examining the actual manuscript documents at the Center for Southwest Research. Thus it was next determined that the manuscripts should be packaged and made available through an eBook or page-turning type application. Nearly a dozen open source and commercial eBook applications were evaluated, and two were selected for use on the Hillerman Portal.

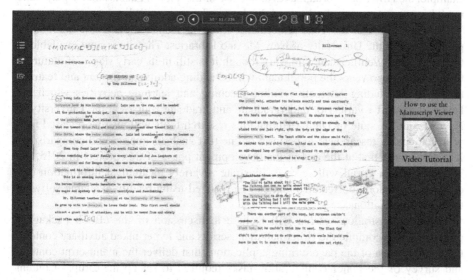

Fig. 2. Digital manuscript viewer showing both original manuscript editing marks and highlighted hypertext links

The commercial eBook application, ePageCreator was selected as the general publishing platform for the majority of the manuscripts, while the open source MegaZine3 platform was selected to provide specialized page-turning features. As discussed below, MegaZine3 can also be integrated into the Drupal Content Management System, which forms the basis of the Hillerman Portal website.

In addition to providing a realistic page browsing experience, another requirement for the manuscript eBook platform was the ability to insert inline hyperlinks into the text of the manuscript pages. As mentioned above, Tony Hillerman's writings include a wealth of ethnographic cultural and religious information about the Navajo and other Native American tribes. Many researchers who are not familiar with the American Southwest are unfamiliar with cultural, historical and geographical references that Hillerman makes in his work. The hyperlink capability provides the ability to enrich the manuscript content, in that definitions, scholarly articles, maps, photographs, audio and video clips can be referenced and made available to users inside each digital manuscript. Thus the Hillerman Portal will serve as both a digital repository of archival materials and an encyclopedia of Native American and Southwest culture, history and geography.

The technological infrastructure of the Hillerman Portal includes a variety of applications that have been integrated to provide a seamless retrieval and access experience for end users. In addition to the eBook packages that deliver the manuscript con-tent, digital audiovisual content hosted on the site is served from a separate Adobe Flash Interactive Media Server. However the core website is a very typical LAMP stack (Linux-Apache-MySQL-PHP) that hosts the Drupal 7.22 Content Management System (CMS). Drupal was selected because of its overall versatility as a CMS and its broad technical and user support community. Drupal can be easily customized with minimal original code, and its modular architecture provides an almost endless variety of plug-ins and add-ons that have already been written by the Drupal community. For example, the Hillerman Portal makes ample use of the Views, Panels and Display Suite modules to create customized record displays and query result lists.

The first phase of the Tony Hillerman Portal was launched on June 14, 2013 at a public event at the University of New Mexico Libraries. The site is now available to the public (http://ehillerman.unm.edu), though it is still in its early stages of maturity. Over the next two years the portal team will be adding additional content and features to the site, including interactive online teaching and learning activities which are keyed to support a variety of undergraduate and graduate courses at the University of New Mexico. A suite of Digital Humanities research tools will also be released next year that enable researchers to perform online text analysis queries and comparisons. It is anticipated that at the end of the development phase of this project in 2015, the Tony Hillerman Portal will serve to illustrate a variety of archival information discovery and exploration features that can be realized using readily available software tools and applications.

This demonstration session will include a discussion of the eBook packaging process used to compile the Hillerman manuscripts and hyperlinked auxiliary content, the configuration of the page turning applications that deliver the manuscript content, and survey of the major configuration tasks required to set up the Drupal Content Types, Views and Panels used in the Hillerman Portal.

Doing More with Named Entities

Turning Text into a Linked Data Hub

Theo van Veen[(⊠)] and Michel Koppelaar[(⊠)]

Koninklijke Bibliotheek, The Hague, The Netherlands
{theo.vanveen,michel.koppelaar}@kb.nl

Abstract. The usability, disclosure and value of digitized full text collections can be improved by linking named entities or events in text to linked data [1]. These data can be used to obtain additional information and it can be used in queries for expressing conditions in terms of semantic relations. When the links are obtained automatically, we need disambiguation by users or by sophisticated algorithms. Providers of full text data will have to deal with all of these aspects. In this paper we discuss our plans and work in progress and propose a common approach to increase interoperability between text data from different providers. We feel that it should be the ambition of every provider of text collections to have as many named entities as possible in text identified with globally unique persistent identifiers, linked to one or more resource descriptions to guide users through the enormous amount of digitized text. Notice: This work reflects the personal view of the authors and does not yet reflect current policies of the KB.

Keywords: Named entities · Linked data · Enrichments · Semantic search · Service integration

1 Introduction

Full text in many cases is a source for relations and a starting point for further navigation. When viewing an online document questions may come up that perhaps can be answered immediately. Linked data can offer navigation to information that might have been missed otherwise. They can also be used at the time of ingest and indexing to apply term expansion. At query time, terms from linked resources may be used to expand or reformulate the query.

To make all of this possible we first have to establish the links from named entities in the digitized text to external resource descriptions, either manually or automatically. This can be done by named entity recognition services and lookup of the named entities in external sources, or the other way around by searching all entries from external resources in the full text and subsequently mark the results. Finding the right criteria for disambiguation will become the very difficult part of this process, especially when using different types of resources [10, 13].

In the linked data cloud there are many links providing data about the same objects with the same as well as different information about a single object. Users might need to access several resource descriptions, possibly in different formats before finding the

Ł. Bolikowski et al. (Eds.): TPDL 2013, CCIS 416, pp. 163–168, 2014.
DOI: 10.1007/978-3-319-08425-1_16, © Springer International Publishing Switzerland 2014

desired information. This variety in sources and formats and the large amount of related information make it necessary to help the user in getting the right information in one step, in a single format and by a standard request. For example, when asking for the birthdate of Einstein we would like to invoke a service with the id of the resource Einstein and id of the birthdate property as parameters and have this service return the birthdate of Einstein in a machine readable format. In this paper we propose a simple API for such a service.

Linked data is often stored in triple stores with SPARQL [2] as query language. Triple stores are very efficient for storing and utilizing relations but not for conventional text searches. Besides that, we cannot expect average users to formulate SPARQL queries because of their complexity. Therefore we propose a combination of conventional search with semantic search as an extension of SRU/CQL [3] which should make it easy for users to formulate semantic relations to restrict or expand queries. The search mechanism behind this should generate a SPARQL query to triple stores only when needed.

With these ingredients we believe that we can benefit from linked data for accessing, enriching and querying the KB full text collections making use of related external information. For now we focus on ANP radio bulletins 1937–1960 and Dutch historical newspapers linked to DBpedia [4], Freebase [5], VIAF [6].

2 The Infrastructure

We use the existing KB infrastructure and the original data and metadata as much as possible with a minimum of replication of data and software. Enrichment is done by adding records into a so called enrichment database with identifiers that are the same as the identifiers of the data to be enriched. For demonstrating the use of linked data we use SIWA [7] (Schema for the Integration of Web Applications). SIWA is a schema to describe when and how external services can be invoked and how they are to be integrated in web applications supporting SIWA. When data are presented to the user the enrichment database is checked for the presence of records with the same identifier as the presented text. Such a service on top of the enrichment database is defined in the SIWA descriptions. By using SIWA, additional functionality does not have to be an integral part of a portal and is more easily reusable by others.

In the enrichment database we distinguish information resources, e.g. text objects, and non-information resources, e.g. persons. The text enrichments contain links to information that is related to named entities in text objects. If a named entity is linked to an external resource description, e.g. in DBpedia, these non-information resources also get an entry in the enrichment database with links to the external resource descriptions.

For information resources a record in the enrichment database consists of the key-identifier of the resource that is enriched and the links to the related resources. In Fig. 1 the two types of enrichments are shown. The enrichments also contain fields like the type of enrichment (e.g. 'sameAs', 'hasVideo'), the mime-type, a status field and the string representing the named entity in the text.

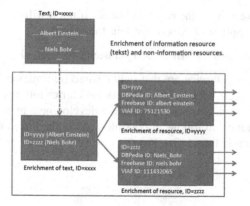

Fig. 1. Enrichments for information resources (left) and non-information resources (right). The solid arrows represent links. The dashed arrow represents a "just in case" link.

There is not a single authoritative identifier for non-information resources and they can take part in different persistent identifier frameworks. Therefore we allow them to be addressed by using the identifier of one of the resource descriptions. For example Albert Einstein is identified in VIAF by "75121530" and in DBpedia by "Albert_Einstein" and can be addressed by both identifiers using VIAF: or DBP: as prefix, respectively.

Web applications using our enriched text collections need to check the enrichment database for each document that is presented and alert the user when there are linked data or other enrichments available (see http://www.kbresearch.nl/xportal).

3   A Proposed API for a Linked Data Service

In the ideal world - ideal in terms of the work described in this article - each name, in text or metadata, is unambiguously related to a specific concept (person, location, event, etc.) by means of a globally unique persistent identification that can be used everywhere for searching information about that specific concept. However, currently this is not the case.

To approximate such a situation we created a so called linked data service to request information from different sources like DBpedia, Freebase, VIAF etc. The response is converted to a single format, currently JSON. The URL syntax for this service is:

http://<base-URL>/<resource-id>?<attribute list>

The resource-id is one of the identifications in the enrichment database and the attribute list are fieldnames being used in the external resource descriptions. The service searches the resource identifier in the enrichment database and searches for the requested fields in the corresponding resource descriptions. If the requested information is not found it will follow the "sameAs" and "exactMatch" links to other linked resources to search for the requested fields. If not it will return an empty string. A request for a description of Albert Einstein looks like:

http://www.kbresearch.nl/ods/DBP:Albert_Einstein?abstract_nl

The benefits of such service are that only desired information is returned without needing to read complete documents, it lowers the barrier for creating applications to request extra information, it speeds up software development by using a standardized API and users don't have to follow all possible links in the linked data cloud until the requested information is found. See Fig. 2.

Fig. 2. The linked data service hides the user from the linked data cloud. In case of the left arrow the user has to follow links by trial and error.

4   The Enrichment Processes

We focus on different types of enrichments:

- links between text objects describing the same events
- links between named entities in text and external resource descriptions
- links between external resource descriptions of the same resource
- links between resources being mentioned in the same document

The first type of enrichment was applied to two text collections of the KB (newspapers and ANP radio bulletins) and a set of descriptions of copyright free videos from the Dutch Institute of Sound and Vision. The similarity between documents was computed as a weighted average of the cosine distance between the two documents and two numbers expressing the overlap in named entities and distance in time. We allowed a time span of one week for the date. The threshold for the cosine distance was such that the precision was 73 %.

Enrichment of articles with named entities linked to external resources is done in two ways:

1. For linking NE's in the ANP radio bulletins in DBpedia we used a text analyzer based on the Stanford named entity recognizer [9] that we trained using the CoNLL-2002 corpus and the NE's were searched in DBpedia. A rough estimation based on the manual inspection is that about 35 % of the NE's found by the NER

were missed as a link to DBpedia and that less than 10 % of the links were incorrect. More precise figures will be presented at the workshop.

2. Linking of NE's in the Dutch newspaper articles was done by searching DBpedia entries in the newspaper collection. It is not possible to establish the recall and precision because the enrichment process is still running. We expect about 2–3 NE's per article. In a later stage we will use the results obtained in the Europeana Newspaper project [8] in which the research department of the Koninklijke Bibliotheek together with the Institute for Dutch Lexicology (INL) optimized the software for historical Dutch material. This will provide us NE's that are candidates for linking.

The next steps will be selecting and adding disambiguation techniques depending on the type of resource descriptions [11, 12, 14, 15]. We recommend the involvement of interested users at an early stage to measure precision and improve disambiguation by verifying or rejecting automatically created enrichments. This type of "socially enhanced linking" will be investigated in the Sealinc project [16], in which we try to measure the quality of automatically created links by means of user assessment.

The third type of enrichment is obtained from the external resource descriptions themselves. For example, if there is a "sameAs" link from a DBpedia record to a VIAF record we will add the VIAF link also to the corresponding record in our enrichment database. In this way we try to benefit from the links that are already available, which is in fact a main principle of the linked data concept.

The fourth type of enrichment is the co-occurrence of resources within a single document. They are not yet part of the enrichment database. We started with the co-occurrence of resources within single ANP radio bulletins but we still need to find out if this will reveal useful unexpected relations.

5   Combining Conventional Search and Semantic Search

In general semantic relations are stored in triple stores and the query language for triple stores is SPARQL. The advantage of SPARQL is that it allows specifying very complex relations in queries. In most cases however, users search for documents by supplying only a few keywords or names. It would be quite difficult for the average user to specify a SPARQL query. To offer the possibility to use the relations stored in a thesaurus or a triple store when needed, we work on combining SRU/CQL with SPARQL queries and added an extension to CQL to allow specifying that part of the search is a relation search by using square brackets like:

query=X and [placeOfBirth=[broader=utrecht]]

The SRU service sends the relation search to a triple store to expand the query. The response is substituted in the CQL query and sent to the SRU service. In this case the search is for X and persons that are born in one of the cities in the province Utrecht. For the less skilled users we leave it up to sophisticated user interfaces to expand or limit the query without the need for users to have detailed knowledge about the infrastructure behind it.

6   Conclusions and Recommendations

We believe that other providers of full text will have to deal with the same challenges and that they also would like to improve the value of their text collections by means of mapping named entities to external resource descriptions. We recommend a common approach with respect to the aspects addressed in this paper to facilitate interoperability between providers of full text collections.

References

1. Linked Data. http://www.w3.org/standards/semanticweb/data
2. SPARQL. Query Language for RDF. http://www.w3.org/TR/rdf-sparql-query/
3. SRU. Search and Retrieval via URL's. http://www.loc.gov/standards/sru/
4. DBpedia. http://dbpedia.org/About
5. Freebase. http://www.freebase.com/
6. VIAF. Virtual International Authority File. http://viaf.org
7. SIWA. Schema for the Integration of Web Applications. http://www.kbresearch.nl/SIWA
8. Europeana Newspapers. http://www.europeana-newspapers.eu/
9. Stanford Named Entity Recognizer. http://nlp.stanford.edu/software/CRF-NER.shtml
10. Sil, A., Cronin, E., et al.: Linking named entities in any database. In: EMNLP-CoNLL '12 Proceedings of the 2012 Joint Conference on Empirical Methods in Natural Language Processing and Computational Natural Language Learning
11. Shen, W., Wang, J., et al.: LINDEN: linking named entities with knowledge base via semantic knowledge. In: WWW 2012, Lyon, France, 16–20 Apr 2012
12. Bunescu, R., Pasca, M.: Using encyclopedic knowledge for named entity disambiguation. In Proceedings of the 11th Conference of the European Chapter of the Association for Computational Linguistics (EACL-06), pp. 9–16, Trento, Italy (2006)
13. van Hooland, S., De Wilde, M.: Named-entity recognition, a gateway drug for cultural heritage collections to the linked data cloud ? Literary and Linguistic Computing, 01/2013
14. Godby, C.J., Hswe, P., et al.: Who's who in your digital collection: developing a tool for name disambiguation and identity resolution. J. Chic. Colloq. Dig. Human. Comput. Sci. 1(2), 116–127 (2011)
15. MacKay, A.W.: Enriching the digital library experience: innovations with named entity recognition and geographic information system technologies (2008)
16. Sealinc. Socially-enriched access to linked cultural media. http://www.commit-nl.nl/projects/socially-enriched-access-to-linked-cultural-media

Implementing Recommendations in the PATHS System

Paul Clough[1(✉)], Arantxa Otegi[2], Eneko Agirre[2], and Mark Hall[3]

[1] Information School, Sheffield University, Sheffield, UK
p.d.clough@sheffield.ac.uk
[2] IXA taldea, University of the Basque Country, Donostia, Basque Country
{arantza.otegi,e.agirre}@ehu.es
[3] Department of Computing, Edge Hill University, Ormskirk, UK
hallmark@edgehill.ac.uk

Abstract. In this paper we describe the design and implementation of non-personalized recommendations in the PATHS system. This system allows users to explore items from Europeana in new ways. Recommendations of the type "people who viewed this item also viewed this item" are powered by pairs of viewed items mined from Europeana. However, due to limited usage data only 10.3 % of items in the PATHS dataset have recommendations (4.3 % of item pairs visited more than once). Therefore, "related items", a form of content-based recommendation, are offered to users based on identifying similar items. We discuss some of the problems with implementing recommendations and highlight areas for future work in the PATHS project.

Keywords: Digital libraries · Recommendations · Europeana

1 Introduction

Increasingly recommender systems are being used to assist users with information discovery by bringing relevant content to users' attention. They are part of a wider set of techniques for providing personalization: the tailoring of systems or services to the specific needs of individual users or communities [1, 2]. Recommendation mechanisms provide advice on objects depending on the user context or profile. They can be broadly classified by the strategy they employ (content-based or collaborative filtering) and by the recipient of the recommendations (individual user or group recommendations). Recommender functionality (and personalization more generally) has been proven useful when providing information access to cultural heritage [3].

The EU-funded PATHS[1] (Personalized Access to Cultural Heritage) project [4, 5] is investigating ways of assisting users with exploring a large collection of cultural heritage material taken from Europeana[2], the European aggregator for museums, archives, libraries, and galleries. A prototype system has been developed that includes novel functionality for exploring the collection based on Google map-style interfaces,

---

[1] PATHS website: http://www.paths-project.eu/
[2] Europeana website: http://www.europeana.eu/portal/

Ł. Bolikowski et al. (Eds.): TPDL 2013, CCIS 416, pp. 169–173, 2014.
DOI: 10.1007/978-3-319-08425-1_17, © Springer International Publishing Switzerland 2014

data-driven taxonomies and supporting the manual creation of guided tours or paths. Another aspect being explored is the use of recommendations to promote information discovery. To date we have been exploring *non-personalized* recommendations based on item-to-item co-occurrences. These provide recommendations of the kind *"people who viewed this item also viewed this item."* Co-occurrence information (items that have been viewed consecutively in the same session) has been minded from a sample of Europeana logs to power the recommendations. Additionally, we provide links to "related items", a form of content-based recommendation, based on identifying 'similar' items and classifying the *type* of relation. In this paper we describe our recommendation work to date, difficulties in implementing recommendations and our plans for future work.

2   The PATHS System

The current PATHS system interface is shown in Fig. 1. At this point the user is viewing an item from the collection indexed in PATHS. This collection consists of approximately 540,000 items from items in Europeana that have English metadata. An additional 1.2 million Spanish items are in the process of being loaded. The prototype system as it stands supports vertical, top-down exploration through the provision of a thesaurus, a tag-cloud, topic map, and faceted search. However, to support the horizontal exploration at the level of individual items, only "paths", manually curated narratives through parts of the collection, are available. To further improve the horizontal exploration facilities, particularly in areas of the collection not covered by "paths", we are investigating non-personalized recommendations. This functionality is shown in Fig. 1 in the dashed box.

2.1   Implementing *"people who viewed this also viewed this"*

We implemented a mechanism to automatically download transaction logs for the main Europeana portal on a daily basis. Currently we use a 6-months sample of logs (1 Jan to 30 June 2012), but have collected almost 2 years of data. We applied standard pre-processing, including the removal of lines not relating to user actions (e.g. cascading style sheets and images), removal of non-human actions (e.g. robots), session segmentation (based on a 30 min timeout between actions) and classification of requests (e.g. viewing an item). A 30 min timeout period of inactivity was selected based on previous research [6, 7], but we recognize that a fixed timeout period does have limitations for reliably detecting sessions and warrants further investigation [8].

In total, the processed data consists of 14,164,379 requests (3,245,766 sessions), with 53.7 % of requests for item views. We filter out those sessions without any request for items that map to the PATHS dataset. This results in 102,525 sessions (3.2 % of the initial log) with 208,584 item requests. For each session we extract sequences of 2 viewed items (ignoring all other request types). For example for the action sequence $item_1 \rightarrow item_2 \rightarrow search_1 \rightarrow item_3$ we would extract the sequences $item_1 \rightarrow item_2$ and $item_2 \rightarrow item_3$. We ignored pairs containing repeated items (i.e. $item_1 = item_2$). This resulted in 55,521 different pairs of items and an average of 1.82 recommendations per item.

Fig. 1. An example screenshot of the PATHS prototype (PATHS prototype system: http://prototype2.paths-project.eu and http://explorer.paths-project.eu (sites visited: 18/12/2013)) when viewing an item

2.2 Implementing "Related Items"

For the "related items" functionality, the similarity between each pair of items is computed using a state of the art approach based on Latent Dirichlet Allocation over the text, allowing users to quickly find related items when browsing. An evaluation dataset was crowd-sourced to enable us to assess this approach [9]. In addition, a typed similarity approach is implemented to determine the 'type' of the relation, such as similar author, location, date, event, people involved or subject. With this extra functionality, users know *why* the system is making the suggestion, an aspect considered as important to recommender systems [10]. The approach is a combination of simple similarity heuristics, based on the appropriate metadata fields, and a lineal regression [11]. The latter method improved the results considerably, obtaining second position among several contenders at an open evaluation exercise[3].

3 Discussion

Like most cultural heritage systems the amount of interaction data generated by users of the PATHS system is insufficient for implementing "people who viewed this also

---

[3] Semeval 2013: http://ixa2.si.ehu.es/sts/

viewed this" functionality, due to data sparseness. Therefore, we exploit usage information from a more widely used system (Europeana), but restrict the data to only those items we index. However, even using data from a more widely used system we can only make recommendations for 10.3 % of items in the PATHS dataset.

A further issue is that only 2,407 pairs of items (4.3 %) are viewed more than once which may be the threshold at which recommendations are acceptable. Therefore, we are also working on extracting more pairs between items based on transitivity (e.g. for the sequence $item_1 \rightarrow item_2 \rightarrow item_3$ we could also assume a relation exists between $item_1 \rightarrow item_3$) and duality (e.g. for the pair $item_1 \rightarrow item_2$ we could also extract $item_2 \rightarrow item_1$). Another approach to deal with data sparseness could be to map each item to a semantic category and then make recommendations at higher levels than item, i.e. suggest pairs of items for the same subject that are viewed consecutively.

One approach we adopt in the current prototype is utilization of additional content-based recommendations. These "related items" help to alleviate the problems of insufficient usage data. Combinations of approaches are commonly used to overcome the limitations in using collaborative filtering and content-based approaches independently [2]. Further work being planned includes evaluating recommendations in a controlled lab-based setting and field trials. Also, we are developing personalized recommendations based on a session-based user model (i.e. the user profile is built up during a session from items viewed) and using PageRank to identify items of interest.

4   Conclusions

This paper discusses the implementation of non-personalized recommendations at the item-level in the PATHS system, which assists users with exploring Europeana. Recommendations of the form "people who viewed this item also viewed this item" are powered by mining co-occurrences of items viewed in Europeana. To complement these recommendations, and alleviate some of the issues with data sparseness, we also implemented "related items" functionality. We discuss some of the issues with implementing non-personalized recommendations, in addition to avenues for further work on personalized recommendations in the PATHS system.

Acknowledgements. The research leading to these results was carried out as part of the PATHS project (http://paths-project.eu) funded by the European Community's Seventh Framework Programme (FP7/2007-2013) under grant agreement no. 270082.

References

1. Smeaton, A., Callan, J.: Personalisation and recommender systems in digital libraries. Int. J. Digit. Libr. **5**(4), 299–308 (2005)
2. Adomavicius, G., Tuzhilin, A.: Toward the next generation of recommender systems: a survey of the state-of-the-art and possible extensions. IEEE Trans. Knowl. Data Eng. **17**(6), 734–749 (2005)

3. Ardissono, L., Kuflik, T., Petrelli, D.: Personalization in cultural heritage: the road travelled and the one ahead. User Model. User-Adap. Inter. **22**(1–2), 73–99 (2012)
4. Agirre, E., et al.: PATHS: a system for accessing cultural heritage collections. In: Proceedings of the 51st Annual Meeting of the Association for Computational Linguistics (ACL'13), Sofia, Bulgaria, 4–9 August 2013, pp. 151–156 (2013)
5. Fernie, K., et al.: PATHS: personalising access to cultural heritage spaces. In: Proceedings of 18th International Conference on Virtual Systems and Multimedia (VSMM 2012), pp. 469–474 (2012)
6. Tanasa, D., Trousse, B.: Advanced data preprocessing for intersites Web usage mining. IEEE Intell. Syst. **19**(2), 59–65 (2004)
7. Catledge, L., Pitkow, J.: Characterizing browsing strategies in the world-wide web. In: Proceedings of the Third International World-Wide Web Conference on Technology, Tools and Applications, vol. 27 (1995)
8. Jones, R., Klinkner, K.: Beyond the session timeout: automatic hierarchical segmentation of search topics in query logs. In: Proceedings of the 17th ACM Conference on Information and Knowledge Management (CIKM'08), pp. 699–708. ACM, New York (2008)
9. Aletras, N., Stevenson, M., Clough, P.: Computing similarity between items in a digital library of cultural heritage. J. Comput. Cult. Heritage **5**(4), Article 16, 1–19 (2013). doi:10.1145/2399180.2399184. http://doi.acm.org/10.1145/2399180.2399184
10. Sinha, R., Swearingen, K.: The role of transparency in recommender systems. In: Proceedings of the Conference of Human Factors in Computing Systems, 20–25 April 2002, Minneapolis, MN, pp. 830–831. ACM, New York (2002)
11. Agirre, E., et al.: UBC UOS-TYPED: regression for typed-similarity. In: Proceedings of the Second Joint Conference on Lexical and Computational Semantics (*SEM 2013), vol. 1: Proceedings of the Main Conference and the Shared Task: Semantic Textual Similarity, Atlanta, Georgia, 13–14 June 2013, pp. 132–137 (2013)

From Access to Use: Premises for a User-Centered Quality Model for the Development of Archives Online

Pierluigi Feliciati[1](✉) and Alessandro Alfier[2]

[1] University of Macerata, Macerata, Italy
pierluigi.feliciati@unimc.it
[2] IBACN - Regione Emilia-Romagna, Bologna, Italy
aalfier@regione.emilia-romagna.it

Abstract. Although the traditional mediation of archivists supplied the necessity of users in accessing archival records and documents, present archives online, i.e. digital environments offering archival content, often require specific competences to be browsed and searched. Differently from most digital libraries, their specialized, separated and hierarchic units of information are not easily accessible for non-expert users. No reference model is currently available to ensure quality to archives online in terms of user needs, experience and satisfaction, and rarely archival projects organize specific user studies to finalize language, interfaces and architectures. After introducing the state of the art and presenting the main issues emerging from user studies applied to archives online, this paper suggests key concepts and methods for creating a quality assessment model centered on final users' engagement, in view of going beyond the simple goal of accessing archives, towards the promotion of their effective use.

Keywords: Archives online · Archival mediation · User experience · User studies · Quality models

1 Introduction

Within the wide context of digital libraries, this paper is focused on web services offering content about archival *fonds*. These services basically provide standardized descriptions –sometimes connected to digital reproductions– and typically achieve two basic requirements: they are based on a hierarchical and multilevel structure (from general to analytic), they provide access by "provenance" (i.e. the origins and contextual information of archival materials). These services are, therefore, material-centric, not subject-based. From now on, they will be named "archives online", to distinguish them from the access environments to active digital-born records ("digital archives"). The effects of the lack of quality reference models for archives online are increasingly evident. When quality is evaluated, users' satisfaction is normally a minor goal. Accessibility to descriptions is often considered their ultimate goal, and there are few published studies based on user involvement to test archives online.

Ł. Bolikowski et al. (Eds.): TPDL 2013, CCIS 416, pp. 174–179, 2014.
DOI: 10.1007/978-3-319-08425-1_18, © Springer International Publishing Switzerland 2014

This paper discusses the challenges of archival profession as a result of the increasing availability of archives on the web and refers to the few user studies applied to quality of archives online as perceived by users. Thereafter, it concludes by suggesting key concepts and methods for the development of a user-centred, quality assessment model.

2 Challenges for Archival Mediation, Between On-Site Reference and Neutral Information Systems

Archival description is traditionally conceived as the activity of producing finding aids (for example guides, inventories, calendars, indexes) resulting from the mediation of archivists [1]. They take as their target a limited audience, selected for its well-established practice with archives, and they adopt a refined technique for document description, based on the descriptive traditions in force among archival communities. This attitude leads to producing finding aids whose use requires often the reference service of archivists themselves. This paradigm of "extended mediation" implies that archives reveal themselves gradually through several stages shaped just by archivists, who produce the finding aids and guide their use.

This model had to come to grips with the massive increase of web services. To what extent are archival finding aids ready to be published on the web, where users are called to act as protagonists of the cognitive process, basically free from any mediation [2]? The North American archival community has dealt with this issue, prompted by several user studies results. From the final users' point of view, archival informative mediation on the web is suffering much more than what archivists usually accept [3–7]. The increased success of archives on line does not imply automatically the increase of their full accessibility [8] and they often perpetuate the paradigm of extended mediation, preserving a material-centric rather than a user-centric approach and just the mediation of archivists seems to take care of translating users' queries into the intrinsic logic of finding aids [9]. The ICA standards, emphasize that the standardization process of archival description generally aims to produce self-explanatory finding aids [10–12], but archival standardization process has privileged decidedly data input, with an "output neutrality" [4]. Compliance to standards is a necessary condition, but not sufficient to guarantee the usability of archives online, under the basic principle that "output is not input" [5, 6, 9].

This situation is worsened by the interfering action of a brand new subject: the software agents. More and more often users have no direct access to online finding aids, taking advantage of the mediation of automatic tools, general or project-specific [13]. Therefore, archives on line should be "two-headed". The first head addresses software agents and has to be built on mandatory metadata to avoid ambiguities caused by blind automatism. The second head addresses human users and should be an easy-to-use information display, no more assiduously assisted by archivists. This challenge requires a reconsideration of the extended mediation model, and the establishment of a new paradigm [14–16]. This assumption opens up the archival world to cross-disciplinary approaches, and the self-explanatory effectiveness of online resources has to be verified empirically, by organizing usability tests and above all articulated user studies.

3   Users' Studies and Archives Online

In North America and more recently in Europe [4–7, 17] the quality of use of archives online has being increasingly tested, no longer merely inferred. Based on the results of these studies, this paper offers a classification of the key issues emerging from the effective interaction of final users with archives online. As regards archival terminology, all the studies show that the language used within online archival finding aids, often too technical, represents a barrier for users not only for description comprehension, but also for the extended search functions. Another core issue is the hierarchical structure: it was widely noticed a sensible difficulty for users to browse the multilevel hierarchy of archival descriptions, even if in some cases the most inexperienced of those users have shown an unexpected ability to learn the structured nature of archival information. Typically, users prefer the available search functions rather than browsing through the descriptive levels. This drive-back effect could be explained considering the interest of final users to what archives are related to, in content *datum*, while archivists concentrate on what composes archives, on the structural *datum*. As regards searching tools, no-expert users tend to be convinced that the query methods are identical for archives online and OPAC. They preferably adopt the default values suggested by the system, thus excluding more refined results. Other critical issues arise from results presentation: archives online adopt usually neutral orders for any list (alphabetical or chronological), while final users expect results ordered according to a semantic relevance rank (such as popular search engines seem to do). When it comes to the use of controlled dictionaries, as well as content visualization issues, the studies carried out so far do not provide univocal results. It has emerged, for instance, that some users prefer minimal descriptions to detailed and analytical content. However, there has been some consensus over the use of displays with short narrative texts linking to more detailed information.

This corpus of user studies, however, reveals several weaknesses. Firstly, they are not based on a common evaluation schema, demonstrating once more how user research in this domain need to be widely shared, to build a more normalized benchmarking framework. Each study applied its own protocol, tailored both on the specific characteristics of the system to be evaluated and on individual research settings. This hinders the possibility to compare data coming from different studies and inhibit the setting of historical series. Secondly, the usual narrowness of panels involved puts in discussion a wide reliability of collected data. Tested panels are typically selected from population layers naturally interested on archives online, like young students, persons with a high cultural background or coming from the same geographical and cultural context to which the archives are concerning. Last, some surveys were conducted without a distinction between novice archival researchers and advanced scholars: this is certainly a relevant issue, because we could guess that the two groups implement very different strategies of interaction with archives online.

4   Applying a New Paradigm for Archives Online: Suggestions for a Quality Assessment Model

A possible quality model to apply the new paradigm for online archival mediation has to be based on some key concepts and should draw from the models adopted in neighboring domains. In the following lines, some of the core concepts and models to achieve this goal are discussed. Starting from the basics, the splitting between archival input and its outputs removes archivists from the final usage stage of finding aids. The operative space thus created, opens up the specific competence of designing the outputs of archives online. A "shared authority" model [18] has to be legitimized even for archival descriptions, opening the evolution of finding aids into "information social phenomena" [16], embedding replacements of human mediations and user generated content [8].

Secondly, the development of archives online have to consider different scenarios of use. Archival use(r)s may be roughly classified according two profiles: the "browsing attitude", which implies knowingly adopting advanced search strategies, and the "searching attitude", i.e. the fishing of single units of information. These profiles, realistic as they may be, should not lead to privileging one over the other.

Another key element in the building of a quality model could be a general classification of the typical issues to be faced for the development of archives online, founded both on published user studies and on some projects on cultural web users:

- *coverage*: users can not easily perceive if what they seek is included in the archives online service they are using, if it could be somewhere else or even if doesn't exist at all in the web (hidden collections). Archives are not that explicit about their effective coverage and do not specify the granularity of descriptions (records? Files? Series? Fonds?);
- *structure/syntax*: archival content structures are often too multifarious, and complexity is sometimes even taken by archivists as a quality requirement;
- *content/language*: projects often adopt excessively technical jargon, internal to the discipline or taken just from the primary sources.

In the perspective of pasting these basic concepts and issues into a model, it has to be reminded that archives online are software products, so they fall under the definition of quality provided by the Quality model included in ISO/IEC 9126-1:200, Software engineering. Thus, the basic entities of a possible model should be users, their context of use and their specified goals, while the basic quality criteria should be effectiveness, productivity, safety and satisfaction.

Considering other available conceptual models to draw inspiration from, the Digital Library Reference Model [19] offers a persuasive representation of the multifaceted DL universe, setting up six domains: Resource, Content, User, Functionality, Policy, Quality and Architecture. However, the User domain does not provide testing and evaluation roles. Moreover, bots, intelligent agents and other machine actors, are not clearly distinguished in the model even if they play special roles and behaviors within the DL. The Resource and the Content domains need special attention in the perspective of their application to the multilevel structure of archival descriptions.

The concepts of identification, quality and format, and especially the distinction between Resource and its expression are fundamental for the archival input/output splitting. We could note that the Functionality Domain does not provide any scenario of User involvement in the view of evaluating the system. The Quality domain is crucial, underlining the necessity of a clear Quality of Service dynamic policy, even if user studies – a basic source to assess quality – are not mentioned at all.

Another model to be considered is the Interaction Triptych Framework: it focuses on the interaction between three entities: user, content and system. Thus, «three categories of metrics are established upon the axes that are formulated by their in-between relationships» [20]. The first categories to be detailed for archives online should be usefulness, to evaluate the interaction between user and content, and usability, on the axis between user and the system.

Coming to a conclusion, apparently the goal of building up an Archives Online Quality Assessment Model has to be shared with a wide community, made of archivists and digital curators but open to digital librarians, user study and information experts. To draft a model, it is useful to focus mostly on the shared characteristics and functions, instead on the (existing) differences with the DL domain [21]. It has to be accepted peacefully that web environments undermined the traditional mediation role between archivists and final users, first of all putting into evidence the distinction of the web output from the encoded input. This re-thinking calls for the contribution of cognitive science, human-computer interaction, web design, other application models and above all should be based on the "users' voice", heard after appropriate user studies [22]. To conclude, the XXI century archivists should build user centric displays, matching their descriptive techniques and standards with human-computer interaction studies, checking their prototypes applying evaluation and testing activities. In this sense, user studies have to be considered as crucial, to finalize archives online and ensure a good quality of use.

References

1. Duranti, L.: Origin and development of the concept of archival description. Archivaria **35**, 47–54 (1993)
2. Vianello Osti, M.: El hipertexto entre la utopía y la aplicatión: identidad, problemática y tendencias de la Web. Trea, Gijón (2005)
3. Duff, W., Stoyanova, P.: Transforming the crazy quilt: archival displays from user's point of view. Archivaria **45**, 44–79 (1998)
4. Scheir, W.: First entry: report on a qualitative exploratory study of novice user experience with online finding aids. J. Arch. Organ. **3**, 49–85 (2006)
5. Yakel, E.: Encoded archival description: are finding aids boundary spanners or barriers for users? J. Arch. Organ. **2**, 63–77 (2004)
6. Chapman, J.C.: Observing users: an empirical analysis of user interaction with online finding aids. J. Arch. Organ. **8**, 4–30 (2010)
7. Daniels, M., Yakel, E.: Seek and you may find: successful search in online finding aid systems. Am. Arch. **73**, 535–568 (2010)
8. Yakel, E.: Impact of internet-based discovery tools on use and users of archives. Comma **2**(3), 191–200 (2003)

9. Gilliland-Swetland, A.J.: Popularizing the finding aid: exploiting EAD to enhance online discovery and retrieval in archival information systems by diverse user groups. J. Internet Cataloging **4**, 199–225 (2001)

10. International Council on Archives: ISAD (G): General International Standard Archival Description (1999). http://www.ica.org/10207/standards/isadg-general-international-standard-archival-description-second-edition.html

11. International Council on Archives: Guidelines for the Preparation and Presentation of Finding Aids (2001). http://www.icacds.org.uk/eng/findingaids.htm

12. International Council on Archives: Principles of Access to Archives (2013). http://www.ica.org/13619/toolkits-guides-manuals-and-guidelines/principles-of-access-to-archives.html

13. Schaffner, J.: The metadata is the interface: better description for better discovery of archives and special collections, synthesized from user studies. OCLC research, Dublin (Ohio) (2009). http://www.oclc.org/content/dam/research/publications/library/2009/2009-06.pdf

14. Meissner, D.: First things first: reengineering finding aids for implementation of EAD. Am. Arch. **60**, 372–387 (1997)

15. Yakel, E., Shaw, S., Reynolds, P.: Creating the next generation of archival finding aids. D-Lib Magazine 13 (2007). http://www.dlib.org/dlib/may07/yakel/05yakel.html

16. Ribeiro, F.: Archival science and changes in the paradigm. Arch. Sci. **1**, 295–310 (2001)

17. Dobreva, M., Mcculloch, E., Birrell, D., Feliciati, P., Ruthven, I., Sykes, J., Ünal, Y.: User and functional testing. Final report. Europeana Foundation (2010). http://pro.europeana.eu/c/document_library/get_file?uuid=1c25ae28-9457-4b0f-be62-654a7cf6c5b7&groupId=10602

18. Duff, W., Harris, V.: Stories and names: archival description as narrating records and constructing meanings. Arch. Sci. **2**, 263–285 (2002)

19. Candela, L., Athanasopoulos, G., Castelli, D., El Raheb, K., Innocenti, P., Ioannidis, Y., Katifori, A., Nika, A., Vullo, G., Ross, S.: The digital library reference model. DL.org (2011). http://bscw.research-infrastructures.eu/pub/bscw.cgi/d222816/D3.2b%20Digital%20Library%20Reference%20Model.pdf

20. Tsakonas, G., Papatheodorou, C.: Exploring usefulness and usability in the evaluation of open access digital libraries. Inf. Process. Manag. **44**(3), 1234–1250 (2008)

21. Feliciati, P., Alfier, A.: Archives on the web and users expectations: towards a convergence with digital libraries. Rev. Nat. Cent. Digitization **22**, 81–92 (2013). http://elib.mi.sanu.ac.rs/files/journals/ncd/22/ncd22081.pdf

22. Toms, E.G.: Models that inform digital library design. In: Dobreva, M., O'Dwyer, A., Feliciati, P. (eds.) User Studies for Digital Library Development, pp. 21–32. Facet, London (2012)

Sound of the Netherlands:
Towards a Pan-European Collection of Sounds

Lizzy Komen[⊠] and Johan Oomen

Netherlands Institute for Sound and Vision, Hilversum, The Netherlands
{lkomen, joomen}@beeldengeluid.nl

Abstract. Sound of the Netherlands makes a sound collection from The Netherlands Institute for Sound and Vision available to a wide audience. This demonstration will showcase the web-based interface as well as the mobile application developed for Sound of the Netherlands. It highlights the thinking behind the design, crowdsourcing aspects, the impact of the project and (re-) use of Sound of the Netherlands datasets and infrastructure, as well as the future work to expand to a pan-European collection of sounds.

Keywords: Sound archive · Crowdsourcing · Soundscapes · Creative industry · Re-use · Creative commons

1 Introduction

There are many initiatives across the world where sounds are collected and distributed. Besides institutional sound collections, crowd sourcing of sounds is becoming increasingly popular. Some examples are UK Soundmap (http://sounds.bl.uk/Sound-Maps/UK-Soundmap) and New Zealand Soundmap (http://soundmap.co.nz/), both are nationwide sound maps that invite people to record and upload sounds of their environment, or 100 Soundscapes of Japan (https://en.wikipedia.org/wiki/100_Soundscapes_of_Japan), a listing of Japanese soundscapes as symbols for local people and to promote the rediscovery of sounds of everyday life.

This SUEDL 2013 demonstrator presents 'Het Geluid van Nederland' or 'Sound of the Netherlands' (http://www.geluidvannederland.nl) which makes a sound archive from the collection of The Netherlands Institute for Sound and Vision (NISV) available to a wide audience. It also encourages users to add their own sounds to the collection and to interact with existing sounds.

2 Sound of the Netherlands

The Netherlands Institute for Sound and Vision is one of the largest audio-visual archives in Europe, with the aim to preserve audio-visual heritage and make this accessible to potential users. The collection totals over 700,000 hours of television, radio, music and film. The sound collection contains over 10,000 sound recordings from the 1950s to the 1990s, showing the evolving soundscape of the Netherlands. Sounds include horse driven trams, street vendors and recordings from the 'Eleven

Ł. Bolikowski et al. (Eds.): TPDL 2013, CCIS 416, pp. 180–183, 2014.
DOI: 10.1007/978-3-319-08425-1_19, © Springer International Publishing Switzerland 2014

Cities' ('Elfstedentocht') ice skating match. Only a selection of 2,100 sounds from the 10,000 existing sound recordings were added to the Sound of the Netherlands interface, mostly due to the lack of metadata or missing location information.

The Sound of the Netherlands interface provides an overview of the national coverage of the sound archive, both in space and time, and is used to encourage users to add their own sound to complement the archive [1]. Since the service launched in September 2012, approx. 250 crowd sourced sounds were added to its repository of 2,100 sounds from the sound archive of NISV. They are available through a 'sound map' (Fig. 1).

We approach field-recording communities and other interested parties and invite them to contribute to the project by uploading their sounds. Users can upload their sounds directly through an easy to use interface. To this end, Sound of the Netherlands makes use of the technical infrastructure of SoundCloud, a widely used social music sharing platform.

The Sound of the Netherlands interface allows navigation in both space and time and by using keywords. It is also possible for users to directly like, share or comment on a sound, either in general or on the sound timeline thanks to the SoundCloud integration. There are plans to improve the interface with a general search entry point.

All sounds (from the archive and contributions from users) are available under either a Creative Commons – Attribution-ShareAlike (CC BY-SA) or a Creative Commons – Attribution license (CC BY). CC BY gives explicit permission to remix and distribute sounds, as long as the creator of the recording is mentioned. CC BY-SA also has this requirement, and adds to this requirement that results of remixes are made available under the same license.

Next to the web-based upload interface, users can use an iOS/Android app created for the project called Soundhunter (Fig. 2) that allows them to create field recordings and upload them directly to SoundCloud and successively, to the Sound of the

Fig. 1. Sound map

Fig. 2. The soundhunter app

Netherlands. It allows users to add metadata and also to attach the desired Creative Commons license. This demonstration will showcase the web-based interface as well as the mobile application developed for Sound of the Netherlands, and the thinking behind its design [1].

3   Impact and Use of Sound of the Netherlands

Over 250 users have uploaded sounds to the platform since the launch and we are currently defining our strategy to foster the existing user base and at the same time ensure it will continue to grow (see also Conclusions and Future work). Using SoundCloud as the underlying technical infrastructure has proven beneficial. It allows us to focus on approaching communities and not invest resources on creating a custom backend infrastructure [1]. Furthermore, SoundCloud has a great reach and offers fine-grained statistics. Until June 2013 there have been nearly 60,000 plays, 11,000 downloads and 2,200 likes of the sounds added to SoundCloud through this project.

The dataset has also been repurposed in new applications for instance the Mix of the Netherlands (http://www.betweencurlybrackets.nl/MixvanNederland/index.html) and Sounds Visual (http://www.opencultuurdata.nl/2013/01/sounds-visual/). The first allows users to make a remix of the collection of sounds. The latter explores visual alternatives to textual tags. Users make drawings that represent the sounds. They are subsequently used as access points to the sounds. Both are created outside of the scope of the project, by third parties and were build on the existing Sound of the Netherlands infrastructure. It showcases how open access to these resources support new and creative services [1].

The sounds have also been made available for re-use on Wikipedia via Wikimedia Commons. Several competitions and workshops were organised, under which an Edit-a-thon where Wikipedia articles were enriched with 'audio illustrations' using sounds from the project. As a result there have been over 190,000 views of 80 Wikipedia article pages, in Swedish, English, Dutch and Catalan, that have made use of sounds from the project (stats for Month 4, 2013).[1]

4 Conclusions and Future Work

The EU funded project Europeana Creative (http://www.europeanacreative.eu), which started in February 2013, provides a new opportunity to expand towards a pan-European collection of sounds. Partners will develop a number of pilot applications focused on design, tourism, education and social networks, demonstrating creative re-use of digital cultural heritage content and associated metadata from Europeana[2].

The 'sounds' pilot will be developed in collaboration with NISV, The British Library (BL), HistoryPin (HP) and Ontotext. NISV and the BL will provide geo-tagged sounds from their archives to Europeana, while HP will provide the needed infrastructure and frontend to present and collect sounds. Ontotext will provide services for geo-referencing of the data contributed to this pilot based on entity extraction [2].

The pilot will enable Europeana metadata to be used by location-based services, and increase the visibility of digitised content in popular location-based search. Secondly, the pilot will support national crowd sourcing initiatives, enabling them to collaborate with a trans-national service [2]. The first results will be presented mid 2014.

Acknowledgements. Het Geluid van Nederland is a project by the Netherlands Institute for Sound and Vision, De Auditieve Dienst and Kennisland. The collection that was made available was digitized in the Dutch digitization project 'Images for the Future'. Het Geluid van Nederland was made possible through the financial support of Stichting Doen and the BankGiro Loterij.

References

1. Oomen, J., et al.: Sound of the Netherlands: crowdsourcing the Dutch soundscape. MW2013: Museums and the Web (2013). http://mw2013.museumsandtheweb.com/proposals/with-help-from-the-public-crowdsourcing-sounds-and-amateur-film/
2. Komen, L., et al. D4.1: pilots delivery plan and content sourcing strategy (2013). http://pro.europeana.eu/documents/1538974/1601973/eCreative_D4.1_NISV_v1.0

---

[1] http://tools.wmflabs.org/glamtools/baglama.php?group=Sounds+from+Geluid+van+Nederland&date=201304

[2] http://europeana.eu/

eCultureMap – Link to Europeana Knowledge

Franc J. Zakrajšek[(⊠)] and Vlasta Vodeb

Urban Planning Institute of the Republic of Slovenia,
Ljubljana, Slovenia
{franc.zakrajsek,vlasta.vodeb}@guest.arnes.si

Abstract. eCultureMap is a geographical knowledge map connecting and visualizing digital cultural objects. eCultureMap is an interactive online map and has been developed in the EU project Carare: Connecting Archaeology and Architecture in Europeana. The pilot map can be browsed at http://carare. eculturelab.eu/. eCultureMap currently displays and links over 1.5 million cultural objects. The map undoubtedly enriches user experience and it proves the added value of Europeana for cultural tourism, creative industries, education, and overall promotion of culture.

Keywords: Digital libraries · Geospatial data · Visualization · Cultural tourism

1 Introduction

Cultural mapping is an assignment of cultural objects and resources to a geographical or non-geographical knowledge map.

European digital library - Europeana[1] is connecting a large number of digital cultural objects (currently about 30 million) from European museums, libraries, archives and multi-media institutions. The content is ready for use by the general public, professionals, students, tourists, ... The eCultureMap is an attempt to re-use this content as a geographical knowledge map. The pilot of the eCultureMap has been developed within the Carare EU project: Connecting ARchaeology and ARchitecture in Europeana[2], funded under the European Commission's ICT Policy Support Programme [1].

There were two objectives when developing the pilot map:

- first, what are the benefits and advances when browsing huge digital cultural content as is Europeana, geographically and the use related spatial tools;
- second, what are the problems and bottlenecks when we geographically "aggregate" digital cultural content from several and different cultural collections originating from different cultural sectors, different institutions, different geographical coordinate systems, and from several different countries.

---

[1] http://www.europeana.eu
[2] http://www.carare.eu

Ł. Bolikowski et al. (Eds.): TPDL 2013, CCIS 416, pp. 184–189, 2014.
DOI: 10.1007/978-3-319-08425-1_20, © Springer International Publishing Switzerland 2014

2   Related Work

The value added with the inclusion of geographical coordinates in the metadata is to enable the inclusion of Europeana data in planning, tourism, education or any web-based service and geo-portals [2]. Europeana data has been reused in numerous ways, also regarding its geographical location. The project Judaica Europeana developed a web based map with Jewish content for Europeana displayed [3, 4]. The Pelagios project developed the Pelagios API for searching and browsing the Pelagios network of place references [5]. Another field where geographical information about cultural heritage items is already recognized is heritage portals displaying heritage locations on a map, as for example an initiative in the digitization of public libraries, museums and archives Ask About Ireland [6]. The UCD Digital Library is another example for exploring cultural heritage in Dublin city and displaying it on a map. Project ATHENA developed guidelines for including geographical information in the meta-data description of digital cultural heritage items with demonstrations on enrichments when geographical coordinates are included in the metadata [7]. The INDICATE project further investigated the possibilities and approaches regarding the use of e-infrastructure in geocoded digital culture [8]. In the Europeana context the value of enriching the datasets with geographical information is noticeable, especially among Hackathon prototypes after 2012 [9].

3   Methods

The first phase of the development of the eCultureMap included the concept, design and structure of the geographical metadata. They included, besides the geographical coordinates and spatial accuracy, also the links to a detailed description of the cultural item on the Europeana and on the local portal as well. The following methods for preparation of the geographical coordinates for digital cultural items were applied:

- Mainly, content providers of the Carare project were providing digital geographical coordinates along with metadata descriptions. Architecture and archeological management systems usually already have geographical data in the metadata. Technical cleaning of this data was necessary to gain compatibility of the data. Further, all data has to be transformed to the WSG84 geographical coordinate system.
- For some collections are used auto generated spatial tags which are made by Europeana.
- A part of the metadata has been enriched by geoparsing with the Europeana Geoparsing Service - v1.0 Beta[3].

---

[3] http://europeana-geo.isti.cnr.it/geoparser/geoparsing

Spatial accuracy of the geographical coordinates of the cultural items displayed on the pilot map are two kinds, first is below 5–10 m in real world which is appropriate for spatial navigation, and the second which is above 10 m.

Second phase of the development of the pilot map included development of the geographical user interface to display and browse digital cultural items. The basic requirement for the interface was being easy to use and intuitive.

Functional requirements for pilot map were:

- to display where Carare digital cultural objects are "located",
- to search Europeana collections and find the location of the selected digital object,
- to use the application also on mobile devices,
- to demonstrate the use of the application in cultural tourism,
- to develop easy to use and intuitive user interface,
- to integrate hyperlinks from displayed centroid on the map to its contexts on Europeana portal and on national /provider level,
- to be a companion of the main Carare web site.

Technological requirements for development were:

- to use open source software,
- to use Europeana search API (Application Programming Interface),
- to use technological components used in the Europeana ICT (Information Communication Technology) as much as possible,
- to be functional with several web browsers "without" exceptions.

4 Results

The pilot map can be browsed at http://carare.eculturelab.eu/ and also accompanied videos are available[4]. It consists of the data ingested to Europeana by Carare project and currently displays 1.488.988 digital objects. The user interface of the pilot map has four main components: mapping, route planning, search, and mobile.

Mapping component is the basic component for displaying the interactive map. The component has several functionalities: basic interactive map functions (zoom to all, zoom-in, zoom-out, pan), switching the basemap layer (available: Google Physical, Open Street Map, Google Satellite, Google Streets, Google Hybrid), and showing the thumbnails of digital objects on a selected location. User can use filter tool to reduce number of digital objects displayed on the map. Because of the different languages of meta data, the authomatic translation from Engish to native languages is provided in background by using Microsoft Translator V2 API[5] (e.g. filter by "castle" displays heritage containing word "château", "Schloss," "slot", "castello" in the title) (Fig. 1).

---

[4] http://www.youtube.com/watch?v=z_xdYGTMjW0;   http://www.youtube.com/watch?NR=1&v= hz6vEbxRy7s

[5] http://msdn.microsoft.com/en-us/library/ff512423.aspx

Fig. 1. eCultureMap, overview (http://carare.eculturelab.eu/)

Route planning component of the pilot map is an easy to use tool for browsing the data along the selected path. After the user finishes digitizing the route by clicking on a map the new browser window opens with self-generated list of digital objects along the digitized route with images, distances and links to detail information on heritage item at the content provider site (Fig. 2).

Search component performs searching by free text among Europeana content and presents the location of the selected object on the map - "Where is what?". The search tool is performed by Europeana search API 2.0[6] which is an efficient tool for searching Europeana collections and for the use with geographical user interface.

Mobile component enables locational services. The component is using geolocation services and is enabled for customization for different mobile devices. All components of the pilot map works also on mobile devices. Functionalities of the mapping, search and route planning component are available.

---

[6] http://pro.europeana.eu/api

Fig. 2. eCultureMap, route planning (http://carare.eculturelab.eu/)

5 Conclusion

The pilot map proves the efficiency of the geographical map as a user interface for Europeana and other cultural portals. The pilot map interface is simple, and is usable also on mobiles, but it depends on the internet connection speed especially when displaying basemap layer. Enhancement of the Carare project website with the map is in giving clear overview of the ingested content within the project and enables easy to use browsing and discovering the content. The pilot map can be already practically used for discovering cultural objects near certain location, even the data base is not complete neither perfect.

Route planning component of the pilot map is interesting and usable tool and could be used in real time when travelling by bus, car or walking with mobile device. Especially is recommended for mobile tablet. The component should be further developed especially by adding selection refinement options.

Quality of the geographical metadata is crucial. It is highly recommended to include and cooperate with content providers when they ingest their data to Europeana and encourage them to enrich their data with geographical metadata. Usually, in case of architectural and archaeological site and other immovable heritage, the quality of the geographical coordinates is quite good because they are part of their documentation and management systems. Museums and libraries have less tradition and experiences in geospatial information. There has been identified the need for raising awareness on benefits of it, more training, geographical tools, and working cases for introducing geographical information in their documentation systems[7].

References

1. Zakrajšek, F., et al.: Map enhancement to project website using Europeana API, Deliverable D 4.7 Project CARARE: Connecting ARchaeology and ARchitecture in Europeana, January 2013
2. Zakrajšek, F., et al.: Report on Europeana GIS services and archaeology/architecture site data, Deliverable D3.5 Project CARARE: Connecting ARchaeology and ARchitecture in Europeana, February 2013
3. Winer, D.: Judaica Europeana: semantic web tools for expressing the contribution of Jews to European cities in the European digital library – Europeana. Article presented at the EVA Florence Conference, 21–23 April 2010. http://www.evaflorence.it/home.php
4. http://www.judaica-europeana.eu
5. Simon, R., Barker, E., Isaksen, L.: Exploring Pelagios: a visual browser for geotagged datasets. In: International Workshop on Supporting Users' Exploration of Digital Libraries, September 2012, Paphos, Cyprus, pp. 23–27 (2012)
6. http://www.askaboutireland.ie
7. Zakrajšek, F., Vodeb, V.: Digital Cultural Content: Guidelines for Geographic Information. Athena project, Roma (2011)
8. Zakrajšek, F.J., Vodeb, V.: Geocoded Digital Cultural Content. Linked Heritage Project, Roma (2013)
9. http://pro.europeana.eu/web/guest/hackathon-prototypes

---

[7] http://www.athenaeurope.org/getFile.php?id=669

An Image Similarity Search for the European Digital Library and Beyond

Sergiu Gordea[✉]

AIT-Austrian Institute of Technology GmbH, Vienna, Austria
sergiu.gordea@ait.ac.at

Abstract. This paper presents an Image Similarity Search service for the European Digital Library and summarizes the requirements of different stakeholders that make use of this kind of service. The current implementation is suited to support public users when exploring the content of Europeana. Further enhancements of this service are required to support design related activities by stimulating and inspiring the creativity of professional designers.

Keywords: Image similarity · European digital library · Creative design

1 Introduction

The European Digital Library (Europeana[1]) provides a single point of access to ca. 22 million cultural heritage objects provided by European Galleries, Libraries, Archives and Museums. This is valuable for the education, research, tourism or creative industries domains, but the heterogeneity of the content objects and poor textual descriptions raise difficulties when navigating and exploring this large repository. This arises mainly because of multi-lingual object descriptions (i.e. using one of 27 European languages), different types of content (i.e. text, image, sound, 3D) and lack of standardized classifications among the 2000+ content providers. Additionally, some of the collections provide poor descriptions of their objects, especially in the case of image content (see objects in photography collections[2]). Within this context, content based retrieval services are providing complementary solutions to overcome the limits of text based search. By using an image similarity search service, the user has the possibility to select or provide a picture and find objects with similar visual content (available within the image index). For example one could search for buildings that are similar to St. Mary monastery in Goranxi, Albania (built in the 16th century). In this case churches or old buildings from different countries having their description in different languages are retrieved (see Fig. 1).

---

[1] See http://europeana.eu
[2] http://www.europeana.eu/portal/search.html?query=title:
Collectie+Heidemaatschappij

L. Bolikowski et al. (Eds.): TPDL 2013, CCIS 416, pp. 190–196, 2014.
DOI: 10.1007/978-3-319-08425-1_21, © Springer International Publishing Switzerland 2014

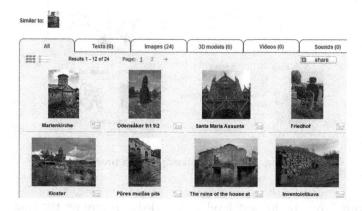

Fig. 1. Searching buildings similar to Goranxi monastery

Within this paper we present a service supporting exploration of the Europeana repository using a content-based image retrieval approach. The service supports well the search strategy of the public user, while on-going work concentrates on extending it to satisfy the expectations of creative design professionals. A new dataset with objects suited to inspire design activities was created and made available for evaluation and demonstration purposes.

2 Image Similarity Search

There are three main categories of stakeholders interested to use content-based search functionality when exploring the Europeana repository: public users exploring cultural heritage assets, professionals in different application domains (e.g. design, history education, art, etc.) and librarians. Typically, they have different levels of knowledge with respect to the Europeana content, different search intentions and different expectations when using an image retrieval service [4,8]:

Public users typically use image search functionality to explore the content of the repositories, eventually searching for objects similar to the ones they know. They expect to retrieve results that present a certain degree of similarity to the query object. This less constraining degree of similarity can be achieved by using global image descriptors like color and edge histograms. Real-time system response is very important in this context [3].

Professional users search for image content able to inspire their work. The employees of creative industries sector are representative stakeholders. They are either interested in the semantic of the image content (i.e. designers, journalists) or in particular geometries and proportions (i.e. architecture designers) [8]. Scalable solutions were proposed recently supporting this kind of search strategies in [2,6]. A trade off between good time performance in favor of search quality is accepted within this group of users.

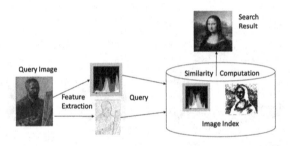

Fig. 2. Image similarity search process

Librarians have the highest level of knowledge regarding the content available in the GLAM collections, consequently they have the highest expectations from image retrieval services. They are interested to perform precise categorizations of the images (e.g. baroque buildings) [7], find multiple copies of the same object (e.g. compare various copies of Gioconda) or recently to find duplicate digitized content in large repositories [5]. The search service demonstrated within this paper was developed in the context of ASSETS[3] project to improve the user experience when exploring Europeana. The implementation is based on open source technologies. The MPEG-7 descriptors are computed by using the LIRE[4] feature extractors and the approximate similarity search algorithm [3] uses the Melampo[5] library. Figure 2 sketches the principle used within the similarity search process. The core of the retrieval process is represented by the computation of the similarities between the query and result images. This is performed by employing the cosine similarity computed on color and shape features extracted from the original images, namely the MPEG-7 Sclable Color, Color Layout and Edge Histogram descriptors.

While navigating through the digital library, users are allowed to use a query image available in Europeana, in Internet or on his/her computer for accessing similar objects in the repository. An usability evaluation was performed in Assets indicating clear interest of public and professional users for image search functionality [1]. The evaluation methodology used a task-oriented and supervised approach. The users were separated in two groups (i.e. public and professional) and interviewed to provide their feedback after interacting with the Assets portal. The conclusions on the image similarity indicated a strong interest and acceptance of the service, but also discovered that the semantics of the similarity is perceived differently by the two groups. In particular, the professional users were not satisfied by the quality of results when using their own query objects that are not available in Europeana. Currently, development efforts are invested

---

[3] http://ec.europa.eu/information_society/apps/projects/factsheet/index.cfm?
project_ref=250527

[4] http://www.semanticmetadata.net/

[5] https://github.com/melampo-vir/

to integrate this service in the Europeana search API. A demonstration of the baseline algorithm and the description of the dataset used are available online[6].

2.1   Content Reuse in Creative Design

Even if most cultural heritage objects have a certain potential to inspire creative design activities, there are several categories of content that present particular interest. Fashion and web designers present use attractive color combinations and particular textures in their daily work. These can be found in nature (e.g. coloring of birds or butterflies), in older ornamental objects or clothing (e.g. court dressing in 19th century). The film and advertisement sectors often use costumes and images of historical characters available in portraits of famous historical characters. Game designers are inspired by mythology and animals, while architects intensively study the symmetry and shapes of older buildings.

3   Experimental Evaluation

By using the Europeana search API we aggregated a dataset of 5125 cultural heritage objects, classified in 14 categories, that present high value for creative design professionals (see Table 1). We set up an experiment having the goal to verify the following two hypotheses:

Hypothesis 1. The current search algorithm presents a level of retrieval accuracy that is able to satisfy the expectations of the public users exploring the Europeana repository.

Hypothesis 2. The image retrieval service may effectively support creative designers in their work by satisfying their expectations in particular search contexts.

In order to verify the given hypotheses, we manually classified the images in the dataset by using two level of categorizations. In order to formalize the different retrieval expectations, we consider that the public users are satisfied by retrieving objects from the same top level category (i.e. Top-Category), while the professionals expect results from the more precise categorization (i.e. Sub-Category). We use the *Precision at N* $(P@N)$[7] metric to measure the accuracy of the retrieval algorithm and we vary N from 5 to 25.

Figure 3 presents the average $P@N$ both, at Top-Categoy and Sub-Category levels (i.e. a search result is considered a hit if it belongs to the same Top-Category or same Sub-Category as the query image). One can identify a tendency of decreasing the retrieval accuracy with the increase of results list. Additionally, the difference between the precision within the *Top-Category* and in the *Sub-Category* increases with N. On average, we can conclude that the search algorithm performs well on the given dataset.

---

[6] see http://image-similarity.ait.ac.at/imagedemo/
[7] http://www.springerreference.com/docs/html/chapterdbid/63595.html

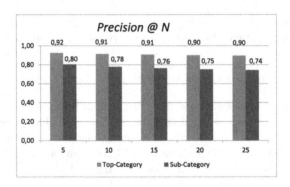

Fig. 3. Average *Precision at N*

Table 1 presents the accuracy of the search algorithm tailored by categories and computed within *Top5*, *Top15* and *Top25* results, respectively. In column headings *P5tc* stands for *P@5* using *Top-Category* matching, *P5sc* uses *Sub-Category* matching, and so on.

Table 1. Image retrieval accuracy using Top- and Sub-Category matching

Top-Category	Sub-Category	#	P5tc	P15tc	P25tc	P5sc	P15sc	P25sc
Birds	Ducks	121	0.77	0.65	0.60	*0.54*	*0.37*	*0.31*
Birds	Eagles and hawks	145	0.93	0.91	0.90	0.72	0.68	0.65
Birds	Parrots	105	0.92	0.86	0.85	0.62	0.39	0.34
Birds	Woodpeckers	210	0.88	0.83	0.82	0.51	0.46	0.43
Drawings	Landscapes	699	0.94	0.93	0.92	**0.96**	**0.95**	**0.94**
Insects	Butterflies and moths	371	*0.69*	*0.67*	*0.65*	0.69	0.67	0.65
Objects	Bottles	144	0.94	0.92	0.90	0.74	0.63	0.56
Objects	Decor miniatures	69	0.97	0.94	0.93	0.65	0.49	0.41
Objects	Electrical engineering	231	0.88	0.82	0.80	0.56	0.39	0.34
Objects	Musical trumpets	1092	0.98	0.97	0.97	**0.92**	**0.91**	**0.90**
Objects	Optical engineering	195	0.81	0.79	0.77	*0.38*	*0.29*	*0.25*
Objects	Porcelain	131	0.96	0.93	0.91	0.83	0.73	0.63
Paintings	Landscapes	425	0.88	0.85	0.83	0.69	0.64	0.61
Paintings	Portraits	1187	0.97	0.97	0.97	**0.90**	**0.90**	**0.89**

Within this experiment one can identify that the matching on Top-Categories provides good results. The lowest precision (i.e. marked with italic font) was identified for butterflies and mots category, which can be explained by the fact that the real nature background is more relevant for the algorithm that the small insect in foreground. By using the Sub-Category matching, the current algorithm (heavily color based) provides best results for drawings and paintings (i.e. marked with bold fonts). The musical trumpets collection contains very similar objects, therefore the high retrieval accuracy. The worst results were obtained for the optical engineering images. The low precision encountered on the ducks category, is obtained because of the similarities with the other categories of birds but also because the nature of images. Many of these contain more than three birds placed with different positions and orientations.

Discussion. With the current experimental evaluation we validate both research hypotheses. The current search algorithm has a retrieval accuracy able to satisfy the expectations of public users navigating through the Europeana repository, and it may satisfy the expectations of professional designers searching for certain types of content like: paintings, drawings, glass or porcelain objects. For other categories of objects, shape-based descriptors and algorithms may perform better. The retrieval accuracy obtained on the current dataset is higher that the regular one, because of the nature of aggregated images. The content was contributed by museums that used a standardized method to generate the physical artifacts and to digitize them. Consequently, the similarity between objects within the same category (or collection) is higher than in other datasets. In any case, the objects were selected by using the Europeana Search API within collections with high quality content that can be reused for supporting creative design work.

4   Conclusions

Within this paper we presented the image similarity search service developed for Europeana using available open source technologies. On-going research activities are related to the reuse of cultural heritage content for inspiring creative design. Several categories of cultural heritage objects were identified to present particular interest in this context. The current version of the search algorithm provides a good overall retrieval accuracy on the given dataset, but there are certain types of images for which search performance doesn't meet the expectations of professional users. Future work will focus on identifying algorithms that are able to maximize the retrieval performance on each of the selected classes of images. We plan to evaluate additional image descriptors (e.g. local and shape-based descriptors) and search algorithms able to better satisfy the expectations of design communities.

Acknowledgments. This work was partially funded by the ASSETS4Europeana and Europeana Creative projects, co-funded by the Commission of the European Communities under the ICT Policy Support Programme (ICT PSP). This publication reflects only the author's/authors' views and the European Union is not liable for any use that might be made of information contained therein.

References

1. C. M. I. E. M. N. P. C. Agnes Saulnier, Preben Hansen. Final report on evaluation of assets services. Project deliverable, ASSETS4Europeana, May 2012
2. Amato, G., Bolettieri, P., Falchi, F., Gennaro, C., Rabitti, F.: Combining local and global visual feature similarity using a text search engine. In: CBMI, pp. 49–54 (2011)
3. Amato, G., Savino, P.: Approximate similarity search in metric spaces using inverted files. In: Proceedings of the 3rd International Conference on Scalable Information Systems, InfoScale '08, pp. 28:1–28:10, ICST, Brussels, Belgium (2008). ICST (Institute for Computer Sciences, Social-Informatics and Telecommunications Engineering).
4. Colombino, T., Martin, D., Grasso, A., Marchesotti, L.: A reformulation of the semantic gap problem in content-based image retrieval scenarios. In: International Conference on the Design of Cooperative Systems, France, 19–21 May 2010
5. Huber-Mörk, R., Schindler, A.: Quality assurance for document image collections in digital preservation. In: Blanc-Talon, J., Philips, W., Popescu, D., Scheunders, P., Zemčík, P. (eds.) ACIVS 2012. LNCS, vol. 7517, pp. 108–119. Springer, Heidelberg (2012)
6. Spyrou, E., Kalantidis, Y., Mylonas, P.: Exploiting a region-based visual vocabulary towards efficient concept retrieval. In: Proceedings of Recognising and Tracking Events on the Web and in Real Life, in Conjunction with SETN 2010 (EVENTS 2010), May 2010
7. Tolias, G., Kalantidis, Y., Avrithis, Y.: Symcity: feature selection by symmetry for large scale image retrieval. In: Proceedings of ACM Multimedia (Full paper) (MM 2012), Nara, Japan, October 2012. ACM
8. Westerman, S.J., Kaur, S.: Supporting creative product/commercial design with computer-based image retrieval. In: Proceedings of the 14th European Conference on Cognitive Ergonomics: Invent! Explore!, ECCE '07, pp. 75–81. ACM, New York (2007)

Talking with Scholars: Developing a Research Environment for Oral History Collections

Max Kemman[1]([✉]), Stef Scagliola[1],
Franciska de Jong[1,2], and Roeland Ordelman[2,3]

[1] Erasmus University Rotterdam, Rotterdam, The Netherlands
{kemman,scagliola}@eshcc.eur.nl
[2] University of Twente, Enschede, The Netherlands
f.m.g.dejong@utwente.nl
[3] Netherlands Institute for Sound and Vision, Hilversum, The Netherlands
rordelman@beeldengeluid.nl

Abstract. Scholars are yet to make optimal use of Oral History collections. For the uptake of digital research tools in the daily working practice of researchers, practices and conventions commonly adhered to in the subfields of the humanities should be taken into account during development, in order to facilitate the uptake of digital research tools in the daily working practice of researchers. To this end, in the *Oral History Today* project a research tool for exploring Oral History collections is developed in close collaboration with scholarly researchers. This paper describes four stages of scholarly research and the first steps undertaken to incorporate requirements of these stages in a digital research environment.

Keywords: Oral History · Scholarly research · User-centered design · Exploration · Result presentation · Data curation · Word cloud · Visual facets

1 Introduction

The digital turn has profoundly influenced historical culture and has led to a rise in the creation of audio-visual archives with personal narratives, commonly identified as Oral History. For the general public, searching these archives by making use of standard search tools may be sufficient. Yet for scholars, the full value of this type of data cannot be exploited optimally as available tools do not enable scholars to engage with the content for the purposes of research.

When working with audio-visual content, the availability of annotations is key to the process of digging up interesting fragments. In the past years, a lot of effort has been put in tools for creating manual annotations and generating annotations (semi-)automatically. But to accelerate scholarly research, tools are required that can take available annotation layers as input and provide means for visualization,

L. Bolikowski et al. (Eds.): TPDL 2013, CCIS 416, pp. 197–201, 2014.
DOI: 10.1007/978-3-319-08425-1_22, © Springer International Publishing Switzerland 2014

compression and aggregation of the data. Thus allowing the researcher to explore and process the data, both at fragment-, item- and collection-level.

However, to develop such dedicated data exploration tools, technology specialists and researchers in the humanities have to engage in a process of mutual understanding and joint development. Taking carefully into account the specific set of practices and conventions commonly adhered to within the subfields in the humanities is a minimum requirement for the uptake of the technology in the daily working practice of scholars. In this paper we present a research tool developed in close collaboration with scholars that enables searching and exploration of aggregated, heterogeneous Oral History content.

2   Four Stages of Scholarly Research

The user interface development is based upon four stages of scholarly research that were defined on the basis of an investigation of use scenarios reported in [1].

Exploration and selection. In the first stage, the focus is on the exploration and selection of one or more content sets within an archive that may be suitable for addressing a certain scholarly issue. The first steps in content exploration by a researcher often come down to searching for material. Research starts with the search for new or additional data. This stage can get the form of plain browsing, but it can also be strongly purpose-driven, (e.g., checking details, searching for complementary sources), item-oriented (e.g., finding the first interview with a specific person), or directed towards patterns in a collection, in which case an entire data set is the focus of attention.

Exploration and investigation. Once the relevant materials have been identified, the focus in the next stage is mostly on the further exploration of the collected materials, the ordering, comparison (by individual researchers or in joint efforts) and analysis, and the documentation of the interpretation. This exploration stage may generate new ideas and perspectives, requiring new searches and inquiries.

Result presentation. After the analysis has been completed, the third stage is the presentation of research results. In the digital realm it has become feasible to link annotations that capture the results of an analytical step to the data on which they are based. Data and annotations can be shared with peers, both during collaboration as well as in publications. Instead of a printed book, one can produce a digital publication with links to audio-visual content.

Data curation. The fourth and final stage of the process is the long-term preservation of the data and the results of the investigation that has been carried out. Especially audio-visual materials that have been processed with digital tools are not the kind of research result that can be stored in a cupboard; they should be deposited in a trusted digital repository [2]. Ideally the depositing of material should be in line with emerging standards for Open Data, as this would allow the data and annotations to be reused by scholars with similar interests. For example, links can then be created to other data sets to place the data in a broader context [3]. Although the actual curation process itself is out-of-scope in this specific research project, workspaces can provide a form of data curation through the individual collecting of interviews, cutting interesting fragments with a virtual cutter and creating additional manual annotations that can be fed into the existing metadata and thereby enrich the collection even further.

3   Oral History Today Research Environment

Visual search. The *Oral History Today* research interface is based upon the four stages described above. As the search process for the *exploration and selection* and *exploration and investigation* stages is reminiscent of Shneiderman's *Visual Information-Seeking Mantra* of *overview first, zoom and filter, then details-on-demand* [5], we developed a visual search interface to provide overview and zooming facilities, as well as support exploration strategies.

Two visualizations were developed to complement the search interface and allow visual searching: *word clouds* and *visual facets*. Word clouds provide a textual insight in the material available, with the additional benefit that a better insight is gained in what terminology is used in the collections explored; an issue identified for keyword search interfaces [4]. Visual facets (Fig. 1) provide a visual overview of the facets. Facets are shown as graphical bars, where the length of each value represents the number of related search results, as demonstrated previously in Relation Browser++ [6]. A difference with RB++ is that the facet values are stacked into a single bar representing the facet. On mouse-hovering a tooltip is shown with a textual description and the number of corresponding items. When the user selects a facet value, the facet bar is moved to the top to allow the user to keep a history of selected facets. Visual facets not only give a more visual overview of the search results, but also allow for faster interactions with the facets.

Evaluation. To allow user feedback to be incorporated in the development process, evaluation is undertaken in multiple cycles. To elicit a broad range of responses with regard to usability as well as applicability to research practices, the first cycle was performed with semi-structured interviews. Five scholars were asked to try research subjects of their own interest. The results of this first evaluation are very positive. Concerning the visualisations described above, it was generally agreed that word clouds enable the searcher to acquire an idea of what material is available. However, they did not think word clouds would provide them with keywords to improve their queries. Visual facets were considered interesting and felt as a very fast way to both acquire an overview of the search results as well as refine search results.

Fig. 1. Visual Facets

Further adjustments. Scholars noted that being able to quickly assess the importance of search results is vital during the *exploration and selection* stage. To enable fast assessments, we added the ability to expand summary-descriptions in the search results, no longer requiring scholars to open each individual search result. After this assessment, scholars need to be able to save important items. Therefore, we developed workspaces, which allow researchers to save interviews in project-specific sets for later analysis, as well as for referencing in publications as needed in the *result presentation* stage described above.

4   Conclusion

The results of the first evaluation are promising. The positive responses of the scholars indicated that the chosen approach for exploring Oral History data is in the right direction. In the near future, this evaluation will receive a larger follow-up in the final evaluation of the research interface. After this final evaluation, the tool will be released to the Oral History research community, allowing us to investigate how it will eventually be used in daily research practices.

Acknowledgements. The work reported in this paper was funded by the EU Project AXES - *Access to Audiovisual Archives* (FP7-269980) and the Dutch national program CLARIAH (http://www.clariah.nl/). We thank Dispectu (www.dispectu.com) and Spinque (www.spinque.nl) for their collaboration in the research project *Oral History Today*.

References

1. de Jong, F., Ordelman, R., Scagliola, S.: Audio-visual collections and the user needs of scholars in the humanities: a case for co-development. In: Proceedings of the 2nd Conference on Supporting Digital Humanities (SDH 2011), Copenhagen, Denmark. Centre for Language Technology, Copenhagen, p. 7 (2011)
2. Jantz, R., Giarlo, M.J.: Digital preservation: architecture and technology for trusted digital repositories. Microform Imaging Rev. **34**(3), 135–147 (2005)
3. Kemman, M., Kleppe, M.: PoliMedia - improving analyses of radio, TV & newspaper coverage of political debates. In: Research and Advanced Technology for Digital Libraries, pp. 401–404. Springer, Heidelberg (2013)
4. Mann, T.: Will google's keyword searching eliminate the need for LC cataloging and classification? J. Libr. Metadata **8**(2), 159–168 (2008)
5. Shneiderman, B.: The eyes have it: a task by data type taxonomy for information visualizations. In: Proceedings 1996 IEEE Symposium on Visual Languages, pp. 336–343. IEEE Computer Society Press (1996)
6. Zhang, J., Marchionini, G.: Evaluation and evolution of a browse and search interface: relation browser. In: Proceedings of the 2005 National Conference on Digital Government Research, pp. 179–188 (2005)

Moving Beyond Technology: iSchools and Education in Data Curation: Is Data Curator a New Role?

Training in Data Curation as Service in a Federated Data Infrastructure - The *FrontOffice–BackOffice Model*

Ingrid Dillo, Rene van Horik, and Andrea Scharnhorst[✉]

Data Archiving and Networked Services, Anna van Saksenlaan 10,
2593 HT The Hague, The Netherlands
{ingrid.dillo,rene.van.horik,andrea.scharnhorst}@dans.knaw.nl
http://www.dans.knaw.nl

Abstract. The increasing volume and importance of research data leads to the emergence of research data infrastructures in which data management plays an important role. As a consequence, practices at digital archives and libraries change. In this paper, we focus on a possible alliance between archives and libraries around training activities in data curation. We introduce a so-called *FrontOffice–BackOffice model* and discuss experiences of its implementation in the Netherlands. In this model, an efficient division of tasks relies on a distributed infrastructure in which research institutions (i.e., universities) use centralized storage and data curation services provided by national research data archives. The training activities are aimed at information professionals working at those research institutions, for instance as digital librarians. We describe our experiences with the course *DataIntelligence4Librarians*. Eventually, we reflect about the international dimension of education and training around data curation and stewardship.

Keywords: Data curation · Data management · Training · Data sharing · Data archive · Digital libraries · Education · Science policy · Documentation

1 Introduction

A research archive can be depicted as a safe haven for research data, carefully selected, documented and stored for future consultation. Accordingly, the core tasks of a data archivist could be imagined to be confined to proper documentation, and the care for material preservation. In short: "Our service starts where others drop the data"[1]. The current practices of archivists seem to deviate from such an archetype to a large extent. This *turn of tables* can best be understood by a recall to the history of archival sciences. In general, for archives of research data the same principles hold as for any other archive. In 1898, in the *handbook*,

---

[1] Personal communication Henk Koning, former Technical Archivist at DANS.

L. Bolikowski et al. (Eds.): TPDL 2013, CCIS 416, pp. 205–215, 2014.
DOI: 10.1007/978-3-319-08425-1_23, © Springer International Publishing Switzerland 2014

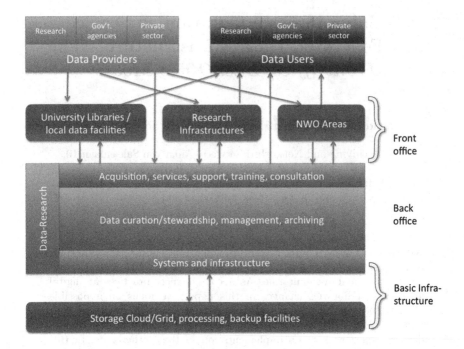

Fig. 1. The federated data infrastructure - a collaborative framework. Scheme designed by Peter Doorn based on the *Collaborative Data Infrastructure* as envisioned in [6, p. 31]

one of the foundational texts in archival sciences [1], Muller, Feith, and Fruin describe the archive as an organic entirety whose function cannot be determined *a priori*. On the contrary, its function needs to be defined and redefined depending on the development of the institution (i.e., a board or government) whose selected traces it is obliged to archive. In other words, Muller et al. describe a *co-evolution* of the institution and its archive. This view applied to a research data archive, the corresponding institution is none other than the science system. From out this viewpoint, it is not surprising that the profound changes in scientific practice [2] and scholarly communication [3] influence the expectations placed on a data archive or, more specifically, a sustainable digital archive (Trusted Digital Repository). The changing modes of scholarly communication and practice alter the form and content of what is seen worth to be preserved. Reference [5] Changing research practices require new negotiations on the division of labor. Who is responsible for setting up digital research infrastructures including virtual research environments - the information service providers such as Trusted Digital Repositories (TDRs) or the research institutions? Who takes care of the preparation of (meta)–data and formats prior to archiving? Who should preserve software tools - the labs which developed them or the archive together with 'data' for which they have been developed?

The high volatility of the environment in which archives are currently operating influences their function as reliable, stable reference point for important information. Open Access, Data Management Plan, Data Stewardship, Data Curation, Trusted Digital Repositories, BigData and SmartData are some of the floating around buzzwords of the last decade. They stand for the struggle to identify and communicate most urgent trends and to coordinate actions across the different stakeholders in the field of data curation. Important to note here is the reference model for Open Archival Information Systems (in short OAIS model, ISO 14721:2012), a model foundational for the discussion of structure and function of any archive. Its key elements are Ingest, Archival Storage, Data Management, Administration, Preservation Planning and Access. Allison emphasizes that the OAIS model is not an architectural model for implementation, but instead offers a shared terminology [4]. Inside of our own organization, Data Archiving and Networked Services (DANS), the OAIS model is often used in discussions about *internal* workflows and their improvement and further development. In this paper, we focus on institutional networks *around* an archive as DANS. Hereby we rely on schemata as depicted in Fig. 1 which sketch the complexity of the *research data landscape*, its stakeholders and infrastructure [6]. Coming back to it later, in a first step we can use this scheme in an exercise to *locate* a TDR such as DANS. Starting at the bottom of Fig. 1 the basic (technical) infrastructure entails storage. In the Netherlands this level of Basic Infrastructure is provided by SURFsara, the Dutch network of computing facilities whose services DANS is using itself. The following three levels could be seen as the heart of activities of an archive of *digital* research data. They form a kind of back-office. The three boxes at the next level, labeled as front office, contain the funding agencies, as NWO[2] in the Netherlands, university libraries, and research infrastructures such as CLARIN[3], or DARIAH[4], which are in themselves complex organizations. They could be seen as 'clients' of an archive. But actually, DANS is also part of them. The same holds true for the top level of data providers and users. DANS as part of research infrastructures harvests information from other data providers. With its own research and development activities it is even part of the data production cycle. In short, DANS plays different roles in different contexts and, therefore, can be located at many places in this scheme. Correspondingly, at DANS a variety of different activities take place. In the next section, we discuss how, together with this increase in complexity, the need emerges to build alliances and to coordinate actions among different institutional players in the *data landscape*. At the core of the paper we propose a specific model to articulate possibilities of collaboration, coordination, and division of labour. We report about steps towards its concrete implementation at the Dutch national level. At the end of the paper we discuss links to international developments.

---

[2] www.nwo.nl

[3] www.clarin.eu

[4] www.dariah.eu

2   The Archivist as a Consultant

DANS is one of the national research data archives in the Netherlands. With roots in the social sciences and humanities back to the 1960s, in its current form, it was founded in 2005 as an institute of NWO - the Netherlands Organization for Scientific Research and the KNAW - the Royal Netherlands Academy of Arts and Sciences. DANS is primarily an information service institute and, despite of a small in-house research group, not a research institute. This makes DANS much more comparable to a classical, stand-alone archive.

The mission of DANS it to promote sustained access to digital research data. For this purpose, DANS encourages researchers to archive and reuse data in a sustained manner, e.g. through the online (self)archiving system EASY[5]. DANS also provides access, via NARCIS.nl[6], to thousands of scientific datasets, e-publications and other research information in the Netherlands. EASY and NARCIS are two services which form the core of DANS. In difference to many other knowledge-domain specific archives, DANS operates cross-disciplinary with a focus on social sciences and humanities. It is also an exclusively digital archive and it is placed - as an institution - outside the Dutch university system. All this together positions DANS as a gateway to the diverse Dutch research data landscape and as a hub in it. Activities and practices at DANS can be ordered along three dimensions:

- *Archive*: selection, preservation, and description of data collections
- *Research and Development*: maintenance and development of the ICT infrastructure for seamless access and exploitation and for long-term preservation
- *Science Policy*: influence on research data policies and data curation strategies on the national and international levels

The first dimension corresponds to a large extent to the image of a traditional research archive. But due to ongoing ICT innovations both in the area of research as well as of information services, a digital archive cannot operate without means to adopt its technological backbone to those innovations. The process of adopting and inventing services entails to a large extent what Andrew Prescott called "tinkering", when he compared practices at digital libraries with the craftsmanship needed in labs and workshops in the high-time of industrialization [7]. ICT is usually depicted as an efficiency engine. What is often forgotten is the existence of a transition period during which old and new forms of practices coexist. On the work floor, this means that traditional services of acquisition, community support, and documentation are pursued in parallel to designing new workflows, testing and implementing them. So, before ICT leads to more efficiency, temporarily the actual workload often increases. Project-based work and external funding for projects can only partly buffer this extension of activities at an archive. On top of archiving and related R&D, the changing environment in which the archive operates requires continuous attention. Hence, a third

---

[5] www.easy.dans.knaw.nl

[6] www.narcis.nl

dimension - science policy - appears. Participation in national and international networks of research infrastructures require substantive investment of time.

The point we make is that the current portfolio of activities at information service institutions is much more diverse than in the past. For DANS this changing role of *an archive* is reflected in its name as *Data Archiving and Networked Services*. Among the increased portfolio of activities, *consultancy* plays a special role [8]. It appears in many forms: in the foundation of a Data Seal of Approval for TDRs[7], in the advisory role in research projects, in contributions to data policy documents, and in training activities. Consultancy contributes to knowledge diffusion around data curation practices and the coordination of data management at a national (partly also international) level. It also supports the emergence of a distributed network structure which we describe in the next section.

3   Strategic Alliance Between Archives and Libraries - the *FrontOffice – BackOffice Model*

Profound and timely data management together with a sustainable storage of data – during and after the research – are indispensable preconditions for sharing data. It is of great importance that universities and other research institutions develop a clear data policy themselves. An adequate infrastructure is needed to coordinate and implement those policies. In the Netherlands, with its rich institutional landscape of information service providers and research institutions, we encounter a discussion around a federated data infrastructure. It is quite clear that no single organization will be able to deliver individually tailored support for all possible data depositors. It also clear that it is not possible for a single organization to provide services across all levels, from storage up to interactions with individual researchers. In order to create a sustainable national infrastructure for data management and curation, it is important to support a network of *local* data stewards close to the actual scientific practice combined with centralized services. Figure 1 designs such a federated data infrastructure. It introduces at the same time a *FrontOffice–BackOffice model* (FO–BO model) as part of it.

3.1   Description of the Model

The FO–BO model clarifies the interaction between researcher and information service provider concerning research data management. It also clarifies the relation among different information service providers. Front offices should be placed at institutions where research takes place in order to support the research community at those institutions. An example could be a front office as part of a university library. The front office is responsible for raising awareness for data sharing and re-use, for taking care of the local data management, and for organizing training for researchers. Virtual Research Environments (VRE's) could be

---

[7] www.datasealofapproval.org

also part of the service at a front office. In particular, temporary data archiving on platforms as Sharepoint or Dataverse could be part of the VRE's. Once a research project is finished the front office - in consultation with the back office - takes care of the transfer of data to a TDR. So, data acquisition is an inherent part of the front office tasks.

The core tasks of the back office consist in the storage and documentation of research data which arrive via the front offices. The back office provides access to data, and possibly enriches and links data. The back office acquires expert knowledge around data management, and the long-term, sustainable and persistent archiving of research data. Part of the back office portfolio is to disseminate this expertise by means of training of information professionals, such as data librarians/managers/stewards, working at front offices. The back office acts as an expertise centrum for the front office and as an innovation centrum concerning new trends in data curation. Figure 2 summarizes the benefits of the model for researchers, front offices and back office organizations. By means of the FO–BO model we also try to reduce the complexity of interactions in the data infrastructure. With this model the role of DANS (and of comparable institutions) is restricted to the back office function. In the next subsection we report about one key element of the model: training for front office personal.

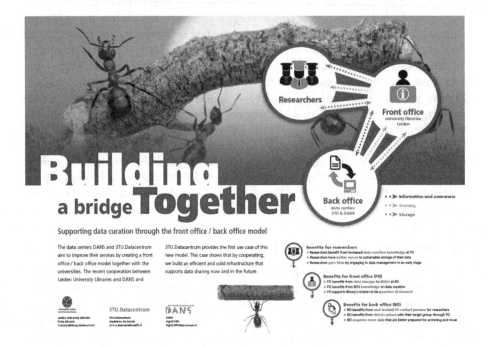

Fig. 2. Poster about the FrontOffice–BackOffice model. Designed by Carolien van Zuilekom, Fieke Schoots, Madeleine de Smaele and Ingrid Dillo

Fig. 3. Snapshot of the website http://dataintelligence.3tu.nl/en/home/ - host of the course "DataIntelligence4Librarians"

3.2 Implementation - the *DataIntelligence4Librarians*

In the FO–BO model training for information professionals is part of the back office portfolio. The *DataIntelligence4Librarians* course is an example for such a training. Organized by the 3TU.Datacenter[8] and DANS, it is based on an earlier course of the 3TU.Datacenter developed for data-librarians. The currently envisioned audience reaches from staff at libraries to everybody interested in the topic independently of the disciplinary background.

Description of the Course. The course design fits into the professional education format. It combines distance learning with four face2face (f2f) sessions and maintains next to an eLearning environment also a public website (see Fig. 3, in Dutch) with background material. Google Plus was used as the platform for the eLearning part. Participants are supposed to study theoretical parts as homework. Between the f2f sessions more homework is assigned. The website contains

---

[8] The 3TU.Datacenter – a network organization of the university libraries of Delft University of Technology, Eindhoven University of Technology, and the University of Twente – offers facilities for the preservation and the sustained availability of technical research data, similar to the services at DANS (see http://data.3tu.nl/repository/).

a description for the first practical task. More of them are distributed in the eLearning environment. Both coach and participants give feedback at f2f sessions as well as on-line. Didactically, feedback and knowledge sharing is used as an important element next to knowledge transfer.

During the first f2f session, an introduction into the course and the eLearning environment is given. An introduction into the module *Data Management* follows and homework is assigned labeled *State-of-Art Map*. This task starts with reading a report, and continues with a number of search tasks using the phrase *research data management* across bibliographic databases (Scopus, Web of Science), but also in Twitter and Google. Participants are advised to subscribe to specific mailing lists to get an impression of the actual discussion around the topic. At the second f2f session participants presents their resulting map. The module *Technical Skills* is introduced and tools (3TU.Databrowser, DANS/EASY) are demonstrated. The third f2f meeting starts with the same scheme of sharing homework and getting feedback. Content-wise the module for this session is *Acquisition and Consultation Skills*. Specific attention is given to the question how to overcome barriers for data sharing. The instrument of a *Data Interview* with possible data depositors is introduced. During the fourth and last session the acquisition assignment is discussed and the course is evaluated. At the end of the course a certificate is issued under the condition that all sessions have been attended and the tasks have been fulfilled. During the modules, different experts from the organizing institutions give guest lectures. Examples of topics are legal aspects, issues of data selection, audit and certification of TDRs, and the FO–BO model itself.

Experiences with the Course. One goal of the course is to sharpen the insight into the role of research data in scientific practices. Eventually, the participant should be able to advise and inform researchers how data curation can enhance data use and re-use. In summary, the goals are rather diverse and broad compared with the limited time of the course.

So far, the course has been run three times: February 2012 to June 2012 (16 participants, organized by 3TU.Datacentre), September 2012 to December 2012 (16 participants), and February 2013 to May 2013 (13 participants). The last two events have been organized in collaboration between the 3TU.Datacentre and DANS. Most of the participants were information professionals, either working at a library or archive, or for one of the network organizations, such as SURF. In the evaluation, the participants named a couple of critical points not unusual for distance learning. Among them are problems with the eLearning environment, or the spreading out of the course over a rather long period. Another critical remark concerns the demonstrations. Obviously the participants did not seek hands-on experiences with a tool, platform, or interface. They seemed to be more interested in guidance and factual information in the area of data curation. This springs also out from the positive reactions. Information about actual developments from experts involved in the practice of data curation have been highly appreciated. Further, a need to get to know each other and to learn from each others practices is articulated. This holds true even for a small country as the Netherlands. One of the suggestions of the participants was to form a *special interest group*.

4   Conclusions

In this paper we discussed changing portfolios of responsibilities for archives and libraries. Data infrastructures emerge in response to data science, open access, and data sharing policies. In the making of a data infrastructure, the division of tasks between different information service providers needs to be re-negotiated. We present a federal data infrastructure with a layered architecture including a *FrontOffice–BackOffice model*. This model allows to articulate different roles in the interaction with research communities, the acquisition of expert knowledge, and the provision of data management services. The model is in line with the *Data pyramid* [6] which classifies data according to permanence and function. Data management is tailored towards certain classes of data and specialization in data curation is allocated to different organizations. Front offices, naturally to be placed at academic libraries, take care of data management for *transient and cyclic data* produced by individuals and research communities. Trusted Digital Repositories as DANS act as back office and take care for *patrimonial data*. They also become expertise center and knowledge transfer hubs for data curation.

Training plays a key role in the FO–BO model. It is a way to disseminate the idea of the model. At the same time, it is an instantiation of the model. The experiences in the Netherlands are encouraging. Several Dutch universities signaled interest in this approach and the challenge is now to implement more front offices there. At the same time, a coordination among possible back office organizations is needed. DANS recently signed an coalition agreement with the 3TU.Datacenter to cooperate more closely and to foster the FO–BO model. This coalition, *Research Data Netherlands*, is open to any other Dutch TDR with at least a Data Seal of Approval. To shape the role of back offices as centers of expertise and innovation is another way to make the model attractive and reliable. To give an example, there is a growing need for auto-ingest of larger data collections. Another shared issue is the question of a sustainable cost model for data archiving. Exploration of these issues needs to be done locally and shared in collaboration.

Returning to the issue of training, as we argue in this paper, in the short run, there is an urgent need for education among information professionals. In the mid term, these efforts could be connected to comparable modules in curricula for future information professionals, e.g. at iSchools. The FO–BO models contains training also as a part of front office activities. This is in line with efforts in the framework of digital librarianship to develop modules for information literacy and data stewardship at many universities. The APARSEN project that aims at establishing a virtual centre of excellence on digital preservation carried out a survey concerning the European training landscape in this area [9]. The DataIntelligence4Librarians course fits very well to outcomes of this survey. A coordination between those different training activities will support further professionalization. Shared textbooks, syllabi, best practices guidelines could also help to keep locally provided on-line material up to date.

Our experiences show that a natural alliance between (digital) archives and libraries exist which is worth to be explored in daily practice. Current science policies emphasizes the role of data and their re-use. The envisioned coupling of funding with data-sharing and archiving, the Linked Open Data movement, and the rise of data science will put more pressure on information service institutions, but at the same time also offers new possibilities. To form alliances and to coordinate actions seems to be the only possible answer. Here, libraries and archives are natural partners because as Ross formulated "when we reflect on the core of digital libraries we easily observe that they may be libraries by name, but they are archives by nature" [10].

Acknowledgements. The following colleagues have been involved in the DataIntelligence4Librarians course. Nicole Potters, Marina Noordegraaf, Madeleine de Smaele, Ellen Verbakel (from the 3TU.Datacenter) and Rene van Horik, Caroline van Zuilekom, Marion Wittenberg, Ingrid Dillo (from DANS).

References

1. Muller, S., Feith, J.A., Fruin, R.: Handleiding voor het Ordenen en Beschrijven van Archiven. Erven B. Van Der Kamp. Groningen (1920). 2ed. Reprinted in: Horsman, P.J., Ketelaar, F.C.J., Thomassen, T.H.P.M.: Tekst en Context van de Handleiding voor het Ordenen en Beschrijven van Archiven van 1898. Verloren, Hilversum (1998)
2. Wouters, P., Beaulieu, A., Scharnhorst, A., Wyatt, S.: Virtual Knowledge: Experimenting in the Humanities and the Social Sciences. MIT, Cambridge (2012)
3. Borgman, C.: Scholarship in the Digital Age: Information, Infrastructure, and the Internet. MIT, Cambridge (2007)
4. Allison, J.: OAIS as a reference model for repositories. An evaluation. Report UKOLN University of Bath (2007). http://eprints.whiterose.ac.uk/id/eprint/3464
5. Doorn, P., Tjalsma, H.: Introduction: archiving research data. Arch. Sci. **7**(1), 1–20 (2007). doi:10.1007/s10502-007-9054-6
6. Anonymous: Riding the wave. How Europe can gain from the riding tide of scientific data. Final report of the High Level Expert Group on Scientific Data. A submission of the European Commission, October 2010. http://cordis.europa.eu/fp7/ict/e-infrastructure/docs/hlg-sdi-report
7. Prescott, A.: Made In Sheffield: Industrial Perspectives on the Digital Humanities. Keynote at the Digital Humanities Congress at the University of Sheffield, 6 September 2012. (The text of this keynote lecture can be found at Andrew Prescott's blog http://digitalriffs.blogspot.co.uk/2012/09/made-in-sheffield-industrial.html)
8. Anonymous. Duurzame toegang tot digitale onderzoeksgegevens. Strategienota DANS (in Dutch). DANS, The Hague (2010). http://www.dans.knaw.nl/sites/default/files/file/Uitgaven/Strategie/DANSSTRATEGIENOTAcompleet_DEF.pdf. A summary in English with the title: Sustained access to digital research data can be found at http://www.dans.knaw.nl/sites/default/files/file/jaarverslagenenstrategienota/Samenvattingstrategienota_UK_DEF.pdf

9. Anonymous. APARSEN report: D43.1 Survey for the assessment of training material. Assessment of digital curation requirements. http://www.alliancepermanentaccess.org/wp-content/uploads/downloads/2012/12/APARSEN-REP-D43_1-01-4_1.pdf
10. Ross, S.: Digital preservation, archival science and methodological foundations for digital libraries. New Rev. Inf. Netw. **17**(1), 43–68 (2012). doi:10.1080/13614576.2012.679446

Putting Museums in the Data Curation Picture

Joyce Ray[1,2(✉)]

[1] John Hopkins University, Baltimore, USA
joyceray202@gmail.com
[2] Humboldt University, Arcata, USA

Abstract. For the past several decades, museums worldwide have recognized the need to digitize their collection records and images. The global reach of the web has increased the urgency of this work in order to make museum collections and information accessible to online users. Museums in Europe and North America are now routinely digitizing all collection objects as they are acquired and loaned, not only for access purposes but also as documentation in the event of loss, damage, or theft of the physical originals. Increasingly, museums are also acquiring born-digital content such as digital media art, historical data in digital formats, and scientific research data. The creation and acquisition of digital assets is expanding at a rapid pace, and museums now have a critical need for professionals in the field who know how to manage and preserve digital assets and who will participate in the development of standards and policies for the creation, management, preservation, exchange, and use of digital data.

The establishment of the Digital Curation Centre in the UK in 2004 and the publication of government reports in the US and Europe calling for the preservation of scientific data (National Science Board 2004; Blue Ribbon Task Force 2008, 2010; High Level Expert Group 2010) has spurred the growth of digital curation. In the US, these developments fortuitously coincided with the creation of a new federal funding program to increase the number of graduates from library and information science (LIS) master's and doctoral programs, and which has supported the development and integration of digital curation into LIS education (Manjarraz et al. 2010).

1 US Federal Funding

The Institute of Museum and Library Services (IMLS) created the 21st Century Librarians (later renamed the Laura Bush 21st Century Librarians) program in 2003 with an initial budget of $10 million. Funding increased substantially over the next several years, providing support for scholarships at the master's and doctoral levels, development of new programs and curricula in the approximately 50 LIS graduate schools in the US, and an early careers program—modeled on a similar National Science Foundation program—to provide research money for untenured, tenure-track LIS faculty at a critical stage in their careers. In 2006, IMLS grant guidelines called for proposals in digital curation in the 21st Century Librarians program—resulting in awards to the University of Arizona, the University of Illinois Urbana Champaign, and the University of North Carolina at Chapel Hill—as well as proposals for research and demonstration projects in digital curation in the National Leadership Grant program,

Ł. Bolikowski et al. (Eds.): TPDL 2013, CCIS 416, pp. 216–225, 2014.
DOI: 10.1007/978-3-319-08425-1_24, © Springer International Publishing Switzerland 2014

which resulted in an award to the Sheridan Libraries at Johns Hopkins University for seminal collaborative work with the National Virtual Observatory. Subsequent grants to numerous LIS graduate programs and to research libraries have contributed to the development of library professionals in digital curation. This sustained funding stream (which, however, has been reduced recently due to federal spending cuts) has helped to reshape the LIS curriculum. It has also helped to build capacity in US libraries for new data services, including data repositories, management planning assistance, and data citation and data management services.

2 Identifying the Gaps in Digital Curation Education

Despite the substantial investment of federal funds, more work is needed to increase the size and scope of the professional data curation community. Because the bulk of IMLS funds have been designated by Congress for libraries and LIS education, funding for museum professional education has remained distressingly limited. Recent studies have drawn attention to the need to expand educational programs in digital curation beyond graduate schools of library and information science, given the wide range of disciplines in need of data curation services.

A 2012 study by Spencer D.C. Keralis found that data curation education efforts "are most often embedded in standard LIS courses (for example, as components or modules of metadata and database architecture courses), and efforts to teach data curation as a discrete set of intelligible practices are both recent and few" (Keralis 2012, p. 38). Keralis found only five LIS schools that offered graduate certificates explicitly in data curation, and, except for the DigIn post-baccalaureate program at the University of Arizona School of Information Resources and Library Science, these were open only to LIS students and library professionals.

Keralis concluded that programs "that are isolated within the standard LIS curriculum or within certificate programs that are exclusive to LIS students are not designed to meet the needs of researchers or professionals who may benefit from these skills" (p. 38). However, he also noted several new and developing data curation certificate programs that cast a wider net. These include:

- the University of North Texas College of Information's Graduate Academic Certificate in Digital Curation, which is open to non-LIS students and to professionals from the sciences and social sciences, computer science, and the humanities, in addition to LIS master's and doctoral students;
- a training program in data information literacy for graduate students in the sciences developed through a partnership between the Purdue University Libraries and the libraries of Cornell University, the University of Minnesota, and the University of Oregon;
- an interdisciplinary Digital Curation Graduate Certificate in the New Media Studies program at the University of Maine; and,
- a program at Pratt Institute's School of Information and Library Science to prepare students as digital managers of cultural heritage collections across libraries, museums, and archives.

Museum studies programs are also beginning to address the specific needs of museums in identifying, preserving, and providing access to digital artifacts, born-digital art, and other assets such as research data.

A workshop supported by IMLS in 2008 brought together 20 leading practitioners engaged with information technology across the cultural heritage spectrum and educators for the library, museum, and archives professions (IMLS 2008). The goals were to explore the ability of educational institutions to support the information needs of cultural heritage organizations and to encourage a closer relationship between education, continuing professional development, and practice in libraries, museums, and archives. Note that the term "cultural heritage" is used here in its broadest sense for convenience, although many collections and activities may not fit well under it.

The workshop tasked participants to (IMLS 2008, p. 1):

- identify the educational goals that LIS, museum studies, and archival studies programs have in common;
- identify the information needs and challenges facing cultural heritage organizations in the 21st century;
- identify other areas of convergence for educators and professionals working to meet the needs of the nation's cultural heritage organizations and the publics they serve; and,
- develop concrete recommendations for innovative approaches designed to improve our ability to meet these needs and challenges.

Perhaps as an indication of where the digital curation field was in 2008, the only concrete recommendations that came out of the workshop were to "keep the conversation going" by providing additional cross-domain opportunities for educators as well as practitioners, and to "document and disseminate the emerging needs of cultural heritage organizations and new methods of meeting them in terms of the number and competencies of students pursuing careers as 21st century cultural heritage information professionals" (IMLS 2008, p. 15). Although these were very preliminary steps, participants were agreeably surprised to find that they had much in common. They identified education as a key avenue for breaking down perceived barriers between museums, libraries, and archives. Many observed that online users are largely oblivious to the domain distinctions made by cultural heritage professionals, and that students tend to be interested in other domains and to oppose "siloization". After much discussion, the group identified four principles that could guide the critical aspects of information access and provision in cultural heritage organizations (IMLS 2008, pp. 12–13).

1. *On the Internet, nobody knows you're a library, archive, or museum.* People want information, and access to information should be as transparent as possible. People who desire access to cultural heritage resources should not be required first to understand and acknowledge the differences that traditionally have divided and differentiated information providing organizations.
2. *Engage your audiences, or lose them.* Providing access to information is only a first step; 21st century cultural heritage organizations must transition from connecting people and information to engaging communities around information

resources. Cultural heritage institutions should take advantage of new information technologies to open up information access for new users and new uses and encourage the growth of new knowledge communities around cultural heritage. Cultural heritage information professionals should play a key role in facilitating the transition within these institutions.

3. *Information wants to be free.* The best way to breathe new life into information is to give it away, opening it up for new uses and encouraging the spark of human creativity. Done correctly, the ultimate outcome is not the erosion of authority but the broadening of it, through the merging of traditional authority with participatory democracy. Cultural heritage information professionals should help their institutions understand and embrace the new philosophies that are transforming traditional notions of control and authority, recognizing that one can give away information while still providing added value and preserving data quality.

4. *Embrace our commonalities, and our diversities.* Finding and promoting areas of convergence between libraries, archives, and museums does not require library and information science, museum studies, and archival studies educators and professionals to discard areas they do not hold in common. Cultural heritage information professionals come from varied educational backgrounds and follow diverse career paths, and it is important that they retain those unique differences over time. In this way, new information technologies can help 21st century cultural heritage organizations work more closely together, while enhancing the unique nature of libraries, archives, and museums.

Five years later, it is interesting to note that each of these four principles embodies a distinct perspective that can inform data curation education in the cultural heritage sector today: (1) the perspective of the online user; (2) the perspective of user engagement (a core value of museums); (3) advocacy for open access to information (a core value of libraries); and (4) recognition that despite their commonalities in the digital age, museums, libraries, and archives have developed differently for reasons that remain valid.

Of eight workshop presenters, only Helen Tibbo from the School of Information and Library Service at the University of North Carolina Chapel Hill outlined a specific curriculum development plan. She described the DigCCur Digital Curation Curriculum project, funded by IMLS in 2006, which aimed to: (1) develop a curricular framework for digital preservation in order to prepare a cohort of educators with a shared knowledge base; (2) build modules rather than full courses; and (3) emphasize core, generalizable modules which could also be adapted for different disciplines.

In 2013, a curriculum framework for digital curation has in fact begun to emerge in LIS schools in the US. This typically includes a course in digital preservation and a "foundations" course that covers aspects of data curation that are not fully covered in the preservation course (such as metadata standards and aspects of copyright not related to preservation issues). In the US, digital curation education has tended to take one of two approaches, depending largely on the expertise and focus of the faculty, that is, either a data life cycle focus (i.e., an archival perspective), or a disciplinary focus, usually though not exclusively emphasizing the sciences. Because museums cover a wide range of disciplines, from art to history to the natural sciences, the data life cycle approach makes sense in the core curriculum, but it is also important to give students an opportunity to acquire disciplinary expertise for the domain they aspire to enter (or, frequently, in which they are already employed).

3 The Johns Hopkins University Certificate in Digital Curation

(http://advanced.jhu.edu/academics/certificate-programs/digital-curation-certificate/)

The Johns Hopkins University (JHU) MA in Museum Studies program launched a mostly online graduate certificate in digital curation in September 2013. It is among the new educational programs aimed at embedding data curation principles and practices into the wider community of cultural heritage and data management. The certificate program draws on the work of LIS schools in the US over the last decade, adapted as necessary to meet the needs of the museum community and to align with the educational principles and practices of the JHU graduate museum studies program.

The JHU museum studies program has been notably successful. It began in 2008 with just 12 students and by 2012 had grown to 900 enrollments. Many museum studies programs in the US have had a mixed record in placing their graduates, in part because the museum career path is based on disciplinary expertise (usually a Ph.D. in a relevant field such as art history or archaeology) rather than a single master's level credential. Because the JHU MA program is "mostly" online and also technology-focused, it has responded to the interests of many working museum professionals who want a better understanding of technology along with the convenience of an online program that they can pursue from anywhere while holding a full- or part-time job.

The digital curation certificate program's learning objectives are to prepare students to:

- Identify and describe the principles of digital preservation and digital curation, including understanding of key terms and concepts.
- Create and assess digital preservation plans and strategies, in the context of the larger museum environment and including assessment of user needs and impacts.
- Demonstrate understanding of archival principles of appraisal and the management of digital content in trustworthy repositories.
- Demonstrate awareness of legal issues that impact museums' abilities to preserve digital content and make it accessible.
- Identify and describe workflows for the creation and management of digital content in museum environments, including communication and cooperation within and beyond the institution that is necessary for efficient and effective digital preservation.
- Demonstrate understanding of research methods and critical thinking skills through the supervised research paper.

The program is designed to meet the needs of all types of museums by preparing students with a broad foundation in digital curation through online core courses, including:

- Digital Preservation - introduces students to the current state of digital preservation, preservation challenges, and basic concepts for designing effective digital preservation plans and programs. Topics include the relevance of digital preservation for museums; archival principles that inform preservation practices; standards and policies; considerations in preservation strategies; issues relating to formats, repositories, and processes; and emerging preservation solutions and services.
- Foundations of Digital Curation - lays a foundation for managing digital information throughout its lifecycle by introducing students to the emerging field of digital curation and by examining the practical issues and tools involved in managing digital collections and repositories over time. Topics include appraisal and selection; principles of records management; resource description; systems design; management of research data; policy issues, and user services.
- Managing Digital Information - addresses technical and practical issues involved in the long-term management and preservation of digital assets, with an emphasis on the unique problems facing museums. Subjects include best practices for digital format conversion, management of digital surrogates and derivatives, practical planning and design of workflow for digital curation, and a survey of the technologies (software, equipment and metadata schemas) required at ingest, storage, access, and dissemination points in the Open Archival Information System Model. These topics are presented in the context of analyzing digital asset management practices (in the broadest sense) of individual institutions, and developing strategies for the curation of these assets.
- One elective from course offerings in the MA in Museum Studies program.

After completing the online courses, students will do discipline-focused work, including an internship at a physical location (which may be repeated once in lieu of the online elective) and a supervised research paper. The internship is a full-credit course that requires 120 h of supervised field experience plus an analytical paper or project (for example, a journal and final report on the internship experience).

The internship and the research course will provide students with both hands-on work and research experience in their chosen field of disciplinary expertise. It is anticipated that mentors of student interns at host institutions might also serve as research supervisors of the research component, resulting in research that will benefit both the host institution and the relevant discipline. A meeting with representatives from leading London museums will be held in London in November 2013 to discuss details of the internship program to ensure that the needs and expectations of host institutions are identified and addressed. (The JHU MA in Museum Studies program requires students to take one on-site seminar, and it has held seminars in London, Barcelona, and Berlin, in addition to Washington and various locations in the US, so it is likely that some students in the digital curation program will be interested in taking internships in Europe). While the MA seminars are 2 weeks, the internship for the digital curation certificate will require at least 3 weeks on-site. Because it is a full-credit course, students will actually have 13 weeks to complete the internship. This means that students could spread out the on-site experience over several weeks, and that they can complete their internship report or other assignments that do not require their physical presence after they have returned home.

The admission criteria for the certificate program are:

- Master's degree in museum studies or related field; or
- Bachelor's degree and at least 5 years' experience in a museum, library, archive or related cultural heritage organization, or
- Current enrollment in the JHU museum studies master's program, after completion of five courses.

4 Community Input on Digital Curation Education

In February 2013, the JHU graduate museum studies program partnered with the LIS schools at the University of Arizona and Simmons College to host a one-day "summit" meeting at the Johns Hopkins' Advanced Academic Programs offices in Washington, DC (supported in large part by an IMLS grant to the University of Arizona). The purpose was to invite input from digital curation practitioners and educators from across the country representing the library, archives, and museum fields. Twenty-two participants attended, including representatives from the Library of Congress, the National Archives and Records Administration (NARA), and the Smithsonian Institutions; library, museum, and archival educators; and leading experts from such diverse organizations as the Chicago Art Institute, the Digital Public Library of America, the Field Museum of Natural History, and the Maryland Institute for Technology in the Humanities.

In addition to the one-day meeting at Hopkins, the summit organizers held preliminary meetings over three days with focus groups at the Library of Congress, NARA, and the Smithsonian, respectively, with participants selected by each institution. The focus groups provided insights into the concerns and priorities of the respective organizations, which then served as talking points for discussions at the summit.

Two overriding issues recognized by all organizations were:

1. the challenges of (and opportunities for innovation in) online discovery and access, and
2. the organizational challenges that institutions face as they try to adapt their work processes and organizational capabilities to the demands of a technology environment that requires shared knowledge, common practices, and collaboration across disciplinary, institutional, and geographic boundaries.

A common theme related to the first challenge—discovery and access—is the demand from researchers for "data", in addition to the general public's interest in ready access to online information. Collections content is increasingly recognized as raw data, and researchers are asking for online access to it, especially when it can be mined and manipulated through automated techniques. For museums, which have traditionally viewed their holdings as "objects" rather than "information", this is a new concept.

In discussions of the knowledge and skills that cultural heritage organizations look for when hiring new professionals, a few practitioners suggested that technical skills, such as knowledge of XML, were important. Most, however, emphasized broader capabilities, such as awareness of the importance of standards and general familiarity with relevant metadata standards, as well as general capabilities such as good organizational and communication skills, and the ability to work in a team of people with different areas of expertise and who often don't speak the same professional language. Some educators and practitioners expressed interest in short-term, informal training programs that might focus on technical skills (such as XML) and that could result in credentials such as "badges", but these were seen as being outside of, and in addition to, a formal degree or certificate program.

As might be expected, despite these commonalities there were many differences identified across different types of cultural heritage organizations. Perhaps the most obvious challenge is semantic. We don't always mean the same thing when we use the same terms. The traditional definition of "curation" in the museum world refers to selection, interpretation, and presentation, in addition to caring for collections and objects. A number of museum practitioners thought that museums are unlikely to hire new professionals with titles such as "data (or digital) curator". They do want people who have the skills that are associated with data curation, but they may call it something else. (Some of the recent online chatter in the museum community has concerned the indiscriminate use of the term "curation" to describe activities such as posting images on Pinterest, or "curating" department store displays, so the use of the term by another professional community that associates it with a knowledge base and a set of principles and practices may be less objectionable to the museum community than it was a few years ago.) Several museum administrators reported that they are hiring archivists and librarians with the skills associated with data curation, even though they would prefer to hire people with museum experience, because they cannot find staff with both museum experience and the requisite digital skills.

5 Conclusion

Museums of all types have a demonstrated need for professionals with data curation skills (Ray 2009). However, they also express a preference for "their own" professionals, that is, people with work experience in museums and a deep understanding of the museum mission.

One of the biggest challenges in designing an educational program in digital curation for museum professionals is the great disciplinary differences in museums. Art museums, natural history museums, history museums, and zoos are very different from each other and require professionals with different education and expertise. This reality demands that a program aiming to provide digital curation education for all types of museums must address basic principles of curation that cut across disciplinary lines, and yet must also provide for specialization by discipline and type of museum. Art museums are acquiring complex interactive digital media works that pose difficult challenges for preservation and re-presentation, while natural history museums must manage research data ranging from archaeology field research to massive quantities of digitized specimens. Many large museums are research institutions in their own right, employing scientists who conduct research on the collections and in the field. Research is one of the four core museum functions, as identified by the US government, along with collections, exhibits, and education (US Office of Personnel Management 1962). If museums don't preserve, arrange for preservation of, their own research data, it most likely will not be available in the future. What disciplinary expertise is needed to curate this research data? This question has not yet been resolved, but it must be addressed. While the core courses can provide an overview of disciplinary distinctions in data curation, students must decide what type of museum they want to work in when they choose their internships and research projects. Leading museums must institute good data curation practices to ensure that the new generation of museum data curators (or data stewards?) acquires the necessary expertise.

Even in terms of aggregating and sharing digitized images and collections information, there are challenging differences between museums, libraries, and archives. This problem is perhaps best exemplified by Europeana because of its large scale and scope (http://www.europeana.eu/portal/). Museum metadata never fit neatly into the original Europeana metadata element set. This has also been a problem for archives, since the Europeana data model is based on the individual item and collection-level descriptions have not been routinely linked to items. Some of these problems might be addressed through the Europeana semantic web initiative, which promises to increase the options for revealing relationships among objects, collections, and external information resources.

Much of the digital curation curricula developed for LIS education in the US that is not specifically library-centric can be adapted to museum education with appropriate museum examples. Among the persistent issues that are museum-centric and should be addressed in museum education are:

- the long tradition of research as a core museum function and the consequent need to preserve research data produced by museum staff;
- the tendency of some museums to overlook the informational value of their collections–as opposed to the evidential value of their objects—which sometimes results in a reluctance to prioritize digitization of collections, plan for long-term preservation of digitized collection images, or provide public access to the non-sensitive information in collections management systems; and
- the tendency of some museums to think of copyright as a mechanism to protect their own rights and revenues rather than as a means to provide access to their holdings, barring legal restrictions that protect the rights of external copyright owners.

There is evidence that traditional attitudes and practices that limit online access to museum data are changing as the result of user behaviors and growing awareness of the value of digital data, but educators can also help to promote greater alignment of principles and practices among collections-holding institutions.

References

Blue Ribbon Task Force on Sustainable Digital Preservation and Access, Sustaining the Digital Investment: Issues and Challenges of Economically Sustainable Digital Preservation. Interim report (2008). http://brtf.sdsc.edu/biblio/BRTF_Interim_Report.pdf

Blue Ribbon Task Force on Sustainable Digital Preservation and Access, Sustainable Access for a Digital Planet : Ensuring Long-Term Access to Digital Information. Final report (2010). http://brtf.sdsc.edu/biblio/BRTF_Final_Report.pdf

Higgins, S.: Digital curation: the emergence of a new discipline. Int. J. Digit. Curat. 6(2), 78–88 (2011)

High Level Expert Group on Scientific Data, Riding the Wave: How Europe Can Gain From the Rising Tide of Scientific Data, October 2010. http://ec.europa.eu/information_society/newsroom/cf/itemlongdetail.cfm?item_id=6204

Institute of Museum and Library Services, Cultural Heritage Information Professionals (CHIPS). Workshop report (2013). http://www.imls.gov/assets/1/AssetManager/chips_workshop_report.pdf

Keralis, S.D.C.: Data curation education: A snapshot. In: Jahnke, L., Asher, A. (eds.) The Problem of Data, Council on Library and Information Resources (2012). http://www.clir.org/pubs/reports/pub154

Kim, J., Warga, E., Moen, W.E.: Competencies required for digital curation: an analysis of job advertisements. Int. J. Digit. Curat. 8(1), 66–83 (2013). doi:10.2218/ijdc.v8i1.242

Manjarraz, C., Ray, J., Bisher, K.: A demographic overview of the current and projected library workforce and the impact of federal funding. Libr. Trends 59(1–2), 6–29 (2010)

National Science Board, Long-Lived Digital Data Collections: Enabling Research in the 21st Century (2005). http://www.nsf.gov/pubs/2005/nsb0540/

Ray, J.: Sharks, digital curation, and the education of information professionals. Mus. Manag. Curator. 24(4), 357–368 (2009)

US Office of Personnel Management, Position Classification Standards for Museum Curator Series (1962). http://www.opm.gov/policy-data-oversight/classification-qualifications/classifying-general-schedule-positions/standards/1000/gs1015.pdf

Sustainability: An Unintended Consequence of the Integration of Digital Curation Core Competencies into the MLIS Curricula

Patricia C. Franks[✉]

School of Library and Information Science, San José State University,
San José, CA, USA
patricia.franks@sjsu.edu

Abstract. The unprecedented expansion of the digital universe presents a dilemma for the digital curation profession: there is a need for professionals with skills and knowledge to provide long-term stewardship of digital assets, but education and training programs designed exclusively to prepare digital curators are inadequate to meet the demand. An infusion of digital curation competencies into the LIS curriculum will ensure that students pursuing related professions—including archivists, museum technicians, librarians, and conservators—are also prepared to serve as stewards of our digital treasure. The unintended consequence of this approach may well be the sustainability of Digital Curation courses and, therefore, Digital Curation curricula. This paper discusses the correlation between SJSU SLIS core competencies and Digital Curation core competencies and outlines the steps being taken as a result of this analysis to launch a Digital Curation Post Master's Certificate program and provide a Digital Curation career pathway for MLIS students.

Keywords: Digital curation · Core competencies · Graduate · Curriculum · Sustainability · Career pathways

1 Introduction

In a paper delivered in Sardinia, Italy, seven Digital Curation pioneers introduced the Digital Curation Centre (DCC) in the UK as a vision for digital curation. They explained that the Digital Curation Center was developed "in response to the realization that digital information is both essential and fragile [1]". And they asserted that the foundation of the Digital Curation Center is the belief that long-term stewardship of digital assets is the responsibility of everyone in the digital information value chain [2]. The year was 2005, the size of the digital universe was 130 EB (135.5 billion GB) [3], and the digital curation value chain was comprised of professionals who "were still developing their expertise" [3].

By 2020, the size of the digital universe is expected to reach 40,000 EB (40 trillion GB). This figure represents more than 5,200 GB of digital information for every man, woman, and child [3]. Digital data is generated by "numerous devices in numerous forms: remote sensors, online retail transactions, text documents, e-mail messages, web posts, camera and video images, computers running large-scale

Ł. Bolikowski et al. (Eds.): TPDL 2013, CCIS 416, pp. 226–238, 2014.
DOI: 10.1007/978-3-319-08425-1_25, © Springer International Publishing Switzerland 2014

simulations, and scientific instruments such as particle accelerators and telescopes" [4]. And everyone in the digital information value chain includes individuals who would not consider themselves digital curators but with whom responsibility for the stewardship of digital assets lie until or unless that responsibility is passed on to someone else.

It is not surprising that there is an increasing demand for information professionals who can manage the burgeoning data generated by the nation's researchers, serve as stewards of the nation's digital cultural legacy, and meet the needs of businesses and government agencies as they manage their growing volume of digital assets. This relatively new and pressing need has created a rising demand for archivists, librarians, and museum professionals who are trained to apply the latest tools and methods to effectively manage and preserve material that is born digital or converted to digital form [5]. This emerging need has also given birth to a new profession: the digital curator.

Although the demand for digital curators is growing, sufficient capacity to educate and train digital curators does not exist. A secondary concern is that the positions currently available for professionals with digital curation education and training are advertised using a variety of job titles, few of them "digital curator," and many of them that involve responsibilities for only one phase of the digital curation lifecycle. Infusing digital curation core competencies into existing curricula is one method to expand the number of professionals prepared to perform digital curation activities in order to protect, add value to, and preserve our digital assets. Preparing students for careers related to but not specifically labeled as "digital curation" will expand the pool of qualified professionals capable of managing and preserving digital data and will increase awareness of the value of digital curation professionals.

The digital curation profession should encourage the integration of digital curation core competencies into the curriculum of other professions. The most obvious place to start is with the Library and Information Science curriculum. The continuing efforts of the faculty of the School of Library and Information Science (SLIS) at San José State University are based upon the thesis that the increase in digital data requires all students to understand the need to be proactive stewards of their own digital data. As we endeavor to infuse digital curation competencies within core courses as well as offer specific elective courses related to digital curation for all students, we have found that we can support both a Digital Curation Post Master's certificate option, which will be offered for the first time in spring 2014, and a Digital Curation Career Pathway for MLIS majors, which will be offered for the first time in fall 2014, without relying upon external funding sources.

2   Digital Curation Profession Growing Pains

"Digital curators manage, maintain, preserve, and add value to digital information throughout its lifecycle, reducing threats to long-term value, mitigating the risk of digital obsolescence, and enhancing the reuse for all purposes" [6]. Digital curation begins during the planning stage and should be a consideration throughout each stage of the digital curation lifecycle.

In 2006, the Institute of Museums and Library Science funded the development of digital curation programs in US graduate schools. The funding supported the development of robust programs (including core curricula, specialized elective courses, and required internships in established digital repositories) in a number of institutions, including the University of Illinois Urbana Champaign, the University of North Carolina at Chapel Hill, and the University of Tennessee [7].

By 2007 digital curation was recognized as a new, umbrella concept that includes digital preservation, data curation, electronic records management, and digital asset management. Digital curators were labeled as the newest type of information professional on the block [8].

According to the Occupational Outlook Handbook, 2010-2011 edition, employment of digital curators in the U.S. was expected to increase by 23 % between 2008 and 2018, much faster than the average for all occupations. However, the 2012-2013 edition of the Occupational Outlook Handbook contains no reference to digital curators or digital curation [9]. The listing for curator provides only a traditional list of duties that does not include digital tasks, and the work environment described focuses on developing physical collections, organizing exhibits, and conducting research. This disparity may be seen as a natural occurrence in the development of a new occupation still struggling for recognition.

Awareness of the importance of managing and preserving digital assets continues to increase, albeit not at the pace one might have anticipated in 2001 when the phrase "digital curation" was first used [10]. The phrase "digital curation" is not clearly understood by those outside of the profession; therefore, confusion exists over exactly what a digital curator does. Qualifications listed for jobs that contain "curator" in the title often vary widely. And job openings that do not contain the term "curator" in the title often require digital curation skills and knowledge.

The diversity of the profession can be understood by studying some of the individuals who hold the position of digital curator. For example, in 2011, Doug Reside introduced himself on his blog [11] as the first Digital Curator of Performing Arts at The New York Public Library and explained that in addition to traditional curatorial tasks, he has made it his mission to: (1) make as much of their collection online as copyright law, professional ethics, and the budget permits; (2) provide contextual information and software tools to make their digital collections as useful as possible; and (3) improve methods for preserving and providing access to the "born digital" materials (word processor files, musical scores, 3d set designs, etc.) that are now part of the creative history of most contemporary works of art.

A search for the term "digital curator" on LinkedIn (LinkedIn.com), a popular professional social network, returned 788 results that included the terms digital and curator in either the job title or description, but very few of the returns placed the terms next to each other. A number of those who were at one time digital curators have moved into other, related positions. For example, Maureen Pennock, ranked first among the results to the query, is the current Head of Digital Preservation at The British Library. Other names returned in response to the query held job titles such as Principal Digital Curator at UC Berkeley and Curator, Digital Research Services at the University of Pennsylvania. Additional job titles included Digital Archivist/Historian at the US Library of Congress, Information Specialist I/Digital Data Curator, Curator Digital Assets, and Manager, Digital Stewardship.

The increase of born digital information has resulted in a convergence of responsibilities for librarians, archivists, museum curators, and records and information managers. Often job openings for positions in those disciplines encompass digital curation duties. For example, a January 2013 announcement for a Museum Curator (Digital and Emerging Media) in the Asian Pacific American (APA) Center of the Smithsonian Institution sought a person to serve as Curator for digital and emerging media (including social media activities) as well as for APA digital and emerging media [12]. The responsibilities for this position include curating digital exhibitions, collections, and programming; preservation is not included among the responsibilities listed.

An analysis of the jobs posted to the Digital Curation Exchange on June 29, 2013, revealed the diversity of the opportunities for digital curators [13]. But of 47 listings posted between January 1, 2013 and April 5, 2013 there were no job titles that used the term "digital curator." However one listing announced a position for a Director of Research Data Curation Service and another announced a position for a Data Curation Librarian. Examples of job titles include: Digital Archivist, Digital Preservation Manager, Electronic Records Specialist, King County Archivist, Institutional Repository Coordinator, Emerging Technologies Librarian, and Digital Asset Metadata and Taxonomy Specialist.

This lack of consistency in the use of job titles and descriptions suggests that, for the time being at least, the core competencies are more demanding of our attention than the job title itself.

3 Sustainability – A Potential Benefit of the Infusion of Digital Curation Core Competencies into the LIS Curriculum

Despite the dollars expended to develop digital curation programs within and outside the US, in 2012, Abreu, Acker, and Hank, acknowledged that "planning and managing digital collections for current and future access and reuse is [still] a significant challenge in our contemporary information landscape, transcending sub-domains under the umbrella of information science, including the fields of archives, digital preservation and curation, and records management" [14].

The call for contributions on the DigCurV 2013 international conference website described digital curation as "a central challenge and activity for libraries, archives, museums and other cultural organizations" [15]. At the conference, Helen R. Tibbo, School of Information & Library Science, University of North Carolina at Chapel Hill, broached the topic of sustainability. Her presentation provided an overview of the following four digital preservation and digital curation grant projects conducted since 2002 and their sustainability potential: [16]. Digital Preservation Program funded by the National Endowment for Humanities (NEH) under the management of Nancy McGovern; DigCCur I and II funded by the Institute of Museums and Library Services

(IMLS) with workshops managed by Helen Tibbo and Christopher Lee; Digital Preservation Outreach and Education Program (DPOE) sponsored by the Library of Congress; and Digital Archives Specialist Curriculum and Certificate offered through the Society of American Archivists.

An analysis of the information presented by Dr. Tibbo reveals that external funding does not equal sustainability. With funding, a dedicated, enthusiastic champion can develop and launch a successful program. But if the capacity to continue the program after the departure of its champion or the end of the grant period does not exist, the likelihood of sustainability is low.

Infusing digital curation competencies into the SLIS curricula can provide at least a partial solution to the challenge of providing sustainable digital curation training and education opportunities. Infusion will result in several benefits, including increased awareness of the digital curation profession, preparation of SLIS students to assume digital curation positions, and assurance that elective courses offered for all SLIS students will be available for students pursuing digital curation career pathways. An added benefit is that graduates of SLIS and other master's level programs who wish to add digital curation competencies to their skill set can do so by enrolling in these same courses as part of a Post Master's Certificate Program. Courses that might be dropped for low enrollment are more likely to be offered if they are useful to students pursuing a variety of career options.

4   Approaches to Identification and Analysis of Digital Curation Competencies Within Existing Courses

Disciplines that once found little common ground, now find their roles converging around the care and preservation of digital assets. When introducing a special selection of articles in the Journal of Education for Library and Information Science that document curriculum development efforts in related disciplines, Jeffrey Pomerantz wrote, "In an era of mass digitization of physical artifacts, and mass creation of born-digital objects, the challenges faced by cultural heritage institutions of all types are increasingly shared." He further stated, "These disciplines—library and information science, archival studies, and museum studies—have come to realize they increasingly share overlapping educational goals" [17].

Various methods can be used to identify the digital curation competencies within existing courses. Such identification can help the institution modify exiting courses and develop new courses and programs to address the needs of students pursuing careers with overlapping educational goals. Three approaches are presented in this section: (1) existing curricula could be analyzed to determine if/how it correlates to the matrix developed by Lee and Tibbo, (2) existing curricula could be analyzed to determine if/how it measures against the ten operational competencies and ten managerial competencies organized by Tammaro, Casarosa, and Madrid, and/or (3) existing curricula could be analyzed to determine how it relates to the various phases of the DCC Curation Lifecycle Model.

4.1   Matrix for Identifying and Organizing Material to Be Covered in Digital Curation Curriculum – Lee and Tibbo

Lee and Tibbo developed a matrix of topics for identifying and organizing material to be covered in a digital curation curriculum. The six dimensions of the matrix are (1) mandates, values and principles, (2) functions and skills, (3) professional, disciplinary, institutional, organizational, or cultural context, (4) type of resource, (5) instrumental knowledge, and (6) transition points in the information continuum [10]. The dimension most useful for curriculum developers wishing to address the essential skills for digital curators is the second, Functions and Skills, which lists twenty-four high-level functional categories and numerous sub-functions. An example of a functional category is Destruction and Removal (the process of eliminating or deleting records beyond any possible reconstruction). This matrix was used by Lee and Tibbo to analyze the curriculum at UNC SLIS in order to identify digital curation elements that were already being taught.

4.2   Ten Essential Operational and Ten Essential Managerial Competencies – Tammaro, Casarosa, and Madrid

A different perspective is provided by Tammaro, Madrid, and Casarosa [18], who organized twenty digital curation core competencies identified through a Delphi Study into ten essential operational competencies and ten essential managerial competencies [18]. These competency statements can be transformed into an evaluation instrument used to link the statements to competencies developed through existing courses.

In a paper presented at the DigCurV 2013 conference in Florence [19], this author described an approach to identify gaps between existing courses and digital curation core competencies by mapping competencies that provide the basis for the MLIS curriculum at San José State University with the ten operational and the ten managerial core competencies organized by Tammaro, Casarosa, and Madrid. One example of each category is presented in Table 1.

4.3   The DCC Curation Lifecycle Model – High Level Approach used by the School of Library and Information Science at San José State University

Because of the volume and variety of courses offered though the School of Library and Information Science at San José State University each term (approximately 100 different course topics) and the frequency with which new topics are added to the course schedule (between 5 and 10 each academic year), a high-level approach to evaluate existing courses for Digital Curation Core Competencies was utilized.

The DCC Curation Lifecycle Model found at http://www.dcc.ac.uk/resources/curation-lifecycle-model includes the following sequential actions: conceptualize; create or receive; appraise and select; ingest; preservation action; store; access, use, and reuse; and transform. It also identifies the following occasional actions: dispose, reappraise, and migrate. Current courses containing content related to archives,

Table 1. Crosswalk between one operational and one managerial core competency and SJSU/SLIS core competencies (http://slisweb.sjsu.edu/current-students/courses/core-competencies)

	Equivalent SJSU/SLIS competency	Existing course(s)	Equivalent Yes/No
Operational competency			
Selects and appraises digital documents for long-term preservation	Use the basic concepts and principles related to the selection, evaluation, organization, and preservation of physical and digital items and collections. (Comp F)	(Two of 36 existing courses that meet this competency) LIBR 259: preservation management—digital preservation only LIBR 284: seminar in archives and records management—digitization an digital preservation	Yes
Managerial competency			
Organizes and manages the use of metadata standards, access controls and authentication procedures	Demonstrate understanding of basic principles and standards involved in organizing information, including classification, cataloging, metadata, or other systems. (Comp G)	(Two of 20 existing courses that meet this competency) LIBR 281: seminar in contemporary issues—metadata LIBR 287: seminar in information science—virtual services	Yes

electronic records, digital curation, and preservation were analyzed to determine how the coursework corresponds to the DCC Curation Lifecycle Model. Table 2 illustrates how eight of those courses support various phases of the digital curation lifecycle.

5   Digital Curation Skills for Managing Personal Digital Objects for All Students

All programs offered through SLIS are taught online. The manner in which the courses are taught utilizing social media and emerging technologies exposes students to the importance of creating, managing, using, accessing, and preserving digital objects—the artifacts they create throughout their program.

Two courses in Table 2 require additional explanation of the ways in which they require all MLIS students to apply digital curation skills to their personal digital objects: LIBR 203, Online Social Networking Technologies and Tools, and LIBR 289, Advanced Topics in Library & Information Science: E-Portfolio.

Students are introduced to the e-portfolio in LIBR 203, the technology course they start even before they begin their first term. They must successfully complete LIBR 203 to remain in the program. Instructors in each course they take after LIBR 203

Table 2. SJSU /SLIS courses mapped to phases of the DCC curation lifecycle model

Course Designator & Title	Course Description and Link to a Recent Syllabus	Phases of the DC Lifecycle
LIBR 203 Online Social Networking Technologies and Tools (Required: 1 unit of credit)	This course introduces students to a variety of new and emerging technologies used in today's online environment. It covers various social networking platforms, content and learning management tools, web conferencing, and other trends in social computing. Link to syllabus: http://slisapps.sjsu.edu/gss/ajax/showSheet.php?id=4976	2 – Create or Receive 6 – Store 7 – Access, Use & Reuse
LIBR 284 Seminar in Archives & Records Management Topic: Characteristics and Curation of New Digital Media	In this course, we will explore approaches to the collection and curation of selected new digital media in libraries and other cultural repositories. In the first stage of the course, roughly the first four weeks, the focus will be on developing an understanding of the characteristics of new media and refining what we mean by the term "curation." The second stage will make up most of the course, consisting of five two-week engagements with five specific media and issues associated with them. Each of the five media will be paired with a specific issue about the impact of games on curation – selection/appraisal, acquisitions, description/archiving, preservation, and access/exhibition. Link to syllabus: http://slisapps.sjsu.edu/gss/ajax/showSheet.php?id=4938	1 – Conceptualize 2 – Create or Receive 3 – Appraise & Select 4 - Ingest 5 – Preservation Action 6 - Store 7 - Access, Use, & Reuse 9 – Preservation Planning
LIBR 284 Seminar in Archives & Records Management Topic: Digitization and Digital Preservation	This course will provide an introduction to the digitization of archival, library, and museum materials, as well as an introduction to the digital preservation of the resulting digital objects. Students will learn about using digital technologies to provide better access to and sometimes to preserve text, images, sound, and video. [Please note: the majority of the course will focus on the digitization of text and image because of the nature of this class and equipment requirements.] Particular topics to be explored in depth include: selection for digitization, legal and copyright issues, digitization requirements for text and images, metadata, and technology issues. The course will provide a broad foundation of the principles, processes and standards guiding the digitization of cultural heritage materials. Link to syllabus: http://slisapps.sjsu.edu/gss/ajax/showSheet.php?id=5144	2 – Create or Receive 3 – Appraise & Select 6 - Store 7 – Access, Use, & Reuse 9 – Preservation Planning
LIBR 284 Seminar in Archives and Records Management Topic: EAD	This class will cover in-depth Encoded Archival Description (EAD), and provide a brief introduction to Encoded Archival Context (EAC), the international standards for the presentation of archival descriptive information and records creator authority records on the World Wide Web. Link to syllabus: http://slisapps.sjsu.edu/gss/ajax/showSheet.php?id=5137	2 – Create or Receive 7 – Access, Use, & Reuse
LIBR 284 Seminar in Archives and Records Management Topic: Electronic Records Management	This course is an introduction to the management and long-term preservation of unstructured content created or maintained electronically. It examines the ways in which new information technologies challenge organizations' capacities to define, identify, control, manage, and preserve electronic records. Topics include the nature of electronic records as evidence; reliability and authenticity in electronic records; electronic records management policy formulation; business continuity planning; information security; the role and nature of recordkeeping metadata; strategies, techniques, and technologies for the long-term preservation of electronic records; individual electronic recordkeeping behaviors, as well as industry, national, and international standards relating to electronic recordkeeping. Link to syllabus: http://slisapps.sjsu.edu/gss/ajax/showSheet.php?id=5141	1 - Conceptualize 2 – Create or Receive 3 – Appraise & Select 4 - Ingest 6 – Store 7 – Access, Use, & Reuse 8 – Transform (for website or display space) 9 – Preservation Planning
LIBR 287 Seminar in Information Science Topic: Virtual Worlds: Life in Tudor Times	This course will immerse students in Virtual England during the reign of the Tudors (1485-1603). Based on research conducted into the events taking place during the rule of Henry VII, through the reigns of Henry VIII, Edward VI, Mary I, and Elizabeth I, students will create and participate in an immersive role-playing experience. The experience will prepare the students to demonstrate the ways in which librarians, and archivists, and museum curators can create community and serve as leaders in portraying knowledge, history and documents in creative and educational ways using virtual world technologies. All activities take place on SLIS Island in Second Life. Link to syllabus: http://slisapps.sjsu.edu/gss/ajax/showSheet.php?id=5630	2 – Create or Receive 3 – Appraise & Select 6 – Store 7 – Access, Use, & Reuse 8 – Transform (for use in SL) 9 – Preservation Planning
LIBR 294 Professional Experiences: Internships (Archival Section)	Experience in a selected public, academic, special library or other information-based organization. (May apply for one of approximately 60 archival on site or virtual opportunities each fall, spring, or summer.) Link to syllabus: http://slisapps.sjsu.edu/gss/ajax/showSheet.php?id=5188	Depends upon the Internship placement.
LIBR 289 – Advanced Topics in Library & Information Science: E-portfolio	This is a capstone course. It involves advanced independent creation of an electronic portfolio demonstrating mastery of all student learning outcomes (core competencies) for the MLIS degree. Evidence for each learning outcome is presented in digital format (e.g., papers, projects, website collections). Must be completed in final or next-to-final semester. Link to LIBR 289 Handbook: http://slisweb.sjsu.edu/current-students/courses/289-e-portfolio-handbook Link to LIBR 289 Syllabus: http://slisapps.sjsu.edu/gss/ajax/showSheet.php?id=5631	1 – Conceptualize 2 – Create or Receive 3 – Appraise & Select 4 – Ingest 6 – Store 7 – Access, Use & Reuse 8 – Transform (for use in e-portfolio)

encourage them to identify, capture, and store examples of their work for use in an e-portfolio they can complete as a culminating experience. When enrolled in LIBR 289, students are required to design their e-portfolio, add content including professional philosophy, appraise the evidence they have collected, select the best examples of their work, transform the digital objects into an easily accessible format for review (e.g., convert word documents to PDF format), and add the evidence to their e-portfolio.

The phases of the Digital Curation Lifecycle to which SJSU/SLIS courses have been mapped are:

1 – Conceptualize
2 – Create or Receive
3 – Appraise & Select
4 – Ingest
5 – Preservation Action (e.g., migration, emulation)
6 – Store
7 – Access, Use, & Reuse
8 – Transform
9 – Preservation Planning

The Electronic Portfolio (e-Portfolio) option is one of two ways (THESIS is the other) in which a student may satisfy the University's requirements for a culminating experience. The goal is to provide a program-based assessment to ensure that each student demonstrates mastery of all program learning outcomes (core competencies) before graduation. Students provide evidence of mastery of the core competencies by uploading files or linking to born digital or digitized examples of assignments created throughout their program.

Students have the option of creating an e-portfolio website or using the e-portfolio system provided by the School (e.g., Angel, Desire2Learn, Canvass ePortfolio programs). The public Electronic Portfolio created by SLIS graduate Mahal Montoya available at https://sites.google.com/site/sjsusliseportfolio/ illustrates the required components: introduction and professional philosophy, competency statements, and conclusion and affirmation statement. Examples are found at the end of each core competency statement and include PDF files and links to presentations.

Current students are required to maintain private e-portfolios and provide access to only their faculty e-portfolio supervisor for grading. The e-portfolio course requires that students engage in activities from all phases of the digital curation lifecycle except for long-term preservation actions like emulation and migration.

6 Internships Provide Opportunities for Students to Apply Digital Curation Skills

One course included in Table 2—LIBR 294, Professional Experiences: Internships—provides an opportunity for students to select placements in which they are interested and to design their own student learning outcomes. More than 600 internship sites are registered in the SLIS Internship Database, and more than 150 unique opportunities, both on site and virtual, are offered each semester.

The key to acquiring digital curation skills and knowledge by participating in an internship is in selecting an appropriate placement and negotiating at least three student learning outcomes with the site supervisor. An example of one listing from the current SLIS database is shown in Fig. 1.

> **JOB TITLE:** EAD Recon Intern
> **JOB DESCRIPTION:** Under the direction of the University Archivist the EAD Recon Intern will convert legacy collection inventories (Word, FileMaker Pro, paper) into EAD using Excel, Acrobat, Oxygen, and Archivists' Toolkit.
>
> **TASK TYPE:** Archival
>
> **WORK TO BE DONE:** Virtual
> **QUALIFICATIONS:** • High level of proficiency with computers and desktop applications, including Microsoft Office suite (especially Word and Excel), Acrobat, MarcEdit, Oxygen, and FileMaker Pro preferred. • Knowledge of Archivists' Toolkit (AT) • Experience using Google Documents • Demonstrated problem-solving ability • Working knowledge of archival repositories and their procedures • B.A. degree or equivalent; enrolled in library degree program or equivalent. • Demonstrated experience in using judgment and initiative • Demonstrated ability to communicate effectively, both orally and in writing • Ability to work independently and collaboratively in a production-oriented, team environment.

Fig. 1. Virtual archival internship opportunity, fall 2013

Student learning outcomes are developed by analyzing the job description and then developing statements that describe what the student will be able to do by the end of the internship as a result of this specific experience. At the end of the term, a report must be submitted by each intern to the SLIS internship supervisor that explains how each student learning outcome was achieved and providing evidence of mastery of each outcome. Examples of student learning outcomes specific to archival internships are:

- Utilize popular archival records management software.
- Evaluate and process legacy collection inventories for conversion to current technologies (EAD).
- Digitize, assemble, and make accessible historical materials in a single-search, online interface.

The existing, robust internship program at SLIS is designed to accommodate students regardless of the career pathway they decide to follow.

7   Designing a Sustainable Digital Curation Pathway for SLIS Students

Each of the three approaches previously described can be used when designing a Digital Curation Career Pathway for students in a Post Master's Certificate Program or within an MLIS degree program.

A gap analysis can be conducted by comparing the digital curation competencies existing within current curriculum offerings with the competencies required of digital curators. The gaps can be filled through curriculum development in the form of modification of existing courses or development of new courses. This approach will contribute to the sustainability of the digital curation curriculum by increasing enrollment in those courses of value to students pursuing a variety of careers in addition to digital curation, such as electronic records management and digital librarianship.

SJSU/SLIS currently offers a Post Master's Certificate with several career pathways, including one in Digital Archives and Records Management [20]. Students take a one-credit required technology course, LIBR 203, plus five additional three-credit courses. Although students pursuing this Post Master's Certificate may obtain positions in digital curation, there are gaps that must be bridged in order to offer a career pathway specifically for digital curators. A team of SLIS faculty have been tasked to determine which existing SLIS courses (as is or modified) can be included in a new pathway for Digital Curators and to develop new courses to fill the gaps.

The following timetable has been set for the design and implementation of a Digital Curation Career Pathway:

- Fall 2013 – Design a program of study, comprised of five three-unit courses, which will include the development of a new Fundamentals of Digital Curation course
- Spring 2014 – Launch of a Digital Curation Pathway for SLIS Post Masters Certificate students
- Fall 2014 – Launch of the Digital Curation Career Pathway for students enrolled in the MLIS degree program

During the curriculum development process, the ten essential operational competencies and ten managerial competencies organized by Tammaro, Casarosa, and Madrid will be used as a tool to ensure the five three-unit courses are designed to allow students to achieve learning outcomes that prepare them for careers as Digital Curation professionals.

8   Conclusion

Digital curators manage, maintain, preserve, and add value to digital data, reduce threats to long-term value, mitigate the risk of digital obsolescence, and enhance the usefulness of digital data for research and scholarship.

Digital curation begins during the planning stage and should be a consideration throughout each stage of the digital curation lifecycle. Although the demand for digital curators is growing, the capacity to educate and train digital curators does not exist.

Students in the School of Library and Information Science's MLIS program are exposed to digital curation competencies throughout their program, through both required and elective courses, including an internship course that provides practical experience. The infusion of digital curation core competencies into the SLIS curriculum expands the number of professionals prepared to perform digital curation activities in order to protect, add value to, and preserve our digital assets.

A high level analysis of exiting courses using the DCC Curation Lifecycle model, leads us to believe that a solid foundation exists upon which to build a Digital Curation Post Master's Certificate option and a Digital Curation Career Pathway for MLIS majors. The ten essential operational competencies and ten managerial competencies organized by Tammaro, Casarosa, and Madrid will be used to ensure student learning outcomes are infused in the courses in order to prepare students for Digital Curation careers.

Our immediate goal is to complete curriculum development activities in Fall 2013 so that students can enter the MLIS Post Master's Certificate program, Digital Curation option in Spring 2014. A second goal is to build upon this work to develop a Digital Curation Career Pathway that will be available to students pursuing the MLIS degree program by Fall 2014. Our approach to curriculum development, leveraging existing SLIS resources (courses and existing faculty), will ensure sustainability of the Digital Curation curriculum at San José State University and can serve as a model for other institutions.

References

1. Rusbridge, C., Burnhill, P., Ross, S., et al.: The digital curation centre: a vision for digital curation. Paper for From Local to Global Data Interoperability—Challenges and Technologies, Mass Storage and Systems Technology Committee of the IEEE Computer Society, 20–24 June 2005, Forte Village Resort, Sardinia, Italy (2005)
2. Rusbridge, C., Burnhill, P., Ross, S., et al.: The digital curation centre: a vision for digital curation. Paper for From Local to Global Data Interoperability—Challenges and Technologies, Mass Storage and Systems Technology Committee of the IEEE Computer Society, 20–24 June 2005, Forte Village Resort, Sardinia, Italy (2005). http://www.dcc.ac.uk. Accessed: 9 May 2005
3. Gantz, J., Reinsel, D.: The digital universe in 2020: big data, bigger digital shadows, and biggest growth in the far east. IDC View (2012). http://www.emc.com/collateral/analyst-reports/idc-the-digital-universe-in-2020.pdf
4. President's Council of Advisors on Science and Technology: Report to the president and congress—designing a digital future: federally funded research and development in networking and information technology, 51 (2010). http://www.whitehouse.gov/sites/default/files/microsites/ostp/pcast-nitrd-report-2010.pdf
5. Franks, P.: Infusing digital curation competencies into the SLIS curriculum. In: Peer-reviewed paper delivered at DigCurV 2013 Conference, Florence, Italy
6. DCC. http://www.dcc.ac.uk/events/idcc13
7. DCEP (Data Curation Education Program). http://cirss.lis.illinois.edu/CollMeta/dcep.html
8. Yakel, E.: Digital curation. OCLC Syst. Serv. **23**(4), 335–340 (2007)
9. Bureau of Labor Statistics, U.S. Department of Labor: Occupational Outlook Handbook, 2012-13 Edition, Archivists, on the Internet. http://www.bls.gov/ooh/education-training-and-library/archivists.htm. Accessed 29 June 2013
10. Lee, C.A., Tibbo, H.: Where's the archivist in digital curation? Exploring the possibilities through a matrix of knowledge and skills. Arch. J. Assoc. Can. Arch. **72**, 126, 139–140 (2011). http://www.ils.unc.edu/callee/p123-lee.pdf
11. Reside, D.: What is a digital curator? (2011). http://www.nypl.org/blog/2011/04/04/what-digital-curator
12. Smithsonian Asian Pacific American Center: Job opening: museum curator (digital and emerging media). http://apanews.si.edu/2013/01/07/job-curator-digital-emerging-media/
13. Digital Curation Exchange.http://digitalcurationexchange.org/jobs. Accessed 6 February 2013
14. Abreu, A., Acker, A., Hank, C.: New directions for 21st century digital collections. In: ASIS&T 2012 [conference proceedings], Baltimore, MD, USA (2012). https://www.asis.org/asist2012/proceedings/Submissions/148.pdf

15. DigCurV: Call for contributions. http://www.digcur-education.org/eng/International-Conference/Call-for-Contributions. Accessed 6 February 2013
16. Tibbo, H.: View from across the pond: opportunities, gaps, and challenges in digital curation lifelong learning. In: DigCurV 2013 Conference [Presentation] (2013). http://www.digcur-education.org/eng/International-Conference/Presentations
17. Pomerantz, J.: Digital library and digital curation education, part two. J. Educ. Libr. Inf. Sci. **52**(2), 77–82 (2011)
18. Tammaro, A.M., Madrid, M., Casaqrosa, V.: Digital curator's education: professional identity vs. convergence of LAM (Libraries, Archives, Museums). M. Agosti et al. (Eds.): IRCDL 2012, CCIS vol. 354, pp. 184–194 (2013)
19. Franks, P.C.: Infusing digital curation competencies into the SLIS curriculum. In: CEUR Workshop Proceedings, vol. 1016, Framing the Digital Curation Curriculum Conference, Florence Italy (2013). http://ceur-ws.org/Vol-1016/paper25.pdf
20. San José State University, School of Library and Information Science: Digital Archives and Records Management. http://slisweb.sjsu.edu/digital-archives-and-records-management

Research Center Insights into Data Curation Education and Curriculum

Matthew S. Mayernik[✉], Lynne Davis, Karon Kelly, Bob Dattore,
Gary Strand, Steven J. Worley, and Mary Marlino

National Center for Atmospheric Research (NCAR), Boulder, CO, USA
{mayernik,lynne,kkelly,dattore,strandwg,
worley,marlino}@ucar.edu

Abstract. The need for the data curator role is being recognized in new institutional settings as research funding agencies internationally extend data archiving mandates to cover more types of research grants. This paper identifies categories of skills required for data curator from the perspective of data professionals within an atmospheric and Earth system science research center. We illustrate how the data curation tasks performed within a research center environment range across a spectrum of required skills. We use this spectrum to discuss implications for data curation education more broadly.

Keywords: Data curation · Life cycle · Metadata · Education

1 Introduction

The title of this workshop asks the question, "Is data curator a new role?" The answer to this question depends on the answer to two related questions, "where it is that data curators work?" and "what is it that they do?" Data management and curation are clearly new topics within library and information science programs, with only a few programs in the U.S. offering specializations in data curation or closely related topics such as digital curation and data science [20]. However, research centers and data centers have long employed individuals with the responsibility to manage, preserve, and curate data sets. The World Data Centre (WDC) system, for example, was created in 1957–1958 as part of the International Geophysical Year project [15]. The WDC system still exists, and is now (since 2008) called the International Council for Science (ICSU) World Data System (WDS). Government agencies in the US, such as the National Aeronautics and Space Administration (NASA) and the National Oceanic and Atmospheric Administration (NOAA), have also long supported data centers dedicated to archiving data collected by government funded science missions. In the social sciences, the International Association for Social Science Information Service and Technology (IASSIST) was formed in 1974 as a professional organization specifically dedicated to advance the practice of archiving social science data [13].

So while "data curator" may be a novel term, the role of data curator – meaning somebody specifically with the responsibility to manage and preserve research data – is not new. What is new is that the need for the data curator role is being recognized in

Ł. Bolikowski et al. (Eds.): TPDL 2013, CCIS 416, pp. 239–248, 2014.
DOI: 10.1007/978-3-319-08425-1_26, © Springer International Publishing Switzerland 2014

new institutional settings, in particular universities and research libraries, as national research funding agencies internationally extend their data archiving mandates to cover more (or all) types of research grants.

In this paper, we present insights into the development of data curation educational programs that draw from our experience within the National Center for Atmospheric Research (NCAR), a federally-funded research center based in Boulder, CO, US. This paper derives from the Data Curation Education in Research Centers (DCERC) program, which provides data curation internships at NCAR for graduate library and information science students. We present the combined perspective of data and library professionals. NCAR has provided access to research data sets, both internally created/collected data sets and data sets brought in from outside organizations, for the geoscience community for decades. Three authors (Dattore, Strand, and Worley) work within NCAR science and computing labs, and are actively involved in managing, preserving, and curating widely used scientific data collections [7, 16]. The other authors (Mayernik, Davis, Kelly, and Marlino) work within the NCAR library and information units, and have contributed to multiple data curation initiatives, both within and external to NCAR [2, 12].

2   Data Curation Training – Why, Who, and How?

Data professionals go by many titles. Swan and Brown define three specific roles that have fine distinctions, data scientist, data manager, and data librarian, but note that these roles might be blurred together in particular situations [18]. Other related jobs might have different titles more appropriate to particular roles, such as data engineer, data specialist, or data curator. In this paper, we use the term "data professional" to encompass the range of possible roles and responsibilities that these diverse titles imply [21].

Whatever the job title, individuals currently working as data professionals typically reach their positions through "accidental" career choices [14]. This brings a variety of skills and backgrounds to data management tasks, which, as we discuss later, is beneficial in the heterogeneous world of research data. Scaling up the pool of data professionals, however, is a challenge when there are few effective ways to prepare for these roles in traditional educational programs [8]. Most often, through practical experience managing and working with data, individuals develop skills and expertise, become sought out by collaborators for guidance, and gain responsibility, either formally or de facto, for data-related tasks [17].

For example, within research libraries, the most common tactic for offering research data services is to reassign existing library staff, not to hire new staff [19].

Data curation educational programs are opening up more direct career paths for individuals to become part of data professional communities. Although still small in size and number, data curation programs are being developed at a number of universities in the US and around the world. Recent reviews and analyses of curricula and programs indicate that most data curation education courses and programs are embedded in traditional library and information science (LIS) graduate programs, generally not available to non-LIS students or professionals [8]. The data curation search tool developed by the University of Illinois reveals nearly 500 courses at 55 institutions with LIS programs [20]. However, upon further investigation, it appears that only 19 % of these courses were deemed to be either exclusively data-centric or data-inclusive, with some portions related to data in e-science and e-research. The larger percentage was on digital topics that were not explicitly focused on research data. And there are even fewer programs targeting data science, informatics and data management for science students [21]. As this range of course curricula suggests, data curation tasks are very wide ranging in scope, and require multifaceted educational programs [11]. In addition, there is growing recognition that data curation is not a single disciplinary practice [9].

From these overviews of education programs and our own experience, the following trends and issues are apparent:

- Professional development opportunities for practicing professionals in libraries and research centers are essential to rapidly growing a cadre of data professionals to meet current demands.
- There is recent growth in data curation certificate programs for both LIS and non-LIS students and professionals in the sciences that will serve an important role in academic preparation and professional development.
- Current data professionals are needed to engage in the educational enterprise, either in formal programs or as mentors in internship programs.
- There is need for internships and other opportunities in data curation that occur outside academic certification and are aimed at students and professionals alike.
- Several opportunities for student internships and professional development for practicing professionals have been funded by the Institute of Museum and Library Services, a US federal funding agency, or as "broader impacts" of large NSF funded projects, such as GEON, NEON, and DataNet (Data Conservancy and DataONE). The challenge remains to institutionalize these educational opportunities after grant funding ends.
- Models that include students and professionals across disciplines will better prepare practitioners to meet the needs of data-intensive research than models that are tightly coupled to any single discipline.

Preparing professionals for data curation positions depends on a clear understanding of potential employers' needs and the challenges in stewarding data coupled with opportunities for aspiring or practicing professionals to experience those challenges first-hand. Building problem solving capacity through curriculum must be met with the acquisition of skills for practical settings [1].

3 Data Curation Within NCAR

NCAR is a National Science Foundation (NSF) Federally Funded Research and Development Center (FFRDC) dedicated to studying the atmospheric and related Earth system sciences. NCAR and its management organization, the University Corporation for Atmospheric Research (UCAR), support scientific research, and provide facilities to support research conducted by the atmospheric and related sciences' university community. These facilities include supercomputers, observational platforms such as radars and aircraft, weather and climate models, and collections of research data. The NCAR data collections range from small scale observational data sets from field programs to high volume reference data sets of both observational and model-produced data.

To address the need to provide LIS students with practical experiences with research data, we developed the Data Curation Education in Research Centers (DCERC) program. DCERC provides a model for educating LIS Master's and doctoral students in data curation through core data curation coursework and field experiences in research and data centers [10]. DCERC is an IMLS funded program to provide library and information science students with internship experiences in a research center environment. DCERC partners include the University of Illinois at Urbana-Champaign Graduate School of Library and Information Science and the University of Tennessee-Knoxville School of Information Sciences.

The focus of the DCERC student internships is to provide students with strong mentoring and first hand experiences in the issues, methods, and challenges of scientific data curation in scientific research contexts. During the summers of 2012 and 2013, DCERC supported five Master's students in internships at NCAR. DCERC will also support two Ph.D. students to conduct doctoral research on data curation topics at NCAR during the 2013–2014 academic year.

DCERC is built around a strong, formal mentoring structure. The DCERC internships utilized a mentorship model that includes scientists and data mentors, as well as a "peer" young investigator mentor and an institutional "community" mentor. The science mentor guides student research practice; the data mentor guides student development of data curation skills and knowledge; and the peer mentor, a Ph.D. information scientist provides general support to students as their projects progress. Within this academic and mentoring structure, students receive intensive formal and practice-based instruction uniquely blended with real world experiences in a world-renowned research center.

The following discussion identifies categories of skills required for data curation, and how those skills might be emphasized in data curation education. Our discussion draws on the extensive experiences of the paper's authors who work as data managers within NCAR, and is supplemented by our DCERC experiences to date [10]. The three authors who are NCAR data managers together have 30+ years of experience in managing and archiving data, and have all served as data mentors for DCERC students. The skill categorization and mapping described below were identified via intensive discussions between the data managers and the paper authors who are based in the NCAR Library.

4 Data Curation Skill Categories and Relations

It is essential for data professionals to have interdisciplinary skills. As Kim, Addom, and Stanton note, the need for interdisciplinary skills derives from the fact that data professionals work with people, data, and physical machines/objects (such as servers, databases, and communication networks) [9].

We break the types of skills that data professionals use down into three categories: skills based in science domain knowledge, engineering skills, and data management skills.

- Science domain knowledge – Data professionals must be able to interact with data providers and users from particular science domains. Understanding how domain scientists create, analyze, and present data is extremely valuable in developing data repository services to meet the needs of individual communities.
- Engineering skills – Data repository systems and tools are complex engineering artifacts. Building new repository tools clearly requires the ability to design and implement systems, but providing repository services also requires the ability to manipulate data files, convert data between data formats, and write scripts to automate routine tasks.
- Data management skills – In addition to scientific and engineering knowledge, data professionals need skill and expertise that is specific to the process of working with, managing, and preserving data.

Table 1 provides a breakdown of how particular data curation tasks map to these three categories from the perspective of data managers at NCAR data archives. This task list is not exhaustive, and each item in the list, such as preservation, encompasses many sub-tasks. Some tasks largely leverage skills from a single category, such as metadata tasks or database design. Other tasks, however, cross categories. Performing data quality control, for example, involves using engineering skills to create and apply automated quality control processes and science domain knowledge to evaluate the results.

Figure 1 illustrates how the overlaps and relationships between tasks and skills from Table 1 can be conceptualized as a spectrum. Each task is placed on the spectrum in accordance with its relationship to science domain knowledge, engineering skills, and data management skills. In addition, the colored bands illustrate how higher level concepts or services span across categories. For example, user services within data repositories typically involve both direct client consultations and community interaction in larger settings such as conferences and meetings, and are used to inform

Table 1. Data curation tasks and required skills

Tasks	Science domain knowledge	Engineering skills	Data management skills
Preservation			X
Metadata creation	X		X
Quality control	X	X	
Formats	X	X	X
Data conversions	X	X	
Access	X	X	
Ontologies/vocabularies	X		X
Interface design	X	X	
User community interaction	X		X
Database design		X	

the design of user interfaces. Similarly, developing access mechanisms primarily involves engineering skills, but also leverages science domain knowledge of the tools and formats appropriate to the user base, as well as data management skills related to metadata and the use of standards.

From Fig. 1, additional themes can be developed that relate to the role of data curators in research center environments. These are: (1) the unique perspective that the data curators have via the data life cycle model, (2) the critical knowledge of metadata that data curators possess and use, and (3) how data professionals act as "data concierges" to translate and transfer knowledge, skills, and resources across multiple communities.

Holistic/life cycle approach to data management and curation.

Data professionals bring a unique perspective that views the curation process as an integrated whole. Technology is critical to the process, but alone is not sufficient to enable long-term usability of data sets. Various data life cycle models have been developed to tie together the processes involved in collecting/creating, using, managing, presenting, and preserving data (see [3] for example). Mentors for DCERC students emphasize the ways that the students' data life cycle perspective allowed

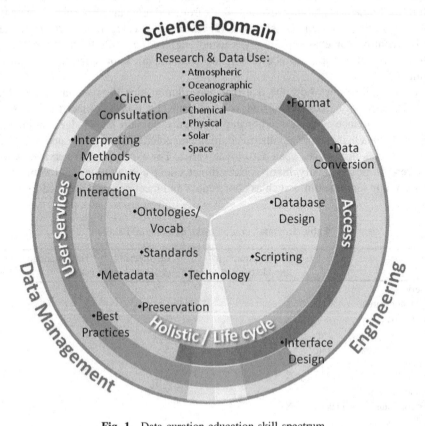

Fig. 1. Data curation education skill spectrum

them to come to the NCAR research center environments with a holistic perspective on the data curation process. Data professionals with science or engineering backgrounds gain this more holistic view through experience in dealing with the interrelations between metadata, preservation mechanisms, access tools, etc.

Metadata, ontologies/vocabularies, and standards.

Having an understanding of the processes and principles specific to metadata generation, standardization, and use is a critical and unique skill for data curation specialists. Students in science programs are typically not introduced to metadata during formal courses, and may only tangentially encounter metadata best practices during their graduate research [6]. Metadata is central to information and data systems, and as such is consistently present in library and information science educational programs. Similarly, the development and use of standard ontologies and vocabularies for describing and categorizing information resources is a skill set unique to information and data professionals. The quality of all data management systems closely relates to the richness of the standardized metadata employed.

"Data concierge".

Data professionals are looked to as experts. They are asked about best practices, about available tools, services, and capabilities. They are regularly required to move between different groups/audiences in order to provide guidance, seek resources, and argue for the value of data services within an organization. Fenstermacher, in a description of a new "data concierge" position developed within a biomedical research organization, provides a concise description of this role, "the Data Concierge is a key link between the researchers, the governing committees, the regulatory processes, data quality, data standards, and IT" [4]. Within NCAR, data professionals provide guidance to data providers on the available data storage and management tools and capabilities, as well as on best practices for metadata descriptions. Keeping up with technological change is also a key role of data professionals, as storage devices, computational tools, and formats are constantly evolving. NCAR data professionals also provide expertise to data users on the appropriateness of data sets for particular uses, and on which data access mechanisms are available for a given repository or data set. These kinds of user interactions draw heavily on science domain knowledge, as noted in Fig. 1. Notably, the importance of user interaction corresponds to the role of librarians in providing reference services to help patrons discover, find, and acquire materials in brick-and-mortar libraries [5].

5 Conclusion

The spectrum of data curation skills and tasks presented in this paper has a number of implications for the education of data professionals. Students who develop combinations of skills centered in one sector vs. another will likely be positioned to pursue different career tracks. The various job titles that data professionals have, such as data librarian, data engineer, and data manager, point to individuals who specialize in specific sectors of the skill spectrum. On the surface, this potential for specialization within the data curation space runs counter to our discussion of the value of taking the holistic life cycle view of data curation, but taking the life cycle perspective does not require all data curators to master every skill. In reality, with the complexity of current digital archiving infrastructures, we cannot expect one person to be expert in all key areas of data curation. The best curation systems, namely the ones that support rapid scientific progress, need multiple people working as a whole, who together have expert knowledge in all key areas.

From the data curation education perspective, data curation programs might benefit from organizing their curriculum based on where they would like to fit within the data curation skill spectrum. Educational programs might also use this spectrum to make it clear to their students and the prospective employers of their students where they fit into the larger set of curation activities. Similarly, organizations hiring data professionals will likely place different emphases on this continuum of skills based on their institution type, and based on the organizational structure of their data curation services. For example, while many university libraries are developing research data services, they typically partner with other campus units, such as computing units, to develop archiving services. University libraries currently developing data-related services typically focus on informational/consultative services [19]. These services would likely be best provided by people with skills that center in the domain knowledge and data management skill sectors of the skill spectrum. In contrast, data repositories in research centers that provide operational data archiving services need well rounded staffs that include expertise in all areas of the skill spectrum.

Our experience and analysis also illustrates the critical importance of domain knowledge within the data curation process within research centers. As Table 1 shows, scientific domain knowledge is essential to performing many data curation tasks. LIS students bring a data life cycle model perspective to data repositories. This perspective is valuable to data managers, and enables the students to gain more benefit from their internship experiences. The life cycle-focused collaboration strengthens the students' practical understanding of how real data curation situations follow or deviate from the life cycle concept, and gives the mentors a defined framework to discuss and analyze their work.

Finally, we note that, as with many things in the digital world, data curation is rapidly evolving. Educational programs that train data professionals must strategically plan for the future. Sustainability of data curation education/training programs is an ongoing challenge. Our DCERC mentorship model, for example, while critical to the success of our program, is intensive and may not scale well were the number of students involved to increase dramatically. With many such programs being funded initially by research grants, institutionalizing and sustaining programs beyond the life of the original grant requires clear illustrations of the benefit of bringing data curators into traditional LIS work settings, and bringing LIS professionals into more specialized data archiving environments. Further development of the model depicted in Fig. 1 can inform the library and information science educational community's understanding of the "data curator" role, and the skills it might emphasize in particular settings.

References

1. Botticelli, P., et al.: Educating digital curators: challenges and opportunities. Int. J. Digit. Curat. **2**(6), 146–164 (2011)
2. Davis, L., et al.: Moving from users, through use cases to requirements. A Data Conservancy white paper (2010)
3. Digital Curation Centre (DCC): DCC curation lifecycle model (2013). http://www.dcc.ac. uk/resources/curation-lifecycle-model
4. Fenstermacher, D.A.: The data concierge. AAMC GIR Viewpoints. n.p. (2009). https:// www.aamc.org/members/gir/gir_resources/138364/viewpoint_aug09.html
5. Garritano, J.R., Carlson, J.R.: A subject librarian's guide to collaborating on e-science projects. Issues in Science and Technology Librarianship, 57 (2009). http://www.istl.org/ 09-spring/refereed2.html
6. Hernandez, R.R., et al.: Advanced technologies and data management practices in environmental science: lessons from academia. BioScience **62**(12), 1067–1076 (2012). http://dx.doi.org/10.1525/bio.2012.62.12.8
7. Jacobs, C.A., Worley, S.J.: Data curation in climate and weather: transforming our ability to improve predictions through global knowledge sharing. Int. J. Digit. Curat. **4**(2), 68–79 (2009). http://www.ijdc.net/index.php/ijdc/article/viewFile/119/122
8. Jahnke, L., Asher, A., Keralis, S.D.: The problem of data. Council on Library and Information Resources (CLIR) Publication 154 (2012)
9. Kim, Y., Addom, B.K., Stanton, J.M.: Education for escience professionals: integrating data curation and cyberinfrastructure. Int. J. Digit. Curat. **6**(1), 125–138 (2011). http://dx. doi.org/10.2218/ijdc.v6i1.177
10. Kelly, K., et al.: Model development for scientific data curation education. Int. J. Digit. Curat. **8**(1), 255–264 (2013). http://dx.doi.org/10.2218/ijdc.v8i1.258
11. Lee, C.: Matrix of digital curation knowledge and competencies. DigCCurr (2009). http:// www.ils.unc.edu/digccurr/digccurr-matrix.html
12. Mayernik, M.S., et al.: Data citations within NCAR/UCP. NCAR technical note, NCAR/ TN-492+STR, National Center for Atmospheric Research (NCAR), Boulder, CO (2012). http://dx.doi.org/10.5065/D6ZC80VN
13. Adams, M.O.: The origins and early years of IASSIST. IASSIST Q. **30**(3), 5–13 (2006). http://www.iassistdata.org/downloads/iqvol303adams.pdf
14. Pryor, G., Donnelly, M.: Skilling up to do data: whose role, whose responsibility, whose career? Int. J. Digit. Curat. **4**(2), 158–170 (2009). http://www.ijdc.net/index.php/ijdc/ article/viewFile/126/133
15. Ruttenberg, S., Rishbeth, H.: World data centres — past, present and future. J. Atmos. Terr. Phys. **56**(7), 865–870 (1994)
16. Strand, G.: Community earth system model data management: policies and challenges. Proc. Comput. Sci. **4**, 558–566 (2011)
17. Strand, G.: The real life of a data scientist. American Geophysical Union, Fall Meeting (2011)
18. Swan, A., Brown, S.: The skills, role and career structure of data scientists and curators: an assessment of current practice and future needs. Report to the JISC, University of Southampton (2008)
19. Tenopir, C., Birch, B., Allard, S.: Academic libraries and research data services: current practices and plans for the future. An ACRL white paper, Association of College and Research Libraries (2012)

20. Varvel, V.E., Bammerlin. E.J., Palmer, C.L.: Education for data professionals: a study of current courses and programs. In: Proceedings of the 2012 iConference, pp. 527–529. Association for Computing Machinery, New York (2012)
21. Varvel, V.E., Jr., Palmer, C.L., Chao, T., Sacchi, S.: Report from the research data workforce summit: sponsored by the Data Conservancy. University of Illinois (2011). http://www.ideals.illinois.edu/handle/2142/25830

Author Index